Beth Henley
A Casebook

Casebooks on Modern Dramatists
Kimball King, *General Editor*

CHRISTOPHER HAMPTON
A Casebook
edited by Robert Gross

HOWARD BRENTON
A Casebook
edited by Ann Wilson

DAVID STOREY
A Casebook
edited by William Hutchings

PETER SHAFFER
A Casebook
edited by C.J. Gianakaras

SIMON GRAY
A Casebook
edited by Katherine H. Burkman

JOHN ARDEN AND MARGARETTA D'ARCY
A Casebook
edited by Jonathan Wike

AUGUST WILSON
A Casebook
edited by Marilyn Elkins

JOHN OSBORNE
A Casebook
edited by Patricia D. Denison

ARNOLD WESKER
A Casebook
edited by Reade W. Dornan

DAVID HARE
A Casebook
edited by Hersh Zeifman

MARSHA NORMAN
A Casebook
edited by Linda Ginter Brown

BRIAN FRIEL
A Casebook
edited by William Kerwin

NEIL SIMON
A Casebook
edited by Gary Konas

TERRENCE MCNALLY
A Casebook
edited by Toby Silverman Zinman

STEPHEN SONDHEIM
A Casebook
edited by Joanne Gordon

HORTON FOOTE
A Casebook
edited by Gerald C. Wood

SAMUEL BECKETT
A Casebook
edited by Jennifer M. Jeffers

WENDY WASSERSTEIN
A Casebook
edited by Claudia Barnett

AUGUST WILSON
A Casebook
edited by Marilyn Elkins

WOODY ALLEN
A Casebook
edited by Kimball King

BETH HENLEY
A Casebook
edited by Julia A. Fesmire

BETH HENLEY
A CASEBOOK

Edited by Julia A. Fesmire

LONDON AND NEW YORK

First Published 2002 by Routledge
2 Park Square, Milton Park, Abingdon, Oxfordshire OX14 4RN
711 Third Avenue, New York, NY 10017

First issued in paperback 2014

Routledge is an imprint of the Taylor & Francis Group, an informa business

Copyright © 2002 by Julia A. Fesmire

All rights reserved. No part of this book may be reprinted or reproduced or utilized in any form or by any electronic, mechanical or other means, now known or hereafter invented, including photocopying and recording or in any information storage or retrieval system, without permission in writing from the publishers.

Library of Congress Cataloging-in-Publication Data is available from the Library of Congress

ISBN 13: 978-1-138-87054-3 (pbk)
ISBN 13: 978-0-8153-3878-9 (hbk)

for my sister, Claudia

Contents

GENERAL EDITOR'S NOTE　ix

INTRODUCTION　xi
Julia A. Fesmire

ACKNOWLEDGMENTS　xxi

Chapter 1
"DANCING ON THE EDGE OF A CLIFF": IMAGES OF THE GROTESQUE IN THE PLAYS OF BETH HENLEY　1
Miriam M. Chirico

Chapter 2
LESSONS FROM THE PAST: LOSS AND REDEMPTION IN THE EARLY PLAYS OF BETH HENLEY　32
Larry G. Mapp

Chapter 3
MOVING BEYOND MISSISSIPPI: BETH HENLEY AND THE ANXIETIES OF POSTSOUTHERNNESS　42
Gary Richards

Chapter 4
***THE LUCKY SPOT* AS IMMANENT CRITIQUE**　64
Rebecca King

CHAPTER 5
ABUNDANCE OR EXCESS? BETH HENLEY'S POSTMODERN ROMANCE OF THE TRUE WEST 88

KAREN L. LAUGHLIN

CHAPTER 6
EXISTENTIAL DESPAIR AND THE MODERN NEUROSIS: BETH HENLEY'S *CRIMES OF THE HEART* 105

GENE A. PLUNKA

CHAPTER 7
SOUTHERN FIRECRACKERS AND "REAL BAD DAYS": FILM ADAPTATIONS OF BETH HENLEY'S *CRIMES OF THE HEART* AND *THE MISS FIRECRACKER CONTEST* 128

LINDA ROHRER PAIGE

BIBLIOGRAPHY 154

LIST OF CONTRIBUTORS 169

INDEX 171

General Editor's Note

Although Beth Henley's first play, *Am I Blue,* was staged at Southern Methodist University in 1974, her first Broadway production (and second play) was performed at the John Golden Theatre in 1981. That same year she won not only the New York Drama Critics Circle Award for best new American play, but also the Pulitzer Prize for drama. *Crimes of the Heart* was subsequently made into a major Hollywood film that introduced her work to an international audience in 1986. Also staples of modern theatre now are Henley's *The Miss Firecracker Contest* (1986), *The Wake of Jamie Foster* (1982), and other plays which premiered in Chicago, London and additional cities. Besides her dozen plays Henley has written five film scripts for Hollywoood. Like so many twentieth-century American artists, Henley is a Mississippi native and will assume her place as a major dramatist in both the twentieth and twenty-first centuries.

Julia A. Fesmire, an Associate Professor at Middle Tennessee State University who received her Ph.D. from Vanderbilt University, specializes in nineteenth- and twentieth-century literature and has taught courses in Women's Studies. She is an ideal editor for a casebook on Henley. Her casebook treats Henley's major plays, *Crimes of the Heart* and *The Miss Firecracker Contest,* and focuses critical attention on many of the lesser known plays, including *The Lucky Spot, Abundance,* and *Control Freaks.* The essays cover a variety of topics, including Henley's vexed status as a Southern writer, her status as a feminist critic of contemporary society, and her use of the comic grotesque. Fesmire has also invited top women playwright scholars to contribute to this volume, including Karen L. Laughlin, whose essay on *Crimes of the Heart* was one of the first critical studies of this important play. Interestingly, the Casebook Series has already published the achievements of Marsha Norman and Wendy Wasserstein, who along with Henley, comprise a triumvirate of the best known and most prolific female playwrights of our time.

Kimball King

Introduction

Although many critics of Beth Henley's work compare her to other southern writers, such as Eudora Welty, Flannery O'Connor, and Tennessee Williams, I always think of her in conjunction with songwriter and singer Christopher Cross, who burst upon the music scene at about the same time Henley achieved her first success in 1979. Cross's first album, entitled simply *Christopher Cross*, was one of the most celebrated debut albums of all time, winning five Grammy awards in 1980 (including Best New Artist and Best Album, as well as Best Record and Best Song for "Sailing"), producing four hit singles ("Sailing," "Ride Like the Wind," "Never Be the Same," and "Say You'll Be Mine"), and selling six million copies worldwide.[1] Beth Henley's introduction to the theater world was equally impressive. Having had a one-act play, *Am I Blue*, produced in college, Henley's next effort, a full-length play entitled *Crimes of the Heart*, was a phenomenal hit. Co-winner of the 1979 Great American Play contest sponsored by the Actors Theatre of Louisville, *Crimes* won the 1981 Pulitzer Prize for Drama, making Henley the first woman in twenty-three years to be so honored. Subsequently, the play moved to Broadway and won the New York Drama Critics' Circle Award for Best American Play in 1981.

How does one follow initial achievements such as these? While accepting one of his Grammys, Cross graciously acknowledged the success of his first album and joked that he hoped he was not a one-hit wonder. In 1981 he won an Academy Award for Best Original Song as a cowriter of "Arthur's Theme" for the film *Arthur*, but, although he has released six additional albums over the last two decades, none have had the commercial and critical success of the debut album for which he is still primarily known. Henley's success seems to parallel that of Cross. Primarily known for both the stage and film versions of *Crimes of the Heart*,[2] as well as the film adaptation of another of her plays, *Miss Firecracker*, Henley has written twelve additional plays as well as several television and movie screenplays, including the films

Nobody's Fool (1986), starring Rosanna Arquette and Eric Roberts, and *True Stories* (1986), on which she collaborated with Steven Tobolowsky and David Byrne. Critical reception of her later efforts has been mixed, and several of her plays have closed after relatively short runs.

The young playwright once expressed dismay that people would come to see a production of her play. Mary Dellasega asked Henley how it felt to have *Crimes of the Heart* performed by the Actors Theatre in Louisville, and Henley responded: "It was so frightening.... It was January and it was freezing and it was snowing. I remember standing in the parking lot, and these people in fur coats were getting out of their cars. And I thought, 'Oh, my God, they paid money, they hired babysitters, and they came out to see this,' and I started crying. I was terrified that I was going to be arrested for fraud. [*Laughs*] It was really scary" (253). Despite initial trepidation, Henley has continued to expand her oeuvre and explore new possibilities. Having confined her earlier plays to southern settings—*Crimes of the Heart*, *The Wake of Jamey Foster* (produced 1982), *The Miss Firecracker Contest* (produced 1980 and 1984), and *The Debutante Ball* (produced 1985 and 1988) take place in small Mississippi towns—Henley's subsequent plays shift, both backwards in time and westward in direction. *The Lucky Spot* (produced 1986 and 1987) signals a transition, taking place in "a small southern town about sixty miles west of New Orleans," which is the setting for *Am I Blue*, but on Christmas Eve, 1934. *Abundance* (produced 1989 and 1990) moves even further back in time to the Wyoming Territory of the late 1860s, covering a twenty-five year period. *Signature* (produced 1990) propels us to the year 2052 in what Alvin Klein described as "a futuristic Hollywood ... a land without mind or heart, ruled by 'celebrity swine' and agents whose religion is ambition" (B12). Expanding creatively, Henley herself directed the original production of *Control Freaks* (1992). *Revelers* (produced 1994 and 1996) moves us to a cottage on the shores of Lake Michigan. *L-Play* (produced 1995) is among the most challenging of her plays due to its lack of coherence, other than being organized around the letter L. One of Henley's friends who attended the first reading of the play noted "how unlike 'Beth' it [is]" (*CPII* xiii). And, although *Impossible Marriage* moves us back to the South, the setting seems largely irrelevant to the themes of the play, which Henley calls "[s]omething like *The Importance of Being Earnest* except by me" (*CPII* xvi). While Henley continues to write and produce new plays, her earlier plays are still performed. *Crimes of the Heart*, for example, was revived in April, 2001 off-Broadway at the Second Stage Theatre in New York. Alfre Woodard, who has acted in earlier and later Henley productions, sums up the experience as follows: "I believe one cannot have a complete life as an actor without having performed or explored a Beth Henley piece.... In the climate of false control, cool minimalism, and forced glibness that often characterizes today's writing, Henley fearlessly lets fly emotionally

Introduction *xiii*

unashamed material and allows us to feel, to question, to argue, to hoot, to mourn" (*CPII* xiii).

Despite the quantity and range of Henley's works, critical scholarship is, until now, somewhat limited. Quite a few newspaper and magazine articles and reviews of her films and various productions of her plays (including the later ones) have been published, along with several interviews with the playwright herself, but there are no full length studies of her oeuvre and surprisingly few scholarly articles.[3] In a 1986 essay, "Criminality, Desire, and Community: A Feminist Approach to Beth Henley's *Crimes of the Heart*," Karen L. Laughlin discusses the Magrath sisters as both criminals and victims of their own self-deception. She asserts that the sisters portray a force that tests the limits society places on female behavior and argues that the play ultimately rejects social oppression of women. The play "provides an alternative to the traditional comic resolution in which women are united with men and consequently prevented from bonding with each other. Though tentative and open-ended, the play's conclusion points toward a significant reorientation of the Magrath sisters' desires and integrates the three women in a brief but wholly affirmative moment of unity" (48). Jonnie Guerra, in "Beth Henley: Female Quest and the Family-Play Tradition" (1989), suggests that Henley's reliance on realism and conventional dramatic forms prevents her from transcending patriarchal structures. Reading Henley's plays as "an attempt to adapt the family play to portray the female quest for autonomy" (119), she notes that in these plays "there exists no marital happiness, nor is there intimacy or mutual understanding in the marriage bond" (121). Guerra concludes that Henley's female characters' "quests for autonomy" are truncated due to Henley's reliance on realism and the formal conventions of the family play. She thus finds that the plays finally "affirm rather than strike out against women's confinement" to a stifling and emotionally bankrupt domestic sphere (128).

Other articles include Nancy D. Hargrove's "The Tragicomic Vision of Beth Henley's Drama" (1984), Billy J. Harbin's "Familial Bonds in the Plays of Beth Henley" (1987), Lisa J. McDonnell's "Diverse Similitude: Beth Henley and Marsha Norman" (1987), Lana A. Whited's "Suicide in Beth Henley's *Crimes of the Heart* and Marsha Norman's *'night Mother*," Lou Thompson's "Feeding the Hungry Heart: Food in Beth Henley's *Crimes of the Heart*" (1992), and Robert L. McDonald's " 'A Blaze of Glory': Image and Self-Promotion in Henley's *The Miss Firecracker Contest*" (1999), all appearing in *Southern Quarterly*. Henley's plays are also discussed as a part of what June Schlueter calls "The Female Canon" in Joanne B. Karpinski's "The Ghosts of Chekhov's *Three Sisters* Haunt Beth Henley's *Crimes of the Heart*" (*Modern American Drama: The Female Canon*, 1990). These pairings of Henley with Chekhov and Norman are continued in articles appearing in *Studies in American Drama, 1945–Present* with Laura Morrow's "Orality and Identity in *'night Mother* and *Crimes of the Heart"* (1988) and Jean Gagen's "Most Resembling Unlikeness, and Most Unlike Resemblance': Beth Henley's *Crimes of the Heart* and Chekhov's *Three Sisters*" (1989). An earlier volume of *Studies in American Drama, 1945–Present* includes Colby H. Kullman's "Beth Henley's Marginalized Heroes" (1993). Additional discussions of Henley's work can be found in Janet V. Haedicke's " 'A Population (and Theater) at Risk': Battered Women in Henley's *Crimes of the Heart* and Shepard's *A Lie of the Mind*," and Alan Clarke Shepard's "Aborted Rage in Beth Henley's Women," published, respectively, in the March 1993 and March 1996 issues of *Modern Drama*.

As this representative list of articles indicates, the vast majority of critical attention thus far has focused on *Crimes of the Heart*, which is hardly surprising considering its critical and commercial success. This casebook includes essays that contextualize and analyze a wide range of Henley's plays from a variety of perspectives. I have attempted to achieve an even balance of objective interpretations to contrast with the earlier criticism, and I have specifically solicited essays discussing Henley's later plays. Just as many music fans consider *Rendezvous* (1992), or even *Walking in Avalon* (1998), to be Christopher Cross's best work, taking his music in new directions, many of Henley's later plays are rich texts for discerning critics. Tony Early's observation about the task facing southern writers, quoted in Gary Richards's article, seems especially pertinent: "My fear is that, eventually, because of our willingness to feed on, without replacing, the tenets and traditions and subjects given to us by our predecessors—Welty, Flannery O'Connor, and William Faulkner most prominent among them—Southern writing will collapse and bury us all, leaving only kudzu, grits, and a certain vaguely familiar voice to mark the spot" (x–xi). Henley's later plays are clearly attempts to create new voices.

Miriam M. Chirico's essay, " 'Dancing on the Edge of a Cliff': Images of the Grotesque in the Plays of Beth Henley," is an appropriate essay with which to begin this collection for both its focus and its range. Henley has often been compared with southern writers largely because her early plays revolve around eccentric, colorful characters in southern settings. Chirico argues that a mixture of comedy and violence exists in all of Henley's works; the fact that critics, readers, and viewers often focus on family struggles and women's issues causes them to see Henley's early plays as primarily realistic rather than experimental. Accordingly, the later plays seem like aberrations. Chirico shows that the elements of violence and the grotesque are present in Henley's plays from the beginning. However, "[a]s her plays move away from the early, quirky tales of female community, they become progressively darker and the use of the grotesque becomes more and more prevalent." Chirico's essay "traces the trajectory" of how Henley uses the grotesque in her plays, "first as a means of developing character," and "later as a subversive tool of rebellion, and finally as a way to force the audience to confront evil," focusing specifically on *Crimes of the Heart*, *The Miss Firecracker Contest*, *The Wake of Jamey Foster*, *The Debutante Ball*, *Control Freaks*, and *Signature*. The grotesque is not a peculiarly southern obsession; indeed, it is a part of all of our lives: "[t]o disregard the grotesque would be to ignore a portion of the human condition, just as ignoring death would prevent us from fully appreciating life."

The next two essays focus specifically on Henley's place in the canon of southern literature. Considering Henley's early plays both in relation to one another and in the context of past and contemporary southern writers, Larry G. Mapp, in "Lessons from the Past: Loss and Redemption in the Early Plays of Beth Henley," makes an excellent case for Henley's inclusion among the more celebrated southern writers as she continues the interrogation into "issues of family and community and with the struggle of individuals to find an identity within a family or community that is oppressive, that is often fragmenting, and that no longer has a center that will hold." Mapp identifies the antecedents for Henley's social critique in such diverse writers as Mary Boykin Chesnut and that "largest bear in the southern forest," William Faulkner, and sees the tradition continuing through Chopin, Hurston, and Lee Smith. *Am I Blue* contains "the seeds of the rest of the plays in volume one," focusing on individuals constrained by families insisting on conformity to socially constructed identities. This first play, along with *Crimes of the Heart*, *The Wake of Jamey Foster*, *The Debutante Ball*, and *The Lucky Spot*, echoes the question Carnelle raises in *The Miss Firecracker Contest*: What can you reasonably hope for in life? Henley's characters differ from their counterparts in other southern texts, however, in that although "each play ends with a scene that offers the women some hope of redemption through love and companionship, both with men and with other women," they "never seem to see their world clearly or as a whole, so we are understandably unsure that their exhilaration over any momentary triumph will be more than momentary." Mapp identifies Henley's response to Carnelle's question as "relentless optimism." "Henley has indicted the traditional southern culture in terms familiar to southern writers and readers. She has not, however, found answers to her own questions about the place of women in it."

Continuing Professor Mapp's inquiry into the "vexed" status of Henley as a southern writer, Gary Richards examines the plays of the 1990s—*Abundance, Signature, Control Freaks, Revelers, L-Play*, and *Impossible Marriage*—a decade in which "Henley self-consciously worked to establish herself as a postsouthern writer, one who has grown out of a southern milieu and indeed has centralized that culture in early writings but for whom that cultural identity no longer remains preeminent in either the writer's daily existence or her artistic expression." Richards pays particular attention to "the wildly comic" *Control Freaks*, which he see as "simultaneously pay[ing] homage to previous southern literature through her citation of texts by Tennessee Williams and Eudora Welty *and* upend[ing] this literature with her brilliant revisionary proofing of these texts." Despite Henley's efforts to redefine herself, she continues to be identified as a southern writer, a problem Richards sees as crucial to her critical reputation. Those who insist upon measuring Henley's later work with the implicit southernness of *Crimes* and the other earlier plays are invariably disappointed. Those who do not will enjoy the richness of Henley's parodies, seeing perhaps in Sister's fate that which is arguably missing from the earlier plays—"ultimately a heartwarming cry of affirmation and female autonomy."

The next article examines *The Lucky Spot*, arguably a pivotal text in Henley's development as a playwright. The debate over Henley's feminism, or lack thereof, as expressed in the plays preceding this one are remarkably like the debate over George Eliot's feminism.[4] It is appropriate, then, to look at this play which moves toward the past with the eyes of a nineteenth-century scholar. Rebecca King does just that in "*The Lucky Spot* as Immanent Critique." Relying on early liberal and capitalist arguments of Hobbes and Locke, King argues that *The Lucky Spot*, because of its southern and temporal settings (Pigeon, Louisiana, on Christmas Eve, 1934), is "an iconoclastic . . . treatment of an American dream predicated on a liberal meritocracy, revealing that, despite their liberatory potential for some, capitalism and liberal meritocracy often result in social and economic dislocations, in homelessness and unemployment." This play, then, functions as a "cautionary tale" decrying the deficiencies of liberal and capitalist ideologies. King also focuses on the feminist critique inherent in this play, noting that Henley "undermines essentialist notions of femininity that ground liberal concepts of family" through Cassidy's lack of domesticity and Sue Jack's maternal failures. Seeing Henley's failure to dramatize solutions to the characters' dilemmas as a realistic response (as was that of Eliot) to an essentially patriarchal and capitalist society as a positive aspect of her satire on contemporary society, King argues that the play "makes clear that certain values and practices promote well-being, while others do not," functioning successfully as immanent critique.

Focusing on Henley's first play of the 1990s, Karen L. Laughlin argues that *Abundance* proposes a postmodern feminist reworking of the Western romance, understood both as a literary genre and as metaphor for American Indian policy and westward expansion. In "Abundance or Excess? Beth Henley's Postmodern Romance of the True West," Laughlin compares *Abundance* with Sam Shepard's *True West* (1980) and invites a rethinking of Shepard's highly masculinized version of the myth of the American West. In contrast with Shepard's contemporary setting, *Abundance* opens in the Wyoming Territory in the late 1860s and spans twenty-five years, offering a late-twentieth-century perspective on nineteenth-century myths of the American frontier. *Abundance* shares with *True West* the sense of unstable identities as its two female protagonists take over one another's personalities and desires much as the brothers Austin and Lee do in Shepard's play. But whereas Shepard construes the West in terms of Hollywood's Western film genre and commercialized creativity, Henley looks to the women's genre of romance in constructing her story of two mail-order brides seeking to make their way in America's "Wild West." In so doing, she shifts emphasis away from finding the "truth" of the West toward recognizing its seductive, ideological power. Henley explores a range of socially constructed desires in *Abundance*—desires drawn from dime novels, popular songs, fairy tales, and myths of heroic frontiersmen and women. Her feminist critique thus interweaves the political and the personal by considering how pioneer romance, rooted in what Diane Elam calls a reality "invested by desire," destabilizes both gender identities and the social structures that support them. Taking issue with Elam, Laughlin's reading also sees this desire in economic or material terms, based in the politics of American territorial expansion as well as in a commercialized construction of self.

Critiquing what is both Henley's first and most recent commercial and artistic endeavor, Gene A. Plunka offers a comprehensive reading of *Crimes of the Heart*. Summarizing the arguments of Laughlin, Guerra, and other critics who have examined the play, Plunka prefers to argue that *Crimes* "represents Freud's notion of the modern neurosis, and the denouement effectively provides a response to the *angoisse* and alienation that permeates throughout society and which typically prevents human beings from achieving happiness." Locating Henley in the tradition inspired by Chekhov, her favorite playwright, Plunka links her black humor to the absurdist theater, deeply rooted in *anomie* resulting from a universe that alienates and isolates us. "What is unusual about Henley's essentially Freudian notion of the search for happiness deterred by the demands of modern civilization ... is that the tradition is rarely represented in Modern American drama." Plunka traces the oral gratification patterns of the sisters, searching for a substitution for the nurture of absent parents and examines the "cultural inhibitions" forced upon them by Old Granddaddy and "the other agent of acculturation," Chick Boyle. Although Lenny's belated birthday celebration is a "communal sharing and outpouring of love ... the play ends in celebration of two oral images—the eating of the birthday cake and the notes of the saxophone—reminding us that alternatives to true happiness always exist, but that the freeze frame of the moment of bonding in 'magical, golden, sparkling glimmer' offers the only fleeting joy of unity that can assuage the loneliness and despair of the otherwise modern neurosis."

This volume would not be complete without an essay discussing the film adaptations of Henley's plays, *Crimes of the Heart* and *The Miss Firecracker Contest*. Linda Rohrer Paige, in "Southern Firecrackers and 'Real Bad Days,' focuses on the relative successes of Henley's films. Noting its critical and commercial success, she sees the film version of *Crimes* as lacking much of the original play's ambiguity, primarily because, for example, the screenplay gives voice and physical presence to Old Granddaddy and Zackery, whose very absence in the play gives them power. In addition, the motives of secondary characters, such as Barnette Lloyd, are overly simplified, reducing them to stick figures and detracting from the play's original social commentary. Paige praises, however, the manner in which the film represents the Magrath sisters' transformations to autonomous human beings, enacted beautifully by Diane Keaton, Jessica Lange, and Sissy Spacek. In her next adaptation, *Miss Firecracker*, "Henley again foregrounds the themes of transformation and autonomy." The change in title, which shifts the emphasis from the context to the individual contest winner, is a signal that the focus is now on Carnelle's relationship with her cousin Elain. Once again, characters in the screenplay, such as Mac Sam, become secondary and lack the complexity that Henley incorporates into the characters of the play. Paige sees Henley's exploitation of fairy tale motifs as the key to unlocking the strengths of *Miss Firecracker*. Interweaving and inverting motifs from "Cinderella," "Snow White," and "The Frog Prince," *Miss Firecracker* "offers the possibility of regeneration, rebirth, and autonomy."

As a final note, all citations to Henley's plays are to Smith and Kraus's two-volume collection of Henley's plays (2000) and are indicated by references to *CPI* for volume one and *CPII* for volume two, followed by the page number. This collection not only provides fascinating prefatory material about productions of each of the plays, it also divides the texts in an especially appropriate way. The plays in volume one, most of which were written in the 1980s, are generally seen as the southern or family plays, and are presented not in the order in which they were written but in the order in which they were produced in New York: *Crimes of the Heart, Am I Blue, The Wake of Jamey Foster, The Miss Firecracker Contest, The Lucky Spot,* and *The Debutante Ball*. Volume two contains the more experimental plays, those basically of the 1990s, that, according to Henley, "are about parts of my life that occurred after leaving Mississippi" (*CPII* vi): *Abundance, Signature, Control Freaks, Revelers, L-Play,* and *Impossible Marriage. Family Week,* produced 10–16 April 2000 at the Century Theater in New York, is not yet available in print.

Julia A. Fesmire

Notes

1. For more information about Christopher Cross, visit his official website at www.christophercross.com and the Grammy Awards site at www.grammy.com/awards/search. The University of Mississippi English department maintains a Beth Henley page at their Mississippi Writers Page website: www.olemiss.edu/depts/english/ms-writers/dir/henley_beth.

Introduction xix

2. The film version of *Crimes of the Heart* was quite successful. Sissy Spacek won the New York Film Critics' Circle Award for Best Actress (1986) and a Golden Globe Award for Best Performance by an Actress in a Motion Picture (1987) for her role as Babe. The film also received three 1987 Academy Award nominations: Best Actress in a Leading Role for Spacek; Best Actress in a Supporting Role for Tess Harper's portrayal of Chick; and Best Screenplay based on Material from Another Medium for Henley's adaptation.
3. Readers should be able to identify the articles mentioned in this introduction in the bibliography at the end of this casebook. Although not intended to be exhaustive, the bibliography includes primary sources for the plays and films as well as major interviews and profiles of Henley and her career. I have included performance reviews of what appear to be the major productions of each of her plays, and have specifically excluded reviews of regional and British productions. The list of scholarly criticism includes those articles available in most major libraries.
4. A key problem with George Eliot criticism, like that of Henley, is Eliot's insistence on placing her heroines within the confines of ordinary and conventional possibility—confines from which George Eliot, herself, escaped. Ellen Moers argues that "George Eliot . . . was no feminist. That is, her aim as a novelist was not to argue for a diminishing of the social inhibitions and a widening of the options that affect the lives of ordinary women. . . ." (194). Kate Millet complains that George Eliot does not offer a positive role model for aspirant women, but simply represents their limitations (139). Kathleen Blake, on the other hand, sees *Middlemarch* as a great feminist work, as does Gillian Beer (Blake 26; Beer 1–29). There is no doubt that George Eliot, and Beth Henley after her, are problematic writers in this regard. Perhaps the answer is that which Professor King suggests: Both Eliot's and Henley's feminisms are closer to a kind of humanism, which extends to freedom for men as well as women and strives for the goal of an improved and enlightened society in which all members may realize their potential capacities. See Gillian Beer, *George Eliot* (Bloomington: Indiana University Press, 1986); Kathleen Blake, "*Middlemarch*: Vocation, Love and the Woman Question," in *Love and the Woman Question in Victorian Literature* (Totowa, N. J.: Barnes and Noble, 1983); Kate Millett, *Sexual Politics* (London: Abacus, 1972); Ellen Moers, *Literary Women* (London: The Women's Press, 1978).

Works Cited

Dellasega, Mary. "Beth Henley." *Speaking on Stage: Interviews with Contemporary American Playwrights*. Eds. Philip C. Kolin and Colby H. Kullman. Tuscaloosa: University of Alabama Press, 1996. 250–259.

Early, Tony. "Preface: Letter from Sister—What We Learned at the P.O." *New Stories from the South: The Year's Best, 1999*. Ed. Shannon Ravenel. Chapel Hill, N.C.: Algonquin Books, 1999. vii–xi.

Guerra, Jonnie. "Beth Henley: Female Quest and the Family-Play Tradition." *Making a Spectacle: Feminist Essays on Contemporary Women's Theater*. Ed. Lynda Hart. Ann Arbor: University of Michigan Press, 1989. 118–130.

Klein, Alvin. "Hooray for Hollywood? More like 'Horrors!' " Review of *Signature*, Passage Theater Company, Mill Hill Playhouse, Trenton. *New York Times,* 12 May 1996, B12 (N).

Laughlin, Karen L. "Criminality, Desire, and Community: A Feminist Approach to Beth Henley's *Crimes of the Heart*." *Women and Performance: A Journal of Feminist Theory* 3, no. 1 (1986): 35–51.

Acknowledgments

This work has been a collaborative effort; many people worked hard to bring this volume together. I especially thank my diligent and punctual contributors, as well as the eagle-eyed editors at Routledge, and Kimball King. I would also like to acknowledge and thank my research assistant Anca Rizea for her good nature, her enthusiasm for literature, and her many hours in the library.

I wish to thank the Faculty Research and Creative Activity Committee at Middle Tennessee State University for providing me with a grant to complete this volume, as well as the English Department for its support and encouragement. I am indebted to Becky King for her technological brilliance and assistance in formatting and printing.

Finally, let me thank my mentor, Will Brantley, as well as my colleagues and friends, Margaret Ordoubadian and Claudia Barnett, for their encouragement and moral support. As always, I am indebted to my husband, Paul, and my son, Graham, who provide me with sanity and good humor.

1
"Dancing on the Edge of a Cliff"
Images of the Grotesque in the Plays of Beth Henley

MIRIAM M. CHIRICO

"You look as if you were dancing for your life," Torvald Helmer tells Nora while she is frantically dancing the tarantella to prevent him from discovering the incriminating letter waiting in his mail box. "I am," she replies, and while we may laugh, it is with the dark recognition that she is telling the truth, that her dance is but a small step away from the spiritual darkness that will soon envelope her. Sue Jack expresses a similar philosophy in Beth Henley's play *The Lucky Spot,* when she realizes that not only is the dance hall her husband has just invested in a financial failure but he has impregnated a young girl he won at a card game as well. "I just feel crazy and lighthearted," she explains. "Like when you're standing on the very edge of a mountain cliff and you're kicking your legs up to t'the sky" (*CPI* 246). The images of these two women—Nora and Sue Jack—dancing in the face of personal disaster combine a gesture we associate typically with happiness—dance—with the emotions of fear, anger, or revulsion, creating a perverse impression. To us spectators, the dance appears to be the wrong response to the imminent disaster; but as witnesses to the incongruity, we are led to understand an uncomfortable paradox: even as the tarantella is a dance of death, Nora's purposeful blundering of the folk dance that Torvald has taught her is a way for her to break free from her bondage to Torvald. Likewise, Sue Jack's dance, on the eve of financial and personal ruin, is exhilarating in its liberation from her husband's unreliability. Incongruous moments such as these, where a frantic dance simultaneously expresses grief, danger, or joy, arrest the viewing mind in order to present the paradox of experience.

    The intricate balance between the affirmation of life and the dangers inherent in living exists within Henley's work, and she often creates a mixture of comedy and violence. Her first play, *Crimes of the Heart,* adroitly balances suicide and attempted manslaughter with laughter and a celebratory embrace of the three sisters at the end, who blow out the candles of a birthday cake. Her plays open up a world of country fairs and funerals, of long-seated hatreds and humorous stories, of violent deaths depicted with a quirky twist. Henley mitigates the horror with a comic tone, placing her firmly in a tradition that thus far has only one other great female practitioner: Flannery O'Connor. Henley's early plays like *Crimes of the Heart*, *The Wake of Jamey Foster*, and *The Miss Firecracker Contest* are so centered on familial struggles and reconciliation that Henley is categorized as a realist playwright, focused on women's issues, rather than an experimental one. This limited understanding, however, prevents viewing Henley's plays as a cohesive whole. *The Debutante Ball*, *Signature*, or *Control Freaks* seem like aberrations that deviate wildly from Henley's early models. The vile characters, the outrageous situations, and the grotesque actions almost seem as if they have been written by another playwright. However, the elements of violence and the grotesque have been present in her plays from the very beginning, and only in recognizing these early grotesque elements can we fully trace her development as a playwright. Reading through Henley's oeuvre, one finds an artistic mind that wrestles with its own nightmarish images and forces us to confront disturbing visions. But her use of the grotesque gradually alters over time. She develops from implied or narrated images of the grotesque in the early works to dramatized human experience at its most violent, lascivious, and gluttonous.

Henley confesses to a particular delight she has in being frightened by morbid or violent images. Her favorite holiday is Halloween, and she will occasionally drip red candle wax over a glass sculpture she owns of a hand holding a knife (Bryer 116). The grotesque for her provides life with a tangible quality of realness, or that sensation of being physically present: "I like to have a big perspective on things: The reason things can be so funny is that they can be so sad; the reason they can be so beautiful is that they can be so ugly. If all there was to life was anguish, it wouldn't be so bad" (Roger 23). Here Henley points out how the mitigation of opposite experiences interests her as a playwright, how one emotion can intensify the experience of its contrary. This paradoxical aspect is specifically what Geoffrey Galt Harpham finds emblematic about the grotesque. He explains that "if the grotesque can be compared to anything, it is to paradox. Paradox is a way of turning language against itself by asserting both terms of contradiction at once." But he is quick to note that paradox, the simultaneous imagining of two opposing ideas, has a purpose other than mere wit, and that is the attempt to arrive at the truth, or even some transcendent belief that cannot be expressed in words. Paradox, because of its rebellious nature, its disrupting of logical and grammatical rules, and its refusal to be any one thing, exposes "new and unexpected realms of experience" and discovers connections and similarities that are obscured or ignored. "This sense of revelation," Harpham continues, "accompanying a sudden enrichment of our symbolic repertory accounts for our experience of depth: it is very nearly synonymous with *profound*" (20). The profound or moving feeling attained at the end of a Henley play may well be due to this paradoxical nature of the grotesque, its twisted and morbid nature, which consequently reminds us of life.

The word "grotesque" comes from the word "grotto," or small cavity in the earth. *La grottesca* was coined to describe the ornamental style which was discovered during the excavation of certain overgrown ruins of Roman villas and baths during the fifteenth century. Mythological scenes where vegetable, animal, and human elements were mixed together decorated the walls and were viewed as shocking contrasts to traditional aesthetics of art, which were modeled on classical patterns of sculpture and architecture. Vitruvius, in his architectural treatise *De architectura,* criticizes the designs as being "monstrous" rather than identifiable depictions of the realistic world, as well as not being feasible according to physical laws; the stems of flowers, he reasons, could never support a roof. Over the years, the word "grotesque" has been applied to other genres besides painting; Wolfgang Kayser's work, for example, *The Grotesque in Art and Literature,* traces exactly this progression of monstrous and inconceivable quality in literature as well as art, identifying key historical periods of the sixteenth century, Romanticism through Sturm und Drang, and the twentieth century as moments of particular fascination with grotesque representation.

In a play by Henley, the grotesque most often serves as the forgotten realm of human existence, acting either in contrast to the comic images of the play or in tandem with them. Jackson Bryer refers to Henley's work as having a combination of a "dark side and the comic side together like two halves of a split image" (117), and Henley herself admits that the "darker side of life" appeals to her: "I've always been attracted to split images. The grotesque combined with the innocent, a child walking with a cane; a kitten with a swollen head; a hunchback drinking a cup of fruit punch. Somehow these images are a metaphor for any view of life; they're colorful. . . . Southerners bring out the grisly details in any event" (Betsko and Koenig 215–216). Henley learned about the potential that this juxtaposition of contradictory emotions could hold for the theater while watching a production of *The Cherry Orchard* starring James Earl Jones. As the working-class character Lopakhin who buys the orchard where his parents have worked as serfs, Jones is both ecstatic over his purchase and devastated at his betrayal of his friends. "All through the speech he was zing, zing, zing, back and forth between despair and joy, madness and sanity, and regret and not caring," Henley relates. "I was screaming in the theater; I thought I was going to be evicted. . . . It was just absolutely a revelation about how alive life can be and how complicated and beautiful and horrible" (Bryer 117). Henley's aesthetic choice to use violence and horror in her plays against moments of beauty or kindness captures the particular kinetic quality inherent in paradox. The rapidity with which Jones can shift between the emotions of anguish and ecstasy so as to appear both, simultaneously, demonstrates a truth central to human existence.

The vacillating movement between opposing extremes of emotions, beliefs, or morals brings us closer to the truth about the human experience. Kayser details the individual reception of the grotesque, which is not mere amusement, but also disgust and fear. For as the grotesque distorts the normal proportions of the accepted world, it raises in the viewer feelings of surprise and horror, or disgust, of "an agonizing fear in the presence of a world that breaks apart and remains inaccessible" (31). Wilson Yates begins his essay "An Introduction to the Grotesque" by carefully defining the field of the grotesque in its various manifestations:

> Grotesque art can be defined as art whose form and subject matter appear to be a part of, while contradictory to, the natural, social, or personal worlds of which we are part. Its images most often embody distortions, exaggeration, a fusion of incompatible parts in such a fashion that it confronts us as strange and disordered, as a world turned upside down ... and it elicits from us paradoxical responses.
>
> The responses to the grotesque are diverse: We laugh at its comic features while sensing its dark implications; we are fascinated and attracted to its power while being threatened by it and compelled to repudiate it; we experience its denial of our canons of truth while glimpsing a truth that our canons deny us; we experience judgment that calls our conventional worlds into question while intuiting that the judgment may be prophetic; we are confronted with the demonic from which we wish to pull back while knowing that we must engage its power to maintain our well-being; we respond with alarm at its distortions and exaggerations, its fusing of organic and inorganic, human and animal aspects of reality, while gaining through those distortions insights into different ways of being and, perhaps, new possibilities for wisdom and wholeness. We experience how the grotesque distorts and ridicules the religious life while posing to us religious questions and the yearning for spiritual transformation. And beneath all of these possible responses we experience the grotesque as a power *sui generis*, an embodiment of demonic or sublime forces—forces that have a double face of darkness and light depending on where we are in the process of appropriating their meaning—while realizing that the works are nothing more than the creations of the artist's imagination. (Yates 2–3)

While Yates focuses on the sinister quality of the grotesque, its distortion of human forms, and its easy subversion of the ordered world, he also emphasizes that it is a form that both repels as well as fascinates. For no matter how much the grotesque disgusts us, we are still drawn in by the surety of its vision. The forays into the bizarre and hideous realms of human existence allow us to recognize the more clearly the nobility of the human spirit. We only understand the human by revealing its animalistic side, and we only perceive the holy through ventures into the debased. But more than that, the grotesque confuses the viewer and prompts the mind to witness the confusion that it must work through in order to attain a higher awareness.

The circumstances of a Henley play concern deformity, death, disease, and decay and often extend to frank discussions of sexuality. Oftentimes deformity or disease is read figuratively in literature as a token of spiritual emptiness. The pathetic character of Brick in Tennessee William's *Cat on a Hot Tin Roof* who shuffles around on crutches with a broken foot is understood as being impotent physically, lacking in sexual desire and spiritual will. Nancy D. Hargrove sees the physical and mental defects in Henley's characters as symbolic attributes that suggest "their moral, emotional, or spiritual imperfection" (63). Hargrove's conclusion relies upon a metaphorical reading of deformity within human beings, showing how their illnesses or depraved actions designate a broken society. She contends that "the repulsive physical and mental afflictions clearly reinforces her theme of the pain and suffering that are inescapable elements of existence as well as her theme of the moral and emotional weakness of human nature" (63). Jonnie Guerra also interprets the grotesque in these plays symbolically. She reads the physical defects as signs of women's frustrations with their circumstances or their selves. Guerra points to Babe's suicide attempts or Lenny's vomiting as indications of "the risk to women of facing up to their empty lives," and describes how the canker sores, loss of appetite and insomnia that Marshael suffers in *The Wake of Jamey Foster* are "self-punishing physical effects" coming from her own "internalized anger and anxiety" (125). Hargrove's and Guerra's readings reveal a significant dimension of Henley's use of disease and deformity; however, these understandings cannot be applied across the board. A character like Mac Sam in *The Miss Firecracker Contest*, for example, is probably the singularly most diseased individual in Henley's repertory, and yet he is the one to offer Carnelle the possibility of eternal grace. To simplify Henley's use of the grotesque as a sign of moral and emotional weakness would be to divide her plays wrongly into characters who are deficient and characters who are whole, without acknowledging that it is only by working through the grotesque that Henley's characters can find redemption or grace.

Henley's deliberate choice to use the grotesque in her plays suggests a specific critical aim toward society. As her plays move away from the early, quirky tales of female community, they become progressively darker and the use of the grotesque becomes more and more prevalent. This chapter will trace that trajectory of how she uses the grotesque in her plays, first as a means of developing character, later as a subversive tool of rebellion, and finally as a way to force the audience to confront evil.

Crimes of the Heart, the play that launched Henley's career and brought her recognition, centers its comfortable realism around moments of human mishap and deformity. The middle sister in *Crimes of the Heart*, Meg, could be the mouthpiece for Henley herself, through her practice of looking at morbid and deformed bodies when she was younger. As the sister who had the misfortune of finding their mother's dead body after she hanged herself, she developed this bizarre behavior as a means of coping with the trauma. She believed that forcing herself to look at the "rotting-away noses and eyeballs drooping off down the sides of people's faces and scabs and sores and eaten-away places" (*CPI* 35) of people's bodies would toughen her in some way and would make her less sensitive to any other horrors life might hurl in her direction. Meg mistakenly defines strength by the ability to view head-on the most gruesome or pitiful images of other human beings, without feeling any sympathy. She stares at the crippled children on posters for the March of Dimes and eats ice cream afterward, as if to indicate that she could cut herself off from feeling human sympathy for any suffering. Her curiosity for these abnormalities of the human form resembles in some ways the anatomical theater during the Renaissance, where scientists would dissect and examine the human form in front of a large group of learned spectators, carefully tearing apart the tendons, displaying bones, or even occasionally parading a living misfit across the room (Kuryluk 28–29). However, while they studied the human form and came to grips with their own mortality, Meg seems determined to inure herself to the personal afflictions in life, strangling her own innate emotional response in the process.

In this early play, Henley incorporates the grotesque as a device for developing a character's storyline. Lisa McDonnell speaks precisely about this use of the grotesque—or what she calls "macabre humor"—as a dramatist's tool that allows Henley to delineate her characters' traits and to advance the plot. She refers specifically to Meg's callous abandonment of her boyfriend, Doc, who risked his own life to stay with her during a hurricane while others evacuated. She writes, "The story [that Meg relates to Doc about being institutionalized in the L. A. County Hospital] makes an important point about Meg's childhood trauma, revealing clearly her loss and the reason for her unwillingness to get close to another human being (Doc Porter). It shows her in the process of developing the gallantry that we admire later in the play at the same time that we see her trying to erect barriers between herself and the suffering of the world" (McDonell 97). Henley has created a character who focuses on the grotesque as a means of separating herself from any emotional connection with the world. Here the grotesque serves as a central motif for the plot.

The play's main incident—Babe's shooting her husband because "she didn't like his looks" (*CPI* 17)—also uses the grotesque to define character and develop, or rather, initiate the plot:

> And there he was; lying on the rug. He was looking up at me trying to speak words. I said, "What? . . . Lemonade? . . . You don't want it? Would you like a Coke instead?" Then I got the idea, he was telling me to call on the phone for medical help. So I got on the phone and called up the hospital. I gave my name and address and I told them my husband was shot and he was lying on the rug and there was plenty of blood. (*CPI* 31)

Babe's shooting her husband is more than momentary insanity; she understands that she needs to defend the black youth with whom she is having an affair. It is the complete discrepancy, however, between the image of her husband lying on the floor in a pool of his own blood and her insistence on acting like a hostess that is the grotesque. Henley juxtaposes the grotesquerie of violence with the macabre humor of offering him a glass of freshly squeezed lemonade after she has shot him. Billy J. Harbin sees the gesture of making lemonade as one "to anesthetize the painful reality of her act," as a way of detaching herself from the awful realness of the event. Her gracious offer to her husband ("Zackery, I've made some lemonade. Can you use a glass?") as he lies shot on the floor, seems "grotesquely inappropriate" for the situation and is an indication of the kind of mental anguish Babe must be suffering (Harbin 86). Joanne B. Karpinski sees this "beau geste turned grotesque" as more than a commentary on Babe's mental state; rather, her offer of lemonade acts as a comic device that highlights the difference between what the audience anticipates Babe will do and how she actually responds (235). One typically expects the wife to correct the situation, apologize, and denounce her own actions as hysterical. But in this case, her grotesque reaction freezes the play, forcing the audience to reconsider the situation. The grotesque as distancing device is a possibility Karen L. Laughlin offers in her reading of this scene, arguing that Babe's erratic response reverses female stereotypes. It is typically assumed that men who commit crimes are classified as "criminals" while women are classified as "sick" because of traditionally held beliefs that women who deviate from expected patterns of passivity and domesticity must be "sick" (Laughlin 43). However, Babe's gesture combines both activity and domesticity; she takes control over her relationship with her husband (who, we later discover, has been beating her) and simultaneously reverts into gentle subservience through her offer of a drink—or at least a mockery thereof. The grotesque in this scene challenges the audience with a paradox—that shooting a husband might not be about feminist hatred, nor about a wife being crazy.

In another early play, *The Miss Firecracker Contest*, Henley's fascination with things grotesque and gruesome lies in odd contradistinction to the play's central topic, the beauty contest. Incorporating the grotesque in a story that defines beauty is a feat which is typically Henley. In the very first scene, Carnelle rattles off a list of relatives who have died from hideous deaths in order to impress her new friend, Popeye. Her Aunt Ronnelle, for example, died from cancer of the pituitary gland, even though the doctors tried to keep her alive by transplanting within her the pituitary glands of a monkey. Carnelle revels in telling Popeye the bizarre side effects: "she started growing long, black hairs all over her body just, well, just like an ape" (*CPI* 151). Not satisfied with this story, however, she proceeds with a litany of all the people who have died throughout her life, from her mother to her father who suffered a fatal heart attack running after the Tropical Ice Cream truck. Her Uncle George died from falling off the roof while trying to remove a bird's nest from the chimney. Like Meg in *Crimes of the Heart*, Carnelle has been deeply affected early in her development by the various deaths of her family members, particularly her parents. She is as intrigued by the nature of death ("It seems that people've been dying practically all my life" [152]) as one would be of the latest fashion or with local politics. Her cavalier attitude in relating the stories is designed to shock Popeye, but it also reveals how stoically she negates the pain of losing these close family members. Her morbid intrigue in the haphazard circumstances that push one over the fine line between life and death quickly disappears in light of the upcoming preparations for the Miss Firecracker contest, but it stands as a curious preamble to the rest of the play. Nor is she the only one affected by grotesque images; her older cousin Delmont suffers from nightmares of dismembered women's bodies. Henley establishes a story of a character who is so plagued by stories of death that she searches for solace and self-identity in a beauty pageant; during the course of the play, Henley inverts the equation, revealing superficial beauty as nihilistic and the grotesque as beautiful. She does this reversal through three characters: Popeye, Mac Sam, and Elain.

The central motif of the beauty contest weighs over this play, and it would be unwise to ignore its importance, even though the actual contest occurs off-stage. The emphasis on physical beauty, the way society values women as objects of beauty, and the devalued sense of self that results are all problems inherent in the beauty contest. Carnelle, who has been termed "Miss Hot Tamale" by the men in town because of her sexual promiscuity, believes that she can change the town's view of her by winning the contest, not realizing that earning the name "Miss Firecracker" still allows the town to determine her self-worth. What she fails to realize is that she is caught in a society that defines and describes women by arbitrary rubrics, and that Carnelle has to learn to define herself. It is not by accident that her older cousin, Delmont, dreams of the chopped up bodies of women; he unconsciously perceives how society has harmed women psychologically by fragmenting their own images of themselves. The very practice of participating in a beauty contest prompts women to harm themselves physically through dieting, hair removal, or by altering their figures in some way. Henley comically reminds us of this fact through the story of one woman who became "hump shouldered from practicing that one Johann Sebastian Bach opus on [the] piano all day long" (*CPI* 176) in order to win the talent part of the beauty contest. The beauty contest, unlike its name, is harmful and disfiguring to women, and while winning the beauty contest is Carnelle's objective, the grotesque characters ultimately show her the danger in this damaging pursuit.

The physical manifestation of the grotesque on stage is represented by two characters in particular: Popeye and Mac Sam. Popeye's brother threw gravel at her eyes when she was younger, then mistakenly gave her ear drops instead of eye drops to flush out the gravel, making her eyes pop out of her head from the burning sensation it caused. From these plausible but far-fetched details, the story then leaps to the ludicrous: her popped-out eyes not only earned her the name "Popeye" but they also allow her to hear "voices." Rather than be embarrassed by this deformity, she revels in her spiritualistic skill, occasionally pausing to hear what the voices in her eyes have to say. Nor is Popeye the only character Carnelle knows who sustains a physical deformity. Mac Sam, a previous lover of Carnelle's, is plagued by so many different diseases that his body is literally disintegrating. He suffers from tuberculosis, alcoholism, and syphilis; he coughs up clots of blood and is painfully thin and stooped shoulder; yet, he still manages to be "extraordinarily sensual" with eyes that are "magnetic" even while bloodshot (*CPI* 175). When Carnelle expresses concern over his health, Mac Sam tosses off her worries, insisting that he enjoys "taking bets on which part of [him will] decay first: the liver, the lungs, the stomach, or the brain" (68). Thus two characters who are misfigured, but oblivious to any limitation this might impose, befriend Carnelle. Not only are they oblivious, but they manage to transform their oddities into a source of attraction or of intrigue; Popeye's eyes provide her access to a supersensory realm, while Mac Sam's decaying body serves him as a gambling arena. Rather than the hardened, selfish, emotionally withdrawn behavior we expect from characters who have been harmed by life circumstances, Mac Sam and Popeye are the two most generous and hopeful characters in the play. These characters, who are comfortable with the grotesqueries of their own bodies, are ultimately the ones to guide Carnelle's growth and transformation.

Carnelle desperately wants to win the Miss Firecracker contest because her cousin Elain, whom she worships, won the contest years ago, and Carnelle believes the title will be her ticket to the respect and admiration Elain receives from the town. Elain delivers a speech at the contest detailing what her "Life as a Beauty" (*CPI* 180) has meant to her, but she never admits that winning the contest has only led to emptiness and meaninglessness in life. She has relied upon her beauty to define her self-worth, and has taken to heart the message her mother gave her years ago—"You've had your spoonful of gravy now go out and get a rich husband" (167)—as the only possibility for self-actualization. She has allowed beauty to limit her potential in life to being a married wife with clocks and face creams. Her inability to develop into an independent woman because of a self-image linked to beauty is most clearly seen in comparison to the characters who fall short of—or rather escape from—society's definition of beauty.

The grotesque characters serve as contrasting figures to Elain in two ways. First, the grotesque focuses foremost on the physical deformities of the body. In this play, both Popeye and Mac Sam have been able to move beyond the constrained practices of physical perfection as the only means of attaining happiness in life. Popeye dreams of moving to the Elysian Fields, an indication that her pursuits in life, while whimsical, are not limited by what society deems possible. She gets fired from her position as a store clerk when she gives away a mirror to a small child in order that she might always know what color her eyes are. Believing that the eyes are the mirror to one's soul, Popeye willingly breaks society's rules so that she might aid someone else's spiritual growth. Likewise, Mac Sam does not allow the fact that he is ill and physically undesirable to prevent him from getting drunk and having sex impulsively; rather, he prefers to take a chance with his body and with relationships with others, "a free roll a' the eternal dice" (*CPI* 178), and he enthusiastically pursues the abundance life has to offer.

Second, and perhaps more profoundly, these characters offer Carnelle a spiritual path, which is also typical of the grotesque. Much has been written on the uses of the grotesque for explaining complex theological issues such as the creation of the universe or the transformation of bread and wine into the spiritual body of Christ. John W. Cooks, in his essay "Ugly Beauty in Christian Art" describes three particular works that are grotesquely ugly in service of such sophisticated thought. The *Roettgen Pieta* (ca. 1370, artist unknown) offers one such ugly presentation of the moment when the Virgin Mary contemplates the dead body of her son in her lap, by realistically rendering Christ's emaciated body and bloody wounds. The consecrated bread of the Eucharist was placed in the elongated hole in Christ's side during Good Friday services, enabling worshippers to comprehend the intangible relationship between Christ's anguish and the sacrament of new life. The combination of the Eucharist and the masterful representation of the physical torture Christ suffered "fulfills the medieval interest in concentrating privately on the evidence of his sacrifice" (132). Kayser explains how the contemplation of the crucified body of Christ pulls the practitioners into an awareness of the horror of the crucifixion while simultaneously enabling them to understand the sacrifice Christ made for humankind's sins.

The physical grotesqueness of the characters Popeye and Mac Sam operate similarly in Carnelle's life. Their presence helps Carnelle to let go of her disappointment about losing the Miss Firecracker contest and to move toward a more spiritual recognition of existence. Mac Sam admits that there is not too much worth living for in life, but he does tell her that there's always "eternal grace" (*CPI* 202), which seems to satisfy Carnelle. Carnelle contemplates herself in a mirror at the end of the play, not so much to ensure her own beauty but to verify her true self. Echoing Popeye's gesture of using a mirror to remember one's true colors, Carnelle looks at her dyed, red hair in the mirror and says, "It used to be brown. I had brown hair. Brown" (203), and in this way she returns to her true self. Popeye also ultimately cures Delmont of his nightmares when the two of them fall in love. His search for a woman possessing traits of "classical beauty" leads him to Popeye, whose beauty comes from within. Thus, the two grotesque characters in the play turn out to be the most psychologically centered and they move Carnelle away from her quest for a public-centered beauty to her quest for beauty within herself.

The Wake of Jamey Foster, another family-centered drama, no longer relegates death offstage, but places it front stage and center in the shape of an open casket. Jamey Foster, the character who lends his name to the play, has recently died and his family members reunite at the house to pay their respects, voice their worries about life, and vent their deep-seated anger at one another. Each of the women in the play has a lot to be angry about. Marshael Foster, while grieving her husband's loss, hates him for having an affair with a twenty-two-year-old woman and abandoning her. "[He] filed for divorce not two weeks ago," Marshael explains, "Now he pulls this little stunt. . . . As you can see, I've got mixed emotions about the entire event" (*CPI* 103–4). Collard, Marshael's sister, estranged from the family by her lascivious and racy lifestyle, regrets the status of her "black, black soul" (103). Marshael's officious but childish sister-in-law, Katty, suffers insensitive comments from a husband who belittles her. And the stray orphan, Pixrose, who has lost her parents in two fire-related accidents, has recently escaped from a third fire at the orphanage where she lived. But the play focuses primarily on Marshael's inability to grieve for a husband who has deeply harmed her. A would-be historian whose dreams of being published exceeded his academic abilities, he jealously attacked Marshael's ability to support the family financially and ultimately pursued a relationship with another woman. The contradictory sentiments of love and hate Marshael experiences are suggested in the opening scene where she bites the ears off of her chocolate Easter rabbits. The gesture, both childish and vicious, of masticating the chocolate animal's ears summarizes Marshael's present emotional state—her spiteful desires harbored underneath a gentle exterior. As with her previous plays, Henley does not invite us into a pristine, sugar-coated world of genteel southern living, but one of pent-up hatred and self-loathing. The grotesque gestures in this play—from exploding hogs to brain damaged relatives to random nose bleeds—become a means to make manifest the violence that often underlies genteel facades. More specifically, the grotesque allows the female characters, who have been harmed for the most part by men, to come to an understanding of their own capacity to do harm.

The sight of the open coffin encasing Jamey Foster dominates the second half of the play, reminding us that death is a prevalent factor in all of our lives; yet, this message comes with a sardonic twist. The corpse wears a ridiculous bright orange-and-yellow plaid jacket, casting it as an object of derision. The characters' reactions to the corpse likewise decry the seriousness of death. At one point Collard examines the corpse and comments on how much weight he has put on, then suddenly drops a piece of ham into the open coffin. A friend of the family, Brocker, takes a photograph of the dead body and does not hesitate to say the customary "Smile!" before snapping the shutter (*CPI* 132). Even the cause of Jamey Foster's death is not without a certain lack of respect: he received a concussion from being hit in the head by a cow one night while on a pastoral tryst, and he died shortly thereafter.

Pixrose, as the girlfriend of Marshael's brother, Leon, introduces the note of the grotesque into the play. In a speech that sounds remarkably similar to Carnelle's matter-of-fact recitation of deaths, Pixrose relates how she became an orphan:

> Well it started out my mama hating the house we lived in. She used t'say it was trashy. She'd sit around in the dark holding lit matches—always threatening to burn this trashy house down—and one day she did it. She lit up the dining room curtains, loosing flames over the entire house and charcoaling herself to death as a final result. (*CPI* 100)

Her grotesquely comic tale points to the notion of female dissatisfaction and the self-destructive horrors that result. The overly theatrical gesture of a woman threatening to burn down the house and lighting matches is manically humorous and may hide the fact that Pixrose describes a self-injurious woman who was vastly unhappy with her life. Pixrose's phrase "charcoaling herself to death" is no less astute for its humor because it points out her mother's responsibility in her own demise. Freud, in *Jokes and Their Relation to the Unconscious*, explains how certain jokes appeal to the ambivalent nature we feel about self-destructive behavior, such as nail-biting, tanning, or smoking cigarettes, but how it is human nature to persist in these activities regardless. Pixrose's flippancy in telling her story echoes society's own unwillingness to question the motivation behind female self-destructive behavior—a process that might have helped Pixrose's mother. This motif of a woman killing herself due to deep-seated anger in her life, while comic in its delivery, becomes the premise upon which the play operates: how do these four women, who have suffered humiliation and pain in their lives, resolve to survive rather than allow their rage to turn into behavior that ultimately destroys them?

The women choose to survive in *The Wake of Jamey Foster* because they acknowledge the grotesque side of themselves and, in so doing, are liberated. A long conversation occurs in Act II in which each woman confesses to the others the worst things that she has ever done. They first share with each other a moment when they have been intensely hurt as a means of coaxing Katty out of the bathroom after her husband, Wayne, humiliates her. She locks herself in the upstairs bathroom and only comes out when the other women reassure her that they, too, have at one time or another been disgraced. After she appears, their stories change direction and, instead, reveal how they have harmed others. Collard explains the rules: "This is supposed to be a story about the cruelest thing *you've* ever done, not that's been *done to you!*" (*CPI* 129). As the stories progress, the women understand themselves as capable of committing violence and cruelty; they perceive that they are not the innocent victims they initially assume themselves to be. When Katty narrates her act of vengeance she receives immeasurable pleasure; she pulls at "her hair with glee" (128), expresses great delight in the telling of the tale, and is rewarded by Collard saying, "Great! Katty, that's rotten. That is really rotten!" (129). Katty worries that the others "won't think [her] sweet anymore," but Collard and Pixrose both refute this vociferously, chanting "We don't care" (184). Their encouragement for one another's evil actions permits Katty to let go of what Alan Clarke Shepard describes as the "conventional commitment to sentimentality imposed upon women by the male characters" (184); Katty is freed from her understood role as a "sweet" southern woman. Collard has no aspirations toward sweetness; she has slept with married men as well as priests, has stolen merchandise, and has cheated at cards. And Marshael tells the others that she refused to help her husband when he was paralyzed, curtly telling him to "hobble home" from the hospital if he wanted some of his papers at the house (129).

The harm that has been done to them colors their identities as women. Katty has just been humiliated by her husband because of his sexual advances toward Collard. She attributes his cruelty to her inability to have children and says, "If only I could have the baby it would give me someone to love and make someone who'd love me" (*CPI* 131). Her ability to acknowledge her own sense of cruelty restores some sense of her pride, but what is peculiar about her story is that it is oddly linked to babies, in the guise of small chicks. Once, when she was younger and some children had shoved her down a mudhole while dressed in her Easter finery, she took vengeance upon them by pulling the heads off of their pet chicks with her bare hands. Collard, too, mentions chickens in the context of the cruelty she has committed—her abortion. After she had the procedure, she went out and ate a ten-piece bucket of fried chicken which she promptly threw up: "First it tasted good and greasy and gooey. Then I felt like I was eating my baby's skin and flesh and veins and all" (131). Alan Clarke Shepard demonstrates how the fowl imagery links to the miscarried babies and aborted fetuses, suggesting that Henley shows us "the cost of women's liberation in graphic images of animal dismemberment" (187). But one of the key elements of grotesque art is the metaphoric association of people with animals. Ewa Kuryluk discusses Hieroynmous Bosch (c. 1450–1516) and Arcimboldo (1527–93) as two painters who create bizarre juxtapositions with the human form; Bosch dissects the human body only to reassemble it with various animals parts attached, while Arcimboldo depicted the seasons as human heads comprised of the vegetables harvested and the animals hunted during that season (Kuryluk 66–73). This perversion of images is actually a form of metaphorical thinking, of layering two images to create one idea. With Collard, her ability to reject her fetus twice—first through the abortion, then by vomiting up the fried chicken—allowed her "to preserve her nascent claim to self-determination" (Shepard 187). Katty's story of killing baby chicks with her bare hands reminds her that her identity is not only tied to her ability to create but to destroy as well. Women often conceive of their identity in terms of maternity, not feeling that they are fulfilled as women if they have not had children. Katty's witnessing that she could kill babies is a refusal to be defined only through her maternal side. In both cases, the narrating of grotesque incidents serves as a liberating function for these women.

Finally, it is Pixrose's assessment of why humans do cruel things that highlights the scene's meaningfulness. Referring to a childhood memory after her house burned down, she tells the others how she put bandages and slings on some of her dolls, even blinding a few of them, and kept them in the cellar where she could control them. "See, just 'cause I was scarred, I wanted them to be too," (*CPI* 129) she explains. Pixrose recognizes that the violent actions the women have each committed comes from feeling hurt or shamed by someone else, and that they, as women, are just as capable of directing that destructive behavior outward as they are at harming themselves.

This conversation is a classic example in southern literature of "priming the pump," of how the candid and honest remarks of one woman's story legitimizes the next woman's revelations of her cruel deeds. Jonnie Guerra explains how this process enables each woman to admit to secrets each has always hidden away due to embarrassment, and how this acceptance and understanding among peers allows each woman to gain a "new sense of self-worth" (124). Yet the connection between telling grotesque tales and the women's renewed sense of esteem deserves to be examined. Cruelty and violence are intrinsic to the human condition. For these women to shift in their storytelling from the cruelty that was done to them to what they did to others is significant because their awareness of the violence within them forces them to acknowledge their own capacity to inflict harm upon others. Recognizing their own grotesque actions shows them that they are not mere victims but have the capacity to harm as well. Ulu Grosbard, who directed the premiere of the play, sees this theme of surviving life's obstacles as central to the play's power: "Henley's vision is not conventional," he says. "Her characters admit to suffering humiliations but also inflicting them. That's far more positive than to pretend that people are only good" (Shewey 37). Katty seems to agree: "... life is so full of unknown horror" (*CPI* 92), she says in the opening scene, anticipating how an accident might prevent Collard from making it to the funeral. But by the time the play is over, one learns that the unknown horror may just as easily come from within.

After such down-to-earth plays as *Crimes of the Heart, The Miss Firecracker Contest,* or *The Wake of Jamey Foster*, with recognizable situations and easily identifiable characters, Henley's later plays come as a shock. The events become wilder, the characters more foreign, and the behavior more extreme. Michael Billington signals this shift from the earlier plays to the later ones by emphasizing the characters' attitudes toward the grotesque: "But where in the past Ms. Henley's characters greeted the grotesque as if it were the everyday," he explains in his review for *The Debutante Ball*, "here they seem to revel in their own eccentricity" (701). The significant difference in Billington's eyes from the earlier plays to *The Debutante Ball* is the role the grotesque plays.[1] The grotesque has moved from the periphery of the characters' lives to the main stage. No longer do characters make minor trespasses into the realm of the bizarre—such as Carnelle's stories of how her relatives died—but rather they embrace the grotesque as the dominant pattern of the play. The trouble in bringing to the forefront the grotesque in these later plays is that there is no longer any way to define the grotesque because there are no stabilizing values by which to judge deviations from normalcy. The uncertainty of a moral compass to direct the viewer's response in these later plays may make it difficult to achieve a successful performance or successful critical response, but it also shows Henley confronting head-on the depravity and malignancy of human nature.

In fact, Henley herself acknowledges the risk she takes moving in this direction as a playwright. Her next play, *The Debutante Ball*, uses the grotesque to dismantle the norms of southern traditional society, such as codified gender roles and specific social rites for courtship and marriage. The debutante ball—like the earlier beauty contest—is a public forum where women are transformed into objects of visual pleasure. It is the quintessential symbol of southern patriarchy, because it is the symbolic moment when the family displays their daughters as wares for the purchase of some male suitor. Henley attacks these known practices and conventions of upper-class, southern society by presenting the antiworld of the Parker family home. Against these established cultural norms of the aristocratic South, the family's behavior is seen as freakish or grotesque. But, as Henley admits in the preface to the play, the distasteful events that make up the very fabric of the play were meant to offend the sensibility of the audience members:

> The consensus was *The Wake [of Jamey Foster]* was indulgent, excessive, even grotesque. I remember wondering what kind of life this new play—which had an onstage miscarriage as its climax and a fifty-two-year-old nude woman covered with psoriasis (sitting in a bathtub) as its final image—would have. I finished *The Debutante Ball* in the late spring of 1984 and gave it to my theatrical agent, Gilbert Parker. Gilbert was supportive but concerned: "Do you have to have the bathroom onstage? Do we have to see the ladies shaving under their arms?" I assured him that, yes, this was a play about facades and secrets and suppressions and longings and that I wanted my characters to be seen as animals fighting to pluck and spray and shave away their true natures—adorning themselves with lies. . . . Gilbert said that the deaf character I'd written was an illiterate lesbian who behaved like a fool and that certainly in the "underpants" scene I'd gone too far. (Henley, "Preface" xi–xii)

The Parker family has carefully constructed a façade in order to be readmitted into society, but their hidden desires and past crimes continually bubble to the surface and disrupt their cool exterior. The grotesque actions and events are the physical manifestations of these secrets. Whereas in *The Miss Firecracker Contest* the physically grotesque characters were emblems of spirituality, in *The Debutante Ball* the grotesque events *are* the reality that threatens idealized notions of beauty. As Henley explains, "The essence of it all is these people trying to look beautiful for this ball, but they're like animals and they're going in and having to pluck out hairs and shave their legs. These people have so many scars, and are trying to be so beautiful, and have so many secrets. It's about secrets as well" (Bryer 117). In other words, the play is about the actuality of the female body in everyday life, a reality that women attempt to hide in order to turn themselves into objects of visual gratification. The damage from tearing away at one's true self and "adorning" oneself with lies is the loss of identity.

Women's bodies have been historically construed as grotesque, in comparison to their male counterparts. Female functions such as menstruation or childbirth have typically been viewed as messy or repugnant and the list of rules in Leviticus instructing menstruating women to remain apart from the tribe is one reminder of this age-old horror of the female body. Likewise, fear of female sexuality prompted the creation of such figures as the female vampire or the vagina with teeth. Kuryluk draws connections between the site where the grotesque first appeared and these popular associations with the female form: "These features of the subterranean [protection and imprisonment] correspond to the perception of woman as one who, carrying the embryo, nurtures as well as imprisons it. Birth liberates the baby from the body of the mother; but when a child does not emerge in time, it dies inside" (20). However, Henley is not continuing to criticize women by joining this tradition of "the female as grotesque." Rather, she examines the extremes that women must go to in order to prevent the public label of their bodies as unseemly.

The plot of *The Debutante Ball* centers around a mother's attempt to reenter society by having her daughter "come out" in the conventional, approved setting of a debutante ball. The mother, Jen Dugan Parker Turner, has been accused of, and tried for, murdering her husband, so that when she is released from jail, she has trouble being accepted back into society. She has remarried a wealthy, naive man who has built her an ostentatious house and she wants the corresponding social connections with this new fortune. Her daughter, Teddy Parker, who in actuality is the murderer, wants nothing to do with her mother's aspiration. She spends the entire play trying to foil her mother's plans for the ball, including engaging in such erratic behavior as wearing socks over her hands, stabbing at her face with tweezers, and gashing at her face with a cheese knife. Jen's first daughter, Bliss, desperately wants to be a debutante, too, and jealously watches as Jen lavishes attention on Teddy. During the course of the play, Bliss rebels in her own fashion, by falling in love with Jen's deaf niece, Frances, who arrives in hopes of finding a husband at the ball.

The play juxtaposes the superficial beauty and hypocritical behavior of southern society with the violence and greed that lurks below this surface. Several critics note how the play's lavishly decorated, marble-encrusted set does not prevent the audience from focusing on the bathroom. The taffeta ball gowns, hairpieces, and makeup cannot hamper us from recognizing the women as they really are: vindictive and hurtful. Teddy, the play's debutante, refuses to be turned into a beauty; in addition to disfiguring her face, she demolishes the ritual of the debutante showcase curtsey by wearing two feet of toilet paper stuck to her heel. She crawls under the dining room tables, smearing cream cheese on the guests' shoes, while her hairpiece ends up floating in the punch bowl. She overturns the process of a coming out ball, disrupts the social order of southern gentility, and saves herself in the process. Likewise her older sister, Bliss, shows a behind-the-scenes, uncensored look at southern women when she takes her underpants off, throws them over the balcony, and relieves herself on stage.

The sight of Bliss urinating is a shock for the audience and becomes Bliss's first gesture of rebellion. The surprise comes from the vision of a peaches-and-cream southerner rushing to the toilet, flipping up her dress, and plunking her posterior on the commode. People, and women in particular, are conditioned to show only that part of themselves that corresponds to society's vision of them. This seemingly distasteful scene exposes the audience to the functions of the body and demonstrates how women hide their dirtier sides from the public. Women often conceal from others their wicked desires for money or sex, but, in so doing, they inadvertently obscure these desires from themselves, preventing any self-knowledge. Bliss's gesture of peeing onstage and of choosing to talk about her bladder (another forbidden female topic) is a movement toward seeing herself as she is. While peeing or shaving one's armpits onstage may not, admittedly, be socially acceptable, what Henley shows in this play is that the constant suppression of women's behavior conditions them to believe that their biological functions are inappropriate, and, in turn, that their natural desires for money or sex are unwomanly. Thus, as they continually hide their behavior and desires from the public, they ultimately deny it to themselves, preventing any self-growth.

Henley uses the shock value of the grotesque in this play to disturb and appall the audiences; nothing short of visceral shock will enable the audience to see how women suppress their behavior. Paul Taylor notes the play's ability to disgust: "the play, whose comedy comes in periodic convulsions of inspired bad taste, has enough off-putting physicality to make you wonder briefly. Well, when was the last time you saw a drama in which a graphically puke-plastered fur-cape was dunked into a bathroom basin?" (700). Henley's play vacillates between the gossamer facade of fur coats and silk dresses and the Rabelaisian world of bodily functions such as shaving, vomiting, urinating—and yes—even miscarrying. This anarchic assault on the audience's sensibilities is designed to show not just the falsity of social decorum, but the grave harm done to the female psyche. Henley admits that it was the hardest play for her to write because of the anger she experienced while writing it: "I was dealing with a very real rage inside myself and looking at what the consequences are of actually acting on that rage. I was also looking at how we try to cover up that feeling; the secrets we all try to live behind" (Henley, "Beth Henley: Playwright" 31). Teddy's rage manifests itself in various self-destructive maneuvers, not least of all her cutting of her face. She has a sexual foray with a disfigured amputee whom she meets on an elevator because she feels sorry for him, but sexual intercourse with a man who physically repulses her is more than likely a way of punishing herself—particularly when she becomes pregnant.

Like any documentary exposing the horrors behind the modeling industry or fashion shows, *The Debutante Ball* provides a behind-the-scenes look at how women mutilate their bodies and their selves in order to fit a prescribed definition of southern gentility and beauty. But Henley also uses this beautiful façade/grotesque reality dichotomy to demonstrate the internal harm that is done to women who embrace this role-playing. She illustrates the popular images of southern women as docile, virtuous, and sweet, and then she undercuts this image by revealing their true feelings of resentment, bitterness, and jealousy that they struggle to curtail. This struggle between outwardly acting as paragons of virtue while inwardly seething leads to destructive self-harm. Teddy's cutting at her face while looking at herself in the mirror suggests not only defiance of the debutante ball, but also represents her hatred toward herself for the murder of her father—a murder that she has not been allowed to admit. Because she has not been able to confess her capacity to kill but instead must masquerade as a pure and delicate flower of youth, she masochistically harms herself. Likewise, the final image of Teddy's mother sitting in the tub of water with her body covered by psoriasis shows her not only stripped of her artifice; it also shows her body rebelling against her. Like poisonous elements, her pettiness, social climbing, and internal bitterness seep out of her soul, to mar the surface of her body. This final glimpse of Jen Parker is a harsh one that may alienate audiences, but it is one that Henley sees as necessary. She wields the grotesque views of women in this play to bludgeon the totalizing belief system of southern gentility and beauty created by society's false ideals of women.

For the grotesque is not some element that exists outside of civilized society like a sideshow at a carnival; neither can the grotesque be relegated to specific moments in time such as Halloween. The grotesque is a force that coexists with human existence. Wilson Yates describes the grotesque as that which does not fit into our daily lives but is present nonetheless as a kind of subconscious, demonic force:

> But whatever we identify as the underlying subject of the grotesque, it will inevitably be about some aspect of life that does not fit, that conflicts with the world as defined by our cultural norms, decorum, and values, by our acceptable ways of being. It will be about that which violates some aspect of the religious, moral, social, or natural world we have constructed and legitimated. In our denial of these aspects of reality, we have relegated them to the edge of our common experience, even though they are about something related to the core of our experience. We have banished the grotesque to the underground of our consciousness, though it remains related to our conscious world. (41)

Henley, through the development of her plays, moves the grotesque from the periphery of her character's lives and places it in direct conflict with her characters. No longer do her characters merely tell tales of sickness and death; they embody the grotesque on-stage through their actions. In this way, her later plays—while seemingly more experimental—may actually be more true to the full range of the human experience by bearing witness to those chaotic and primitive forces in ourselves and in the world that we rarely acknowledge, but that exist in spite of our ignorance. For in *Signature* and *Control Freaks*, plays written later, the characters are less aware of the distortions and irregularities in their lives than the audience is because the grotesque has become the very fabric of their world. Now it is the audience members who must carry the normalizing standards of behavior by which to judge the characters' actions as freakish or bizarre. Consequently, the experience of watching these plays prompts a personal revelation within the viewer, rather than the character, about the grotesque. These plays are less about a character's transformation than the audience's encountering the grotesque through the dramatic form. "If the grotesque image is monstrous or horrifying," Yates explains, "we know that horror and its meaning in the moment of participation" (44). Henley invites the audience to participate in the grotesque.

Furthermore, what Yates also makes clear is that the grotesque operates on two levels: formally, by its means of representation, and symbolically, by the content that it represents. "In effect, it *literally* reveals in its formal imagining of composition and subject matter, in its exaggerated, comical, frightening, often inexplicable presentation, the reality of grotesqueness" (41). The grotesque forms and images that Henley chooses to dramatize point to the dark realms of human experience or the human psyche. Her choice of form reflects the content. Up until now, Henley has written plays in which the characters confess to these dark drives; she has allowed the content of the grotesque to speak. But with *Signature* and *Control Freaks* (and to a certain extent *Debutante Ball*), which are stylistically different from her naturalistic plays, she uses the grotesque as both content and form. Unlike the familiar characters such as Meg or Carnelle whose worlds readily resemble our own, these later characters lead us into an alien world of deformed beliefs and violent behaviors that we are forced to acknowledge and accept as our own. Both *Control Freaks* and *Signature* rely upon images that violate the audience's sensibilities. They portray the human form, in the words of Wilson Yates, as a "monstrous caricature" of itself and the characters behave in ways that are vicious and "foreign to our world of self-perception" (45). What is crucial about this direct portrayal of the grotesque is that it engages the audience; the vile natures of the characters are made manifest to us viscerally through the provocative images. We are not resorting to a character's description of someone's cruelty or nastiness; we are witnessing it firsthand. We are not hearing about evil, we are experiencing it through performance.

Signature depicts the future. In Henley's own words, it offers a "strange, chaotically horrifying, deathly beautiful, sadly silly world" (*CPII* 58). The energy of the play comes from the grotesque's extravagant, explosive, and frenzied character, qualities which Geoffrey Galt Harpham attributes to the internal struggle of the grotesque's disparate parts (8). No longer set in small-town locales such as Hazlehurst, Mississippi (*Crimes of the Heart),* Henley's next play takes place in the jet-set haven of Los Angeles, in the year 2052. The characters are not the marginal wallflowers of the old-moneyed South;

rather they represent the hippest-of-the-hip in the social strata, ricocheting off the latest fads, languages, and clothing like pinballs in a material world. The three central characters, Boswell, an artist-philosopher, Maxwell, his brother, and L-Tip, his brother's ex-wife, are interested only in furthering their own mercenary goals by stomping on the souls of others. Their desires and behavior are suffused with the grotesque and this futuristic setting warns the audience that human nature will progressively become more greedy and self-centered the more fads and media attention preclude human relationships. It is a brave new world with all the current turn-of-the century problems exaggerated: homelessness, environmental waste, HIV, and air pollution exist alongside romanticized versions of suicide complete with talk-show airtime. People are estranged from the very experiences of living; unable to gaze upon the night sky, they instead marvel at the stars through a video monitor. Instead of dying quietly, they receive publicity in the up-and-coming obits. And even in a technologically advanced society, homeless waifs are only partially cared for; they receive government-issued food boxes, but they must eat them out on the streets.

Boswell T-Thorp, the main character, is a has-been conceptual artist; he developed an artistic theory know as Boxdom, which permeated the pop-cultural scene years ago, but his popularity is on the wane. His live-in tenant, a woman by the name of William, shows him profound love, but he disparages her because she is not of the right class. L-Tip acts as his manager, successfully manipulating his previous fame to gain her a larger clientele. She dumps him as soon as she attains success with other personalities, as she dumps his brother, Maxwell, by divorcing him. Maxwell spends half the play groveling after her; he writes love poems for her which are eventually published, transforming him from the impoverished wretch living on the streets, to a well-dressed poet of some renown. He runs into his ex-wife at a point when she is destitute—having been fired and unable to find work—and gives her a hand up; she later turns on him. This play perverts the Horatio Alger tale, fraught as it is with rags-to-riches and back-to-rags scenarios that depend not upon hard work but on taking advantage of another person in order to achieve wealth and success—however fleeting.

Henley revels in depicting Hollywood's depraved morality, from the desire to claw one's way to the top to the emotion-numbing drugs to the obliviousness of the soul. Boswell recognizes the inauthenticity in the lives around him, but he still insists on the value of notoriety: "I should have consorted with celebrity swine," he bemoans, "I should have been a grinning, glad-handing salt lick for the press." Celebrities behave as if the camera were ever-present: they manufacture joy because "Up is in," and they even go so far as to have their faces surgically fixed into a permanent smile (*CPII* 64). L-Tip deadens the experience of living with "emotional equilizers, soul-sedatives, and pain executioners" (88). But the pain of repressing one's human emotions comes at a price: lack of self-knowledge. "Of course, I'm terrifically unhappy," she admits. "Before I started going to my therochief I never even suspected how unhappy I was. Now I'm totally aware of my misery. It's a big improvement" (107). Henley uses gross satirical behavior to point to the inadequacy of the human experience within a media culture that is based entirely on simulation and performance.

She furthers this sense of a culture alienated from its own human essence by her creation of an alternative language for the play, a vocabulary built on hyperbole and sound effects, much in the same way Theater of the Absurd playwrights incorporated a language devoid of meaning. "Oh you reindeer you," L-Tip tells Boswell, relishing his compliment before getting off the phone. "Well, click, click, Box. We gotta go slide, spill, splatter, and burn! It's suck time. Jacka, jacka, jacka!" (*CPII* 61). Language is deformed and unable to unify individuals, serving rather as a performance of sophistication than a method of communion. Even the over-used sentiment "Have a nice day," has been reduced to an abbreviated "H.A.N.D." that the characters wish each other (68). When Max calls for his euthanasia appointment, the attendant slides into a euphemistic jargon, "So you're calling to euth yourself, not a friend or relative?" (80), a device that distances him and Max from the reality of the suicide.

The corrupt, selfish behavior in *Signature* is exaggerated in order to reveal the disintegration of society's artificially constructed moral guidelines. Wilson Yates contests that the grotesque offers a paradigm of the human being's metaphysical placement in the world, because it reacts against those arbitrary value systems that people rely upon to designate good and evil for themselves:

> People create systems of norms, of decorum to protect against the threats of the low and the marginal, to keep them in their place whether they are political, cultural, or psychological in character. In so doing they tend to make themselves vulnerable to the 'imps of the indeterminate,' to ambivalence, to ambiguity, in life. This is the dilemma with which we are faced. It is in response to this that tyranny is born (excessive order) and revolutions occur (the search for a new order), and it is in the face of this dilemma that the grotesque appears warning us of our dilemma. (35)

The characters in the play have adopted such false values of success and failure, that when they are faced with "imps of the indeterminate"—crises such as the loss of popularity, poverty, or divorce—they react inappropriately, such as Maxwell's application for suicide. The grotesque acts as a confrontational tool, deliberately attacking those destructive norms by which society defines "the good life." The grotesque questions these paradigms and ruptures categories, demanding that we create a new, more thoughtful, and acceptable order. The grotesque behavior in *Signature* is only an exaggerated version of the current culture's self-interest—the "cult of me" run amuck. *Signature* brings under scrutiny what we have come to accept as the norm: the abhorrent repercussions of capitalism, with its corresponding habits of egoism and competition.

The character of the graphologist, known simply as "Reader," prevents the play from becoming a simple moral tale of superficial, money-grubbing Hollywood types. Henley describes meeting a graphologist in London who offered a belittling analysis of her signature. Stunned not only by his reading but by her willingness to let herself be assessed by a complete stranger, she discovered her impetus for the play (*CPII* viii). This bearded woman at the center of the play is part lunatic and part poet, a woman who has the intuition to perceive Boswell's destructive personality, but who is also certifiably insane (Greene). She informs him that he is a selfish dolt who has wasted his life and who has never learned to live. Describing him as "shallow, self-absorbed, antisocial, conceited, cruel, and cowardly," with a heart like a raisin and a life like "an empty cereal box infested with microscopic bugs," she insists that he transform himself ("Change your writing; change your life") and offers him bizarre writing activities that are in actuality exercises in meditation and generosity (*CPII* 82–83). When he welcomes a homeless teen into his apartment and proposes marriage to the previously scorned William, it appears that Boswell has turned over a new leaf.

But the Reader is like a pernicious troll in a skewed fairy tale who—under the guise of extending wisdom—offers Boswell recommendations which in truth lead him astray. She symbolizes the female grotesque, the witch or siren who lures men into her power, and then misleads them in some way, harming or confusing them. Physically repugnant, with breasts that ooze blood, milk, and mud, she appears in one scene in a sleeveless shirt, her armpit hair long enough to weave with pink ribbons. In another scene, distraught with love for Boswell, she rips open her shirt, exposing her two blood- and mud-caked breasts that she asks Boswell to feel. When Boswell shares with her his upcoming marriage to William, she informs him that this is not the woman she has envisioned as his beloved. Because he believes in her clairvoyancy, he breaks off the engagement, throws the homeless child back on the streets, and returns to creating his last art piece, which ultimately is destroyed by the public.

The Reader is the perfect example of the boundaries society has set up between insight and insanity. This bearded woman with mud and blood oozing from her breasts resembles a painting by Hieronymous Bosch, and yet Boswell trusts her implicitly because she taps into his greatest fear: his transience. The characters' obsession with fame, which prevents them from truly living their lives, is most threatened by the presence of death, because death reduces the self to nothing and eradicates any chance of "making a name" for oneself. Parodying Keats, Boswell boasts of himself, "Here lies one whose name was drilled in granite" (*CPII* 83). Rather than securing a place in people's hearts, he prefers that his signature be fixed in stone. The Reader reminds Boswell about the cost of such public fame, but this warning is problematic coming from the mouth of the play's most inhuman character. The fact that such wisdom comes from an insane woman—an "imp of the indeterminate"—demonstrates how this soulless culture of trends and fashions can be guided by the madness of fools.

The grotesque operates within this play in two aspects: in both the moral egregiousness of the characters and the image of the eponymous character after whom the play is named. The first warns against the cruelty of humankind through exaggerated behavior while the later cautions that a society not secure in itself can be misled by any mad whispers masquerading as wisdom. Henley does, however, intersperse the grotesque with humane models of existence. Alvin Klein, in his review of the play for the Passage Theater Company in May 1996, notes that "this is not a Doomsday play, but an exploration of caring" (12). Williams, the toxic-waste worker who rescues animals from bad environmental spills, repairs the mistakes that others have made. In a particularly striking scene, Maxwell places a call to be euthanized, and, as he is giving all his vital information, Williams cleans an animal damaged by material waste. This glimpse of Maxwell so afraid of experiencing his own grief that he treats death as a refuge is made all the more poignant by the sight of William restoring an animal to health. The two contrasting individuals signals a society capable of repairing external damage, but not inner emptiness.

Control Freaks, on the other hand, offers no such moments of reprieve. The play breaks, violates, and explodes theatrical boundaries. This is no longer the festive world of the *Miss Firecracker Contest* or the rebellious world of *The Debutante Ball*. *Control Freaks* explores the grotesque side of human nature at a point where *The Debutante Ball* and *Signature* left off. Complete with a multiple personality disorder, incest, sexual molestation of a minor, and murder, Henley considers it her most daring play (Bryer 117), in which she focuses on "the darker side of the human spirit and passions" (Dellasega 258). Referring to the Los Angeles performance she directed, she describes it as "grotesque ballet of a poem that never stops" (Cullum 44), beginning in a controlled fashion but gradually erupting into chaos (Bryer 114). The characters are wholly evil creatures and their actions are outrageous. *Control Freaks* reveals a dangerous world of anarchic desires and nightmarish visions that forces the audience to contemplate the nature of evil.

The absurd tone and plot of the play demonstrates that Henley has strayed far from her beginnings in realism. Kayser indicates mental insanity as one area popular for explorations of the grotesque, simply because "it is as if an impersonal force, an alien and inhuman spirit, had entered the soul" (*CPII* 184). Certainly, in the character of Sister, this deviation of human nature is taken to an extreme since she suffers from a multiple personality disorder, in which *two* "alien and inhuman" spirits inhabit her body without her knowledge, bickering back and forth. She serves her brother, Carl, bubbles for breakfast and sensuously feeds him M&M's by hand. Weird screams and the sounds of shattering glass come from the blender, unnoticed by everyone except Sister, furthering the belief that she is mentally disturbed if only she can hear such sounds. Betty, Carl's new wife, is having an affair with her former lover Paul behind Carl's back, so Carl begins to plot how he can murder Paul to avenge his honor. Betty, in a perverse moment, wonders whether they will kill him "before or after hors d'oeuvres?" because she needs to know for "shopping purposes" (123). Carl also demonstrates his beastly nature when he defecates behind the bushes onstage, blames it on the neighborhood dog, and then rolls about in his own feces. Their lust after money and sex and their willingness to kill one another are unmitigated and unrelieved. Paul chastises Betty for her sordid past when he tells her: "you were a whore and burnt apartment buildings for money and drowned your son in a bucket" (130). Henley deliberately constructs a ludic world that prevents any audience empathy with her characters, as one could with Meg, for example, in *Crimes of the Heart*. Rather, *Control Freaks* employs the grotesque in order "to invoke and subdue the demonic aspects of the world" (Kayser 188)—to invite the grotesque on stage for a direct encounter with the audience.

Part of what makes the play so disturbing is the characters' strong sexual rapacity, which is expressed through a repertory of lascivious gestures and sadistic meetings. Sister, for example, experiences a sexual climax while refusing Paul's marriage proposal. The more she says "no," the more turned-on she becomes, until she is writhing on the stage, the "no's" coming fast and furious, her body "convulsing with orgasms all alone on the ground" (*CPII* 135). In an earlier scene, Betty runs her hand under her skirt and smears her scent across Paul's face, providing a particularly strong sexual gesture for the stage. Paul and Betty "leap on each other" (138) and roll behind the bushes to make love. Later on, Paul "starts slowly kissing and licking [Betty] from her ankles to her thighs" (139) and she lets out slow, orgasmic moans. Both of these scenes exhibit the practice of dominating another both physically and psychically. To control another's sexual responses is to control that person. Sister cannot stop the passionate swells her body experiences any more than Betty can prevent herself from moaning at Paul's kisses.

Finally, at the play's end, Carl and Betty have double-crossed everyone, including each other, by poisoning the celebratory wine they offer to Sister and Paul. The characters reel around the stage, clutching their stomachs in pain, until Carl produces an antidote to save himself, which he stirs with a large vibrator. He commands that Paul crawl toward him on his hands and knees while he holds the vibrator out to Paul. Carl then abases Paul by making him lick the antidote off the "rubber cock" (*CPII* 143) so that he is effectively performing fellatio on Carl. Far from being a loving gesture, sex has been reduced to its most sadistic state in this play, where the characters sexually stimulate one another in order to humiliate them in turn.

Sadism and masochism have a central place in the literary tradition of the grotesque. Kuryluk's definition shows how sadism in particular comes from a desire to control the other sexually: "The sadistic desire to torture and to destroy is connected to a belief in masculine power which can subdue the woman as well as the earth, while the masochistic dream of female dominance aims rather at a return to mother earth and a reconciliation with her" (148). Each character in this play strives to control another without losing control over him or herself, and the form of control is usually sexual: wiping one's vaginal fluids on the face of an ex-lover to seduce him or compelling someone to lick a vibrator to save his life. Carl, making Paul crawl toward him, comments, "I just liked seeing that slime crawl to me. It was nice. I had him under control" (*CPII* 144). A conversation between Paul and Betty shows their attempts to manipulate each other as each tries to gain the upperhand:

PAUL: You told me you wanted to suck me dry. You said you wanted to make me cry like a little baby. You said you wanted me to come through your nose.
BETTY: . . . I didn't mean it.
PAUL: What? You didn't mean what?
BETTY: Anything I said or did.
PAUL: It felt like you meant it. It felt exactly like you meant it. It felt like you lost control.
BETTY: No. I was acting. It was all an act.
PAUL: I don't believe you.
BETTY: I just did it so you'd give Carl a good price on the building.
PAUL: Yeah?
BETTY: Yeah.
PAUL: I don't believe you.
BETTY: Why not? It worked, didn't it? You're selling the place to him for peanuts. (*CPII* 129)

The conversation begins with two strong images of sexual control: either Betty reduces Paul to "a little baby" through his own sexual ecstasy or Paul reminds Betty that she at one point wanted to abase herself to him through the act of fellatio. Betty quickly regains ground by implying that her words were untrue, only a performance to maneuver Paul into doing something against his will. Betty wields her sexually suggestive comments as a tool to exploit Paul against his will. Paul counters her statement by implying that she spoke those words when *she* was out of control—insinuating that Betty, far from controlling another, revealed her true self to him when sexually excited. Thus control, sexuality, and self-truth, which are inextricably linked in this brief dialogue, become significant in the larger context of the play.

Understanding another's sexual desires is one way to gain knowledge over the other person. In her exploration of the grotesque, Kuryluk finds that often artistic depictions of sexuality are pathways toward inner truths. She discusses how both men and women understood the symbol of underground caves—the original seat of the grotesque—as a symbol for "the internal space enclosed by the body . . . the residence of one's unique mind, spirit, or soul." She further explains that "the soul was conceived in the European tradition as a volatile female, [which] added further complexity to the symbolism of the cave and led to the creation of metaphors which linked sexual drive to the exploration of one's own or another person's self" (317). Since the act of penetrating into subterranean grottoes, or the grotesque, was akin to exploring the human's soul, what better metaphor for penetration into a warm, enclosed space could exist than the act of sexual intercourse? Freud certainly relied upon the metaphor of exploring subterranean passages of the human conscious in his applied practice of psychoanalysis. Kuryluk describes Freud's psychoanalytic sessions as exploratory work in the grotesque: "During the psychoanalytic sessions the semi-dark, richly decorated rooms of the well-to-do Viennese bourgeoisie and Freud's own office turned into grottoes of wild reverie which deeply linked the doctor to the patient and, not surprisingly, led them to the discovery of eroticism" (93). In this way, Freud helped the patient to obtain self-knowledge, but it is also apparent that he governed the access and the interpretation of such knowledge.

The discovery of sexuality at the root of the patient's neurosis seems a heavy-handed application of Freud, but it serves well in understanding the basic plot of *Control Freaks*. In this play, Henley has invited the audience to penetrate the roots of a very disturbed psyche, Sister's, whose several personalities, indicated by the abbreviations in brackets below, control her and protect her from knowing the truth about herself.

SISTER (SPAGHETTI/PINKIE): [SP] I gotta be careful. I gotta watch my mouth. Speaking in evil./ (*She slaps herself.*) [P] Don't hit me!/ [SP] Shut up! I will if I want to!/ (*She slaps herself and pulls at her hair.*) [P] Ow! Ow! Ow! Stop it! You're hurting me./ [SP] Then, shut up. (*She stops beating herself and sighs with exhaustion—as Sister.*) Oh goodness. Goodness. (*Tiptoeing around the yard.*) I don't know who I am anymore. There's this real sense I am lost. I have gotten lost. The path has disappeared and the berries have been eaten by the wren. (*CPII* 128)

In this conversation, Sister, who has no knowledge of the other personalities within her, shows a lack of control over herself as she strikes and harms herself physically. She clearly admits not knowing who she is. But what is more significant than this avowal are her self-abusive gestures that demonstrate that she has no control over the fragmented selves of her own identity. In providing this image of a woman beating herself up onstage, Henley requires the audience to contemplate the devastation and cruelty that Sister has suffered at the hands of her brother Carl, who has sexually molested her over her lifetime. Her multiple personality disorder—the three voices warring over her body—is the result.

Henley's play relies upon knowledge of how multiple personalities form. Often this disorder is a result of years of repeated and sustained sexual abuse experienced as a child. In order for the young child to disassociate him or herself from the sexual or physical abuse the adult is inflicting, the child will sometimes create another personality to experience the abuse in his or her stead. Robert A. Phillips, the psychiatrist who treats the patient with multiple personality disorder in the book *When Rabbit Howls*, writes that "Multiple personality . . . is the responses of a creative mind seeking to escape the saturation of childhood terror and pain" (xi). What Henley has done in this play is to re-create the psychological turmoil Sister experiences for the audience, to show them the world from her injured perspective. The fact that Henley describes her play as "dream real" (*CPII* 112), and that only Sister hears the odd noises in the kitchen, hints at the play's expressionist qualities, and suggests that we are viewing the internal angst of a character projected outwardly on the stage. Her curious behavior of wearing various wigs during the play or tossing her dress out the window as if she herself were jumping indicates a fragmented self-identity, as do such lines as "there are scars on my tonsils from silent screaming" (144) and "pain was like glass stuck inside, but it didn't hurt . . . because we were not home" (146). The sexual sadism and scatology in this play re-create for the audience the only image of the world that Sister has ever known, and the visceral shock is necessary to convey her own operant mode of fear and self-loathing. In *Control Freaks* Henley has combined the content with the structure; the subject matter of the play—sexual molestation of a child and the means of expressing it—and the crude onstage behavior are both grotesque. The grotesque in this play forces the audience to experience the confusion and shock of sexual perversion when it is used repeatedly to control another person's soul.

Wilson Yates, in his "Introduction to the Grotesque," suggests that the grotesque in art and literature allows us to contemplate the nature of evil within the human condition (26). As he explains, "The grotesque refers to aspects of human experience that we have denied validity to, that we have rejected, excoriated, attempted to eliminate and image as a distorted aspect of reality" (40). Because we may wish to ignore topics such as incest, physical and emotional abuse, or sexual molestation, does not mean that they do not exist. Yates later describes the artist as a "midwife" who brings forth those "expressions of reality" that do not fit in our day-to-day world:

> They are our children, our cast-outs now returned not as prodigals but as monstrosities; and the artist is the midwife that brings them forth. They are children of strangeness that frighten, confuse, defy. They are not welcome. They have violated the way we have ordered and rationalized our world, and they continue to violate what we deem rational, good, appropriate. But, still, they are our children even as they return in masks, and in mockery, in defiance to disrupt our well-being. (41)

Yates's description of grotesque characters corresponds to the characters of Henley's world, misfits who exist in the "boundary of experience." The grotesque has always played a role in Henley's plays, moving from the boundaries of reality in the early plays, in which the grotesque forms the basis of a wild yarn, to its more predominant place in the later plays, such as *Control Freaks*. Time after time, Henley reminds us of that dimension of the human experience that people would prefer to forget, a dimension that either reveals the pain that humans have experienced or exposes the cruelty that humans inflict upon one another. Sometimes, the grotesque serves as a means of transcending societal beliefs and constructs to get at more primitive truths. Sometimes it merely reveals the terror of the unfathomable, the ghostly, the sadistic, the obscene, and the mechanical so that we can examine these terrors with a cold, objective eye.

We do not court the grotesque in our lives, but it is there in the form of accidents, mishaps, and cruelties. To disregard the grotesque would be to ignore a portion of the human condition, just as ignoring death would prevent us from fully appreciating life. Henley admits that she turns to the theater because it is like a sanctuary from the real world for her, and that the passions of the actors and the people involved help her to forget about death: "It was such a magical world where everyone was passionate about something; they felt so alive when they were there, and they really cared that their water be set exactly here and not here. It made you not think about dying" (112). For Henley, the small idiosyncrasies of the actors regarding their roles or the way their props are set signifies a fervent belief in their own existence—"I hold this glass, therefore I am." The fact that the actors can transform a world of artificial lighting and plywood sets into real life is tangible proof for Henley of the existence of the life force. Into this living world Henley invites the grotesque, through the suicide with a cat, a character's popped eyeballs, or a bearded graphologist, because these quirks or oddities come within the purview of human experience. The grotesque, in its awareness of the terrors of the living and the finitude of the body, is perhaps the closest we can come to contemplating death while remaining just this side of the footlights, after which all is darkness.

Notes

I would like to thank my former students Lois Winkler and Martha White for joining me in reading Henley's plays and explaining the "southernisms," and my friend Kelley Crisp for showing me where to laugh.
1. The play had its world premiere at the South Coast Repertory on April 9, 1985, and was subsequently produced by The Manhattan Theatre Club on April 26, 1988. The production Michael Billington reviewed took place at the Hampstead Theatre, London, May–June 1989.

Works Cited

Bennett, Barbara. *Comic Visions, Female Voices: Contemporary Women Novelists and Southern Humor.* Baton Rouge: Louisiana State University Press, 1998.

Betso, Kathleen and Rachel Koenig. "Beth Henley." *Interviews with Contemporary Women Playwrights.* New York: Beech Tree Books, 1987. 211–222.

Billington, Michael. "A Cracked Belle." Review of *The Debutante Ball. Guardian,* 1 June 1989, 24.

Bryer, Jackson R. "Beth Henley." *The Playwright's Art: Conversations with Contemporary American Dramatists.* New Brunswick, N.J.: Rutgers University Press, 1995. 102–122.

Cook, John W. "Ugly Beauty in Christian Art." *The Grotesque in Art and Literature: Theological Reflections.* Eds. James Luther Adams and Wilson Yates. Grand Rapids, Mich.: William B. Eerdmans, 1997. 125–141.

Dellasega, Mary. "Beth Henley." *Speaking on Stage: Interviews with Contemporary American Playwrights.* Eds. Philip C. Kolin and Colby H. Kullman. Tuscaloosa: University of Alabama Press, 1996. 250–259.

Green, Alexis, ed. *Women Who Write Plays: Interviews with Contemporary American Dramatists.* Lyme, N.H.: Smith and Kraus Publishers, 2000.

Guerra, Jonnie. "Beth Henley: Female Quest and the Family-Play Tradition." *Making Spectacle: Feminist Essays on Contemporary Women's Theater.* Ed. Lynda Hart. Ann Arbor: University of Michigan Press, 1989. 118–130.

Harbin, Billy J. "Familial Bonds in the Plays of Beth Henley." *Southern Quarterly* 25.3 (1987): 81–94.

Haller, Scot. "Her First Play, Her First Pulitzer Prize." *Saturday Review* 8 (1981): 40–44.

Hargrove, Nancy D. "The Tragicomic Vision of Beth Henley's Drama." *Southern Quarterly* 22.4 (1984): 54–70.

Harpham, Geoffrey Galt. *On The Grotesque: Strategies of Contradiction in Art and Literature.* Princeton: Princeton University Press, 1982.

Henley, Beth. "Preface." *The Debutante Ball*. Illus. Lynn Green Root. Jackson: University Press of Mississippi, 1991. xi–xiv.
———. "Beth Henley: Playwright." *New York Times*, 3 January 1988, sec. 2, 31.
Kayser, Wolfgang. *The Grotesque in Art and Literature*. Trans. Ulrich Weisstein. New York: McGraw-Hill, 1966.
Karpinski, Joanne B. "The Ghosts of Chekhov's *Three Sisters* Haunt Beth Henley's *Crimes of the Heart*." *Modern American Drama: The Female Canon*. Ed. June Schlueter. London: Associated University Press, 1990. 229–245.
Klein, Alvin. "Hooray for Hollywood? More Like 'Horrors!' " Review of *Signature*. *New York Times*, 12 May 1996, B12.
Kuryluk, Ewa. *Salome and Judas in the Cave of Sex: The Grotesque—Origins, Iconography, Techniques*. Evanston, Ill.: Northwestern University Press, 1987.
Laughlin, Karen L. "Criminality, Desire, and Community: A Feminist Approach to Beth Henley's *Crimes of the Heart*." *Women and Performance: A Journal of Feminist Theory* 3, no. 1 (1986): 35–51.
McDonnell, Lisa J. "Diverse Similitude: Beth Henley and Marsha Norman." *Southern Quarterly* 25.3 (1987): 95–104.
Phillips, Robert A. *When Rabbit Howls*. New York: E.P. Dutton, 1987.
Roger, V. Cullum. "Beth Henley: Signature of a Non-stop Playwright." *Backstage*, 24 March 1995, 23, 44.
Shepard, Alan Clarke. "Aborted Rage in Beth Henley's Women." *States of Rage: Emotional Eruption, Violence, and Social Change*. Eds. Terry L. Allison and Renée Curry. New York: New York University Press, 1996. 179–194.
Shewey, Don. "A Director with an Eye for the Telling Detail." *New York Times*, 10 October 1982, 28, 37.
Taylor, Paul. Review of *The Debutante Ball*. *London Theatre Record* 9 (1989): 700.
Waters, Mark. "Violence and Comedy in the Works of Flannery O'Connor." *New Perspectives on Women and Comedy*. Ed. Regina Barreca. Philadelphia: Gordon and Breach, 1992. 185–192.
Yates, Wilson. "An Introduction to the Grotesque: Theoretical and Theological Considerations." *The Grotesque in Art and Literature: Theological Reflections*. Eds. James Luther Adams and Wilson Yates. Grand Rapids, Mich.: William B. Eerdmans, 1997. 1–68.

2
Lessons from the Past
Loss and Redemption in the Early Plays of Beth Henley

LARRY G. MAPP

In the introduction to the 1993 collection of essays *The Female Tradition in Southern Literature* the editor Carol Manning points out that established literary theory has ignored the "motifs and themes" in the work of women writers and the "threads that connect some writers—threads that reveal a female tradition in southern literature" (2). Manning points out that lists of major southern writers usually contain important women writers, including Ellen Glasgow, Katherine Anne Porter, Caroline Gordon, Eudora Welty, Carson McCullers, and Flannery O'Connor. Perhaps, she argues, the inclusion of so many southern women writers has made it seem that southern literature can be spared the attention of critics bent on revising the canon to reflect accurately the contributions of women writers. But as Manning then explains, this assumption is false.

Southern women writers were, from the beginning, treated according to the same double standard applied to other women writers. Nineteenth-century women writers were almost completely excluded from discussion because their work was deemed to be sentimental and lightweight or, even worse, because it was popular. Many critics easily dismissed later writers such as Glasgow, Porter, Gordon, Welty, and McCullers because they failed to treat the same themes as men writers. Critics wanted writers who dealt with large cultural, political, and social themes. After Faulkner established himself as the largest bear in the southern forest, every writer (male or female) has been measured against his reputation, and women especially have found themselves criticized for not meeting the criteria associated with Faulkner's greatness. If a writer's themes apparently lack the heft of Faulkner's themes, some critics dismiss the writer as a lightweight. One remedy for this kind of thinking, as Manning notes, is to identify in the work of southern women writers the themes and motifs that they share with the writers who preceded them and with their contemporaries. Those themes and motifs take on the heft of being eternal and large when they live across time and cultural changes. Beth Henley's plays repay this kind of attention because they contain thematic echoes that link her to writers, both male and female, who preceded her or who are her contemporaries.

The six plays in volume one of Henley's collected plays are set in the South and explore the range of issues that preoccupied Henley from 1972 until 1989. In the six plays she deals with issues of family and community and with the struggle of individuals to find an identity within a family or community that is oppressive, often is fragmenting, and no longer has a center that will hold. In all of the plays tensions arise when women, and sometimes men, begin to challenge the traditions that have constrained them. And each of the plays ends with a scene that offers the women some hope of redemption through love and companionship, both with men and with other women. A brief examination of the plays reveals this recurring pattern in her plays, as women who are constrained by very southern traditions in a highly patriarchal society attempt in various ways to escape or overthrow it.

While *Am I Blue* was produced in New York in 1982, a year after the production of *Crimes of the Heart*, it is the product of Henley's years as a student at Southern Methodist University, where she first saw it produced by her fellow students in 1974. The play presents a conversation between seventeen-year-old John Polk and sixteen-year-old Ashbe and is set in a New Orleans bar and in Ashbe's rundown apartment. John Polk is having a bad day because he is trying to make his fraternity brothers happy by doing what they expect of him. Ashbe's life has been twisted because her mother and sister have moved away leaving Ashbe to live with her father, who is out of town but who may return in a few days. Ashbe copes with her losses by being relentlessly optimistic, outrageous in behavior and dress, imaginative, and happy. By the end of the play her personality dominates John Polk's conventional personality and enables him to assert himself in refusing to visit the prostitute whom his fraternity brothers have bought for him. Instead, he and Ashbe decide to dance all night and wait for the rats to come out. This ending seems at least temporarily to resolve the play's tensions and to offer some hope as the two lonely young people take comfort in each other and, by dancing together, create a kind of beauty in a rat-infested world. While this is a play written by Henley the student, it contains the seeds of the rest of the plays in volume one. Behind the problems of these two characters lie families who do not serve them as one supposes families should. John Polk's family simply does not see who he is, and the fraternity acts as an extension of the family in insisting that he behave stereotypically and not according to his own developing sense of self. Ashbe's family seems almost to have forgotten her; she is cut loose at the age of sixteen and knows too much about the life of Bourbon Street. The single, brief conversation with her father suggests that she is acting more like an adult as he is losing himself in alcohol in order to deal with the breakup of his marriage. Yet amidst this sadness and loss Ashbe displays the relentless optimism that many Henley characters possess. The actor Carol Kane says that when she has "the honor to be one of Beth's characters" she feels "a rare and exquisite freedom. This could be thought odd because all of Beth's characters, while gifted with extraordinary dialogue, are shackled with emotional weights the likes of which no human should ever have to carry" (*CPI* xv). Kane recalls being reminded by director Norman Renee that Henley's "characters are filled with hope. Insane, unstoppable hope against all reason" (xv–xvi). This hope releases them "to fly free in the face of doom" (xvi). As we look for the source of this "unstoppable hope against all reason," we might also wonder if it is both the strength and the weakness of the plays.

Crimes of the Heart explores the same issues. The three women at the heart of the play have been ruled by men who tell them what to do and enforce their wishes either by fiat or by appealing to traditions that dictate how women (and men) should behave. The oldest sister Lenny has subjugated her life entirely to that of her ailing grandfather, even moving a small bed into the kitchen so she can be more responsive to his calls during the night. Middle sister Meg fled Mississippi and the family history and Old Granddaddy; but as she tells Doc, "After a while I just couldn't sing anymore.... I went nuts. I went insane" (*CPI* 44). The youngest and aptly named sister Babe has dutifully endured Old Granddaddy's dictates and married the wealthy, powerful, and abusive Zackery. By shooting Zackery she rebels against Old Grandddaddy's reign and forces herself and her sisters to deal with the legacy of their mother who killed herself in loneliness and despair after her husband abandoned her. The play concludes with a communal scene in which the three women demonstrate their sisterly resolve and mutual support as they gather around Lenny's cake and laughingly tear into it, a symbolic rejection of convention. Babe is not going to jail, Meg has regained her singing voice, and Lenny has talked to her old beau Charlie. But one wonders what gives rise to the riotous laughter other than the exhilaration of the moment. What has happened to these women that can sustain optimism—except a resolve to be relentlessly optimistic?

The Wake of Jamey Foster takes place over a day and the following morning as a family assembles in Jamey's house for his wake and burial, an occasion that emphasizes the manners and traditions of society. Jamey left Marshael four months earlier and then died after being kicked by a cow as he and his lover gamboled in a field. Much of the play's tension comes from Marshael's refusal to conform to the role of bereaved widow and to tolerate the dictates of Jamey's family. The quarreling between Marshael and various family members sets the tone of the play, but it ends with a very calm scene. While everyone is at the funeral, Brocker, who seems to love Marshael, lulls her to sleep by playing the spoons and singing the children's song "This Old

Man." The quiet and ironically serious tone of this play's ending gives the characters depth and perhaps makes them more believable. Marshael seems mature enough to know what she has done in flaunting tradition, and Brocker may just be mature enough to companion her in this revolt. As Brocker plays the spoons and sings a children's song, he and Marshael seem to affirm the necessity for play, the necessity for imagination, and the necessity for sharing. The ending of the play reminds us of the ending of *Am I Blue* in which Ashbe and John find in their companionship and in their dancing a moment of beauty and solace.

The Miss Firecracker Contest is an ambitious play that expands the questions Henley asks about family, tradition, custom, and the plight of an individual unable to find an identity within those settings. Henley centers the play on a beauty and talent contest, an apparently meaningless custom that unduly rewards physical appearance and a modicum of talent. Carnelle Scott hopes that winning the contest will provide a triumph and an identity that will permit her to leave Brookhaven, Mississippi, in a burst of glory. Her cousin Elain is a former Miss Firecracker and still derives much of her identity from being the "beauty" who won the contest eleven years earlier; yet Elain finds herself unhappy and perhaps drifting out of her marriage. Carnelle is not a beauty and lacks even a modicum of the talent rewarded by such contests, but her struggle to win and to be acknowledged and valued publicly only points out the relative emptiness of Elain's distant triumph. Carnelle's comic and often sad attempts to measure up to the beauty and talent of Elain provide much of the tension of the story. The other characters—Mac Sam, Popeye, and Delmount—provide commentary on the tragicomic striving of one tiny human trying to find or make meaning of her life. Popeye, the seamstress, has the earnest and ironically innocent sense of wonder and joy of other Henley characters, perhaps best demonstrated by her practice of sewing costumes for frogs, a not-so-subtle commentary on Carnelle's costuming of herself for the contest. The contest contains a parade, a more public version of the contest's earlier displays of beauty and talent. Delmount comments, "I mean, for Christ's sake who would want to ride in a parade? It's so pitiful. Man parading his ridiculous pomposity down his pathetic little streets, cheering at his own inane self-grandeur" (*CPI* 186). Mac Sam, Carnelle's former lover and a carnival worker, adds new depth to this play. Mac Sam has tuberculosis and syphilis, a disease he contracted from Carnelle; and he has not sought treatment for either disease. Mac Sam often coughs up bright pink pieces of lung and offers to show them to other characters. He also makes no effort to protect other characters from his illnesses, even offering Delmount a drink from his flask after he has coughed all over it (186). He plans to share his syphilis with Elain near the end of the play when he exits to meet her secretly. Sam seems to need nothing from life and to expect nothing from it. He accepts his diseased state as a matter of course because he expects life to be unpredictable, uncontrollable, and, finally, hard and indifferent. Mac Sam intrigues us because he seems almost Christ-like as he takes on the diseased condition of human life and bears it uncomplainingly. One could say he even tries to instruct the characters as he shares his body and blood when he coughs. Mac Sam also is the character who mentions the idea of "eternal grace" when he and Carnelle discuss what one can expect of life (202). Although with Mac Sam Henley broaches the topics of religion, grace, and forgiveness, Mac Sam is neither savior nor satan. But he resonates with readers of southern fiction because he reminds us of both; and when Mac Sam speaks of eternal grace, he mentions it as if he is a member of a culture that only faintly recalls having been Christian.

With *The Lucky Spot*, Henley creates a love story involving the former rumrunner Reed Hooker and his wife, the former taxi dancer Sue Jack. The back story comes out as Sue Jack is released from prison and she and Hooker reunite at his dance hall in Pigeon, Louisiana. Their married life mirrored their single lives as they drank heavily and lived wild lives. The accidental death of their child changed everything as Sue Jack blamed herself and they both grieved. Sue Jack was sent to prison after she tossed a woman she found in bed with Reed from a balcony. Despite the seedier setting for the play and the characters who live hard lives, this is a play about two people who love each other and whose lives are disrupted by their own choices and by chance. Near the play's end Sue Jack's and Hooker's love brings them together again, and Hooker says, to Sue Jack, "Well, we sure could use some dumb luck" (*CPI* 262). Hooker and Sue Jack hope that luck can provide the safe haven so absent in their lives.

There is a wonderfully gothic element to the last of the six plays, *The Debutante Ball*. At its heart is the scheming mother Jen who is forcing her pregnant daughter Teddy to participate in the Hattiesburg Debutante Ball because Teddy can help her reclaim the family's rightful place in high society. Jen is ruthless in her dealings with her daughters and has married her new husband, the lawyer who defended her when she was tried for murdering her first husband, just to get his money. But she is full of secrets and lies, the most important being that Teddy is the murderer and that Jen lied to protect her. The other characters are healed to some degree as the truth becomes known, but at the end there is a richly conflicted scene in which Jen, gradually being abandoned by everyone, begins to take a bath. Teddy notices that Jen's psoriasis has recurred and Jen says, "God, look how the ravages of time have conquered me. All the cracks and sores and ugliness" (*CPI* 314). Teddy applies ointments to Jen's ravaged body and tells her she is leaving, too, but that she no longer fears being held in the grip of a snapping turtle, a beast reputed to hold its grip until it hears thunder. Teddy says, "Yeah, and that ole snapping turtle's gonna let loose and I'll just be standing there in the rain and in the thunder and these arms will want to hold onto somebody and have their

Lessons from the Past

arms holding onto me." Jen can only reply, "Hmm. Well. I hope so. I, well, I . . . Yes. Good. Yes" (315). Teddy believes in love and can hope as can her sister Bliss who has "this sort of hole inside me. This desperate longing to love and be loved" (306). So the Mother, perhaps too corrupted by lies and manners and traditions and defeats to save herself, seems to be erupting from within as her body breaks apart, a condition reminiscent of Mac Sam's.

Of course, the family quarreling common in all of these plays and the tradition-bound society against which the women rebel rings true for all audiences, but in southern literature we can find an early, unexpected, and revealing antecedent for it in the writings of Mary Boykin Chesnut. Chesnut wrote her diaries in the years 1861–1865. Her husband James, a senator from South Carolina, resigned in the fall of 1860 after Lincoln's election and returned home to help draft the document of secession for South Carolina. Throughout the war he and Mary were at the center of the war effort, James as an adviser and combatant, and Mary as an interested observer, supporter, and critic. She began the diaries on 18 February 1861 and made her last entry on 26 July 1865. For years afterward she revised the diaries, often by adding material that some historians have regretted because it fictionalizes the diaries. Whatever the judgment of historians, when C. Van Woodward edited the diaries and published them as *Mary Chesnut's Civil War* in 1981, the book received the Pulitzer Prize for history. The thread that links Chesnut with Henley is the portraits of women, family members, and friends. Men of course, run the war, but early on Chesnut signals her willingness to dispute their wisdom and authority. When James resigns and comes home to initiate secession, Chesnut supports him but notes that "going back to Mulberry to live was offering up my life on the altar of country" (5). Many of the entries explore the relationships of women, either members of her family or close friends. In this passage Chesnut records a conversation between two women:

"So Mrs. _____ thinks Purgatory will hold its own—never will be abolished while women and children have to live with drunken fathers and brothers."

"She knows."

"She is too bitter. She says worse than that. She says we have an institution worse than the Spanish Inquisition—worse than Torquemada and all that sort of thing."

"What does she mean?"

"It is your own family she calls the familiars of the Inquisition. She declares they set upon you, watch and harass you, from morn till dewey eve. They have a perfect right to your life night and day. Unto the fourth or fifth generation. They drop in at breakfast. "Are you not imprudent to eat that? Take care now, don't overdo it. I think you eat too much so early in the day." And they help themselves to the only thing you care for on the table.

They abuse your friends and tell you it is your duty to praise your enemies. They tell you all your faults candidly—because they love you so. That gives them the right to speak. The family take interest in you. You ought to do this, you ought to do that. And then—the everlasting "You ought to have done." That comes near making you a murderer—at least in heart" (180). . . .

"Then for hurting you, who like a relative? They do it from a sense of duty. For stinging you, for cutting you to the quick, who like none of your household? In point of fact, they only can do it. They know the raw. And how to hit it every time. You are in their power" (181).

The Magrath sisters would feel at home in this conversation, as would Marshael Foster, Carnelle, or Jen's daughters, Teddy and Bliss. Chesnut's women, however, speak more directly and more incisively to the point and have a power behind their words that so often seems to be missing in Henley's women. If we look again at *The Miss Firecracker Contest*, perhaps we can explain the differences more clearly.

The plot of *The Miss Firecracker Contest* focuses on Carnelle Scott, a twenty-four-year-old woman determined to win the Fourth of July Miss Firecracker contest so that she can leave Brookhaven, Mississippi, in triumph. With the aunt who raised her now dead Carnelle is cast out again and feels the uncertainties and rootlessness that she felt as a child when she was dropped off to live with her aunt. Her cousin Elain is the former Miss Firecracker whom Carnelle wishes to emulate. Although other characters still see Elain as "the most beautiful thing in the whole wide world" and continue to shower her with roses she both expects and demands, Elain has left her husband, her children, and what she terms her "dreary, dreary life" (*CPI* 199). Elain also carries the burden of her mother differently than does Carnelle—all the characters seem to agree that Mrs. Jackson was mean, but Elain practices the same meanness on her brother Delmount and on Carnelle, and her actions often echo the description of families in Chesnut's diaries.

Like Carnelle and Elain, Delmount lives an incomplete existence. He wishes for perfection in women; but, since such perfection is unattainable, he looks for perfect parts—a single perfect feature to hold his attention. The seamstress Popeye is equally odd—she hears voices in her head and occasionally converses with them. She developed her skills as a seamstress by making outfits for frogs. Later in the play she decides to visit the Elysian Fields and seems only mildly discomfited when Delmount reveals that the Elysian Fields exist only in myth. When Delmount and Popeye fall in love shortly after meeting, we are left to wonder about the basis and meaning of this relationship. Perhaps Delmount sees in Popeye a perfect innocence and optimism. Perhaps Popeye sees in Delmount a frog ready for a costume.

These are deeply flawed and fragmented characters, all of them stumbling through life without a plan or a purpose. Perhaps the most interesting

Lessons from the Past

character in the play is Mac Sam, one of Carnelle's former lovers. Henley describes him as "in his mid-thirties. He is amazingly thin, stooped shouldered, and in drastically poor health. Yet there is something extraordinarily sensual about him. His eyes manage to be magnetic and bloodshot at the same time" (*CPI* 175). Mac Sam has tuberculosis and regularly coughs up pieces of his lungs, bright pink pieces that he inspects and offers to show to others. And he has syphilis, a disease that Carnelle passed to him. Carnelle has been cured, but Mac Sam has not sought treatment. He knows he is dying piecemeal, but he walks about displaying his own fragmenting self. A character similar to Mac Sam appears in Lee Smith's epistolary novel *Fair and Tender Ladies*. Ivy Rowe leads an adventurous life not unlike Carnelle's early life. But after Ivy marries, she and Oakley move back to the mountains and Sugar Fork Creek to raise their family and farm the family land. Several years of hard manual labor cause Ivy and Oakley gradually to lose contact with each other emotionally and sexually. And Ivy loses touch with herself, particularly with her imagination and her love for storytelling. When Oakley decides to establish some beehives, he invites the itinerant beekeeper Honey Breeding to collect the bees for the new hives. Honey is as sensual, magnetic, and mythically empty as Mac Sam. Ivy runs off with Honey and spends days with him atop Blue Star Mountain making love and telling stories. Ivy stays with him until she falls ill and cannot resist Honey's bringing her home. They come down the mountain with Honey in the lead, "light-hearted it looked like, sure-footed, whistling a little song" (Smith 237), a description that fits Mac Sam. In a letter to her sister Silvaney, Ivy says "Sometimes now when I think about Honey Breeding, it is almost like I made him up out of thin air because I needed him so bad. I can't think of him as real, somehow" (247).

In Mac Sam Henley creates a grotesque character whose physical deterioration and fragmentation mirror the fragmentation of the other characters, perhaps even the fragmentation of their culture. Mac Sam literally comes apart on stage as he coughs up and disposes of parts of himself. Yet he also speaks the most intriguing line in the play in this exchange:

CARNELLE: ... I thought maybe I was the victim of broken dreams but then I thought maybe I wasn't. I was trying so hard t'belong all my life and ... I don't know.... Anyway, I just don't know what you can, well, reasonably hope for in life.
MAC SAM: Not much, Baby, not too damn much.
CARNELLE: But something—
MAC SAM: Sure. There's always eternal grace.
CARNELLE: It'd be nice. (*CPI* 201–202)

Mac Sam's reference to Grace interests because it completely lacks context. There is nothing in the play, no framework of experience or ideas that prepares the reader (or Carnelle) for the comment and Carnelle clearly lacks a context within which to discuss Grace, hence her cryptic response: "It'd be nice." A reader versed in southern literature will have noticed from the outset that Henley's characters seldom refer to religion and that the word "Christ" only occurs as an epithet. Just after Carnelle leaves Mac Sam, Delmount and Popeye climb out atop the tent and Delmount's first comment when he looks out at the sky is "Holy Christ" (202), an expression without reference to anything either religious or spiritual and highlighting the absence of those elements in the play. Carnelle briefly muses on the term while she is alone in the dressing room as she repeats, "Grace. Eternal grace. Grace" (203). But the play provides no reason to believe that she develops the idea beyond her brief musing. Ivy Rowe provides an interesting contrast here because she does not think of herself as formally religious, yet she lives a deeply spiritual life. Smith says that Ivy "is unable to find a religion that suits her—an organized religion. She makes up her own. Writing for her is . . . a sort of a saving thing. Almost a religion of its own" (Ketchin 51).

So within the context of southern literature, the families and culture of these plays are quite familiar. We find the same families and the same patriarchal society in southern literature from the very beginnings of the form, as Mary Chesnut demonstrates. Similarly, in Kate Chopin's *The Awakening*, Edna Pontellier fights for her need to be an individual, but the patriarchal culture drives her to her death, either a suicide or an ultimate form of self-realization. And in Zora Neale Hurston's *Their Eyes Are Watching God*, Janie struggles against patriarchal and racial impediments and retains her dignity and develops a powerful sense of self. Perhaps an essential difference between Henley's characters and those of Hurston and Chopin is that Henley's characters never seem to see their world clearly or as a whole, so we are understandably unsure that their exhilaration over any momentary triumph will be more than momentary. At the conclusion of *The Miss Firecracker Contest*, Carnelle speaks to Delmount about the disappointment of the contest: "It's just I was upset about not being able to leave in the blaze of glory. Of course, I know it doesn't matter. I mean, the main thing is—well the main thing is . . . Gosh, I don't know what the main thing is. I don't have the vaguest idea" (*CPI* 204). Neither Edna nor Janie would ever learn so little from experience.

The Kentucky writer Wendell Berry often writes about the loss of community in American society. Berry speaks eloquently of the consequences of our losing a connection to the land on which we live and he argues that only by restoring that connection can we rebuild connections with each other and rebuild our communities (Berry 46–63). Henley's characters do not live in communities; or if they do, the communities seem decidedly unhealthy. Wherever they are, they wish to escape it, but they have no real alternative in mind, nor any method of arriving at an alternative. This characteristic brings to mind Lena with whom Faulkner opens *Light in August*. She sits beside a dirt road awaiting the arrival of a wagon whose approach she has been observing for some time through the hot air of a Mississippi summer day. Lena has walked from Alabama to this point, clad in a "mailorder dress," bare-footed, and carrying her shoes wrapped in a piece of paper (3). Lena will move through this long novel relentlessly, at first searching for and finding the father of her unborn child and then, when he rejects her, continuing to travel, "determined to see as much as she c[an]" before biology and other necessities force her to take root (506). The novel explores the passions of men and the great havoc those passions exact on a town not unlike the settings of Henley's plays. But rising somehow above them is the slight figure of Lena, driven by wonderment, by the need to see and to experience life while time permits, and by an unfailing trust that somehow people will be kind. Here is a direct link between the two Mississippians Henley and Faulkner. While much time has passed between the writing of Faulkner's novels and Henley's plays, the solidly patriarchal world has changed little. Lena trusts in her bare feet because they remind her (and us) of her rootedness in place, and she trusts in the kindness of strangers. Henley's characters are not rooted in place, families, or communities; so they have not found anything to trust, not even themselves. With these six plays, then, Henley has indicted the traditional southern culture in terms familiar to southern writers and readers. She has not, however, found answers to her own questions about the place of women in it.

Works Cited

Berry, Wendell. *Another Turn of the Crank*. Washington, D.C.: Counterpoint, 1995.
Chesnut, Mary Boykin. *Mary Chesnut's Civil War*. Ed. C. Vann Woodward. New Haven: Yale University Press, 1981.
Chopin, Kate. *The Awakening*. New York: Modern Library, 1994.
Faulkner, William. *Light in August*. New York: Vintage, 1985.
Hurston, Zora Neale. *Their Eyes Were Watching God*. New York: Harper, 2000.
Ketchins, Susan. *The Christ-Haunted Landscape*. Jackson: University Press of Mississippi, 1994.
Manning, Carol S. *The Female Tradition in Southern Literature*. Urbana: The University of Illinois Press, 1993.
Smith, Lee. *Fair and Tender Ladies*. New York: G.P. Putnam's Sons, 1988.

3
Moving beyond Mississippi
Beth Henley and the Anxieties of Postsouthernness

GARY RICHARDS

Beth Henley's status as a southern writer has been a vexed one since she burst upon the literary scene in the 1980s with a series of plays memorably set in contemporary Mississippi and the surrounding areas. For many theatergoers and theater critics alike, the young author seemed all too southern, as both the settings of her plays and her biography ostensibly confirmed. In her early works she repeatedly favored Mississippi's small towns—Hazlehurst (*Crimes of the Heart*), Canton (*The Wake of Jamey Foster*), Brookhaven (*The Miss Firecracker Contest*), and Hattiesburg (*The Debutante Ball*)—to contextualize her characters' lives, and when she strayed geographically, she did not go far. Pigeon, Louisiana, "a small southern town about sixty miles west of New Orleans" (*CPI* 207), sets *The Lucky Spot*, while the action of Henley's apprentice play *Am I Blue* takes place in New Orleans itself. Her early life had been no less focused on the South. Born in Jackson, Mississippi, in 1952 and raised there, she attended Southern Methodist University in Dallas and did not permanently leave the South until 1976, when she moved to Los Angeles to pursue a career in acting. Henley thus spent the first two and a half decades of her life rooted in the very geography that had arguably produced the South's three most critically acclaimed twentieth-century writers. Not only was she reared in the hometown of Eudora Welty, to whom Henley has frequently been compared, but she was born at the height of fellow-Mississippian Tennessee Williams's Broadway successes and only two years after William Faulkner won the Nobel Prize for his transformation of his northern Mississippi county into the mythic literary Yoknapatawpha. By the early 1980s, when Henley's work began to appear, Faulkner's canonization was complete, Williams reigned with Arthur Miller as the preeminent postwar American dramatists, and Welty's magisterial body of writing was garnering renewed praise, all of which prompted critics to position Henley within the long literary shadows of these figures.

Certain staid scholars of southern literature were, however, less eager to embrace Henley without reservations. Consider, for instance, the treatment of Henley in the encyclopedic *The History of Southern Literature* compiled under the general editorship of Louis D. Rubin, Jr., in the mid-1980s. In the chapter "The Future of Southern Writing," Donald R. Noble foregrounds Henley among the emerging writers of the region but only insofar as she complicates preconceived notions of southern literature and southernness in general. While Noble ultimately—and, as history has proven, rightly— deems Henley "the premier Southern playwright of the 1980s" (579), he begins his essay by focusing on her, along with Barry Hannah, to emphasize just how variegated contemporary writers' relations with the South are. Using the codified literary production of the 1920s through the 1950s (the so-called Southern Renascence) as his touchstone point of comparison, Noble asserts:

> There is no point in expecting writers raised in the fifties and sixties to write in the mode of Faulkner, Caldwell, Wolfe, and Warren. These writers came of age in a different South, so their subjects, characters, and concerns and the voices they use to express them will of necessity be different. The ways in which this new writing will partake of the new and the old together may be seen in the work of all the writers under discussion here, but particularly in the work of two of the younger writers . . . Beth Henley and Barry Hannah. (579)

While Noble here seemingly seeks to clear a valid critical space for contemporary southern writers, justifying that they cannot—yet also need not— write like William Faulkner and Robert Penn Warren, Noble potentially undercuts his stance by citing these very figures. Because *The History of Southern Literature* so valorizes the work of these and other Renascence writers as representing the acme of southern literary production, the difference that Noble ascribes to Henley, Hannah, and the likes translates as, at best, deviance from a norm and, at worst, inferiority. Indeed, the only way that Noble can bring Henley and *Crimes of the Heart*, her play of "modern young women" (579), safely within the fold of southern literature is through her attention to southern idiom, which she ostensibly shares with Renascence writers. "[T]he stuff of this play," Noble offers, is not its feminist underpinnings but rather "the gossip and stories Henley asserts she can hear in abundance any day in her childhood home in Jackson" (579). Henley's southernness thus stands in *The History of Southern Literature*, albeit tentatively and tangentially to the dominant understandings of the region and its literary production.[1]

As conflicting as these early negotiations of Henley's regional identity may seem, they merely anticipated the greater complexities of the negotiations in the 1990s. It was in this decade that Henley self-consciously worked to establish herself as a postsouthern writer, one who has grown out of a southern milieu and indeed has centralized that culture in early writings but for whom that cultural identity no longer remains preeminent in either the writer's daily existence or her artistic expression. In the plays of this decade (*Abundance, Signature, Control Freaks, Revelers, L-Play,* and *Impossible Marriage*), Henley consistently—if not always successfully—explores new concerns and preoccupations refreshingly unshackled from southern environs: gender roles in the nineteenth-century American West; the future of an ego-driven, media-controlled society; the complex relations of family, power, and eroticism; the dynamics of theater production itself; the inherent instabilities of the postmodern moment. The omnipresent southern settings of the 1980s here all but disappear, replaced by the likes of the Wyoming frontier, the shores of Lake Michigan, even a surreal futuristic Los Angeles. In fact, only one of the dozen scenes of *L-Play* is specifically set in the South, and the Savannah of *Impossible Marriage* seems largely irrelevant to the overarching thematics of the play. Thus, for Henley, her South of the previous decade truly seems gone with the wind.

This radical change in Henley's work appears to have fostered three dominant critical responses in regards to her southernness or lack thereof. Some persons commendably assess each play and the ever-evolving Henley who has produced it on their own terms, neither denying the regional investments that structure so many early works and no doubt continue to influence Henley herself nor making those investments the necessary validating components of every artistic expression. For those critics of southern literature typified in the 1980s by Noble, however, Henley's evolution away from a regionally based set of concerns seems to have snapped whatever tenuous links there were between her and a codified southern literary identity. As a result, with the possible rare exception of *Crimes of the Heart*, Henley's plays do not at present figure prominently either in the scholarship of southern literature or in its classroom teaching.[2] Finally, perhaps the most complicating—and, I suspect, for Henley the most anxiety-inducing—responses are those of critics who refuse to remove from her the label of southern writer and instead continue to use this designation as the requisite starting point for assessing her work, even though this mode is now profoundly anachronistic. Of these three responses, it is the last that potentially demands the most careful consideration, since it may help to explain in part the troubling and not necessarily fair narrative frequently imposed upon Henley's career: the thrilling fresh young voice of a wunderkind has given way to stridency, confusion, and even ineptitude, leaving high expectations more or less unfulfilled after an initial flash of brilliance.

Like any categorization reflecting an identity reduced to only one or two constitutive axes of the individual's whole, the label of "southern writer" is a problematic one, and it has as often been feared, avoided, or endured as it has been coveted and embraced. While this anxiety may spring from a number of interrelated sources, such as regional biases, highly subjective personal concerns, the economics of literary production, and so forth, the dismay is perhaps most often contingent upon uneasiness with the pervasive monolithic understandings of the South's literary production. While these understandings, whether held by critics or by popular audiences, have changed in light of the recent pressures of multiculturalism and canon reformation, the monoliths are indeed proving hard to dismantle. Granted, some have waned, such as the "moonlight and magnolia" school of romance and sentimentalism, supposedly epitomized by Margaret Mitchell's *Gone with the Wind*, and the "southern temper" school that helped to formulate the Southern Renascence in the 1950s. Few critics now, for instance, would offer with the assurance of Robert B. Heilman the inanely broad assertion that the "southern temper" is, quite simply, "the coincidence of a sense of the concrete, a sense of the elemental, a sense of the ornamental, a sense of the representative, and a sense of totality" (3). But other southern monoliths remain amazingly resilient. At mid-century, for instance, Flannery O'Connor groused in her essay "Some Aspects of the Grotesque in Southern Fiction" about the pervasion of the "School of Southern Degeneracy" (38) in popular understandings of the region's literary output, and maintained in another essay that the very phrase "southern writer" "conjures up an image of Gothic monstrosities and the idea of a preoccupation with everything deformed and grotesque. Most of us are considered, I believe, to be unhappy combinations of Poe and Erskine Caldwell" ("Fiction Writer" 28). Nearly thirty years later, Shannon Ravenel, an editor who has worked diligently to undermine notions of southern canons, could nevertheless still confidently identify the same set of cultural presumptions at work when, in her introduction to *New Stories from the South*, she cites the quip of Pat Conroy's mother that all southern literature is a variation on but one narrative: "On the night the hogs ate Willie, Mama died when she heard what Papa did with Sister" (vii). Even today many persons no doubt hold the region's literature to remain singularly preoccupied with social deviancy and sexual aberration, especially as reinforced—intentionally or not—by contemporary texts along the lines of *Bastard out of Carolina*, *Pulp Fiction*, and, in fact, Henley's early plays themselves.

While one might expect multiculturalism and canon reformation, rooted as they usually are in postmodern skepticism of monolithic structures, literary or otherwise, to undermine these reductive paradigms for southern literature, these recent forces have in some significant cases ironically fostered new, equally reductive understandings of this writing, ones that emerge phoenix-like from the ashes of the culture wars. The editors of Norton's 1998 *Literature of the American South*, for instance, achieve the useful and appreciated task of destabilizing the paradigms mentioned above, contextualizing representative works from these "schools" with counternarratives and omitting texts that too emphatically reveal romanticized or gothic preoccupations.

(Indeed, William L. Andrews and his coeditors limit Poe's fiction to one tale and omit Mitchell and Caldwell altogether.) And yet, when taken as a whole, the anthology reveals that in the place of these deposed paradigms is a new touchstone for assessment: the negotiations of racial difference. Too long neglected in matters of southern canon formation, race here, however, becomes omnipresent to the near exclusion of other categories of identity and reduced solely to relations between African Americans and European Americans. Moreover, the anthology's selections present an adroitly manipulated metanarrative in which the South moves from the shameful days of slavery through the trials of Jim Crow to a halcyon contemporary moment when the region has finally righted its racial wrongs or at least, in the case of the white South, become guiltily aware of past sins. The range of selections within this tripartite structure affirms the valorization of the late twentieth century, since these scant sixty years receive the lion's share of pages and include a proliferation of voices, all at the particular expense of the pre-1880 section, that cover approximately two centuries yet are quarantined to less than a fourth of the anthology's pages. What remains amazingly consistent, though, throughout the compilation is a focus on racial difference, so that the ostensibly appropriate question to pose of southern writing seems no longer how does it reinscribe a mythic past or partake of gothic extremes but rather what comment does this writing make on race relations. Thus, when juxtaposed against the earlier schools, the contours of this monolith are new, but its scope is as restricted as those of the previous schools' paradigms.[3]

It is these culturally ingrained, often competing paradigms, whether old or new, that potentially create so much anxiety within literary figures who are associated with the South and that, of course, continue to impact the critical reception of their work. How, Henley and other writers must ask themselves, does their work fit within these oversimplified understandings, if at all? Which of these competing paradigms seems to provide the most appropriate context or discourse for critical assessment? What are the benefits and liabilities of this position? What complexities of both the authors and their texts are necessarily diminished when these works are forced to stand within or outside a particular paradigm?

Again, Flannery O'Connor, a writer whose work was—and often still is—far too neatly pigeonholed within that "School of Southern Degeneracy," offers useful comments on the issues giving rise to these questions. "Most readers these days must be sufficiently sick of hearing about Southern writers and Southern writing and what so many reviewers insist upon calling the 'Southern school,' " she carps in "The Fiction Writer and His Country." "No one has ever made plain just what the Southern school is or which writers belong to it" (28). Horrified though she would be with having her sentiments characterized as such, O'Connor here displays precisely that postmodern skepticism of reductive literary monoliths alluded to earlier, bridling at the notion of a codified southern literary production. Any writer's work, she implies, defies such categorization (which, in turn, is itself uncategorizable), yet that writer must function within—or in spite of—the overlaid presumptions that arise from that particular set of limited discourses. "If you are a Southern writer, that label, and all the misconceptions that go with it," O'Connor offers, "is pasted on you at once, and you are left to get it off as best you can" ("Some Aspects" 37), regardless of whether the label springs from, say, the romantic or the gothic paradigm of southern literature. "Southern identity," she asserts with acerbity in "The Regional Writer," is no more "connected with mocking-birds and beaten biscuits and white columns any more than . . . with hookworm and bare feet and muddy clay roads" (57). Uniting all these salient O'Connor essays is, therefore, an adamant stance that her fiction—and, by extension, her own identity—is far more complex than any regional paradigm grants.[4] But even O'Connor herself now threatens to become part of the newest southern literary monoliths, as contemporary fiction writer Tony Earley, like others, acknowledges: "My fear is that, eventually, because of our willingness to feed on, without replacing, the tenets and traditions and subjects given to us by our predecessors—Welty, Flannery O'Connor, and William Faulkner most prominent among them—Southern writing will collapse and bury all of us, leaving only kudzu, grits, and a certain vaguely familiar voice to mark the spot" (x–xi).

While Henley has yet to articulate her opinions about regional literary identity as fully as O'Connor—or even Earley—has, Henley's work of the last decade strongly implies parallels between her sentiments and O'Connor's. The younger woman seems to find the label of southern writer just as limiting as the older one did. However, unlike O'Connor, whose fiction remained firmly fixed in a southern milieu despite anxieties about a dictated regional identity, Henley has, as already mentioned, worked deliberately in the past decade to move beyond these limits by almost consistently abandoning southern settings for her plays. But this particular marker of her post-southernness assumes even greater significance in the context of Henley's introduction to the second volume of Smith and Kraus's recent collection of her plays. Here she immediately foregrounds geography and draws the explicit contrast between the southern settings of her early plays and the non-southern one of the plays of the 1990s:

> The first five plays in Volume One take place in the present/past. By that I mean they are contemporary plays but not quite set in the here and now. They deal essentially with obsessions and concerns from roughly the first twenty years of my life. All of them, with the exception of *Am I Blue* (set in New Orleans) are set in Mississippi, the place I grew up. These plays seem to have an amber quality to them; they search to make sense of observations made long ago. To nick a term from Tennessee Williams, they are memory plays.

> The final play in Volume One, *The Lucky Spot*, takes place in Louisiana in 1933. The first play in this volume takes place in the Wyoming territory beginning in the 1860s. By setting these plays in period, I was able to take some active control of the amber glow, move out of Mississippi, and start heading west. These are plays written about parts of my life that occurred after leaving Mississippi. . . . (vi)[5]

And, indeed, as if to mirror the body of her writing for the last decade, the portions of this introduction written by Henley make no further mention of her native region after establishing its early centrality.

This deliberate westward trajectory stressed by Henley's comments here may seem strained, however, to the reader of volume one of her collected plays or even to the avid theatergoer who recalls Henley's productions of the 1980s, since both scenarios end not with *The Lucky Spot* and its setting of Louisiana's distant past but rather with *The Debutante Ball*, set in small-town Mississippi. Yet, as Henley carefully explains in the first of her two introductions to the collected plays, "The plays in this volume are not presented in the order in which they were written, but rather in the order in which they were produced in New York. The actual order they were written in is as follows: *Am I Blue, Crimes of the Heart, The Miss Firecracker Contest, The Wake of Jamey Foster, The Debutante Ball*, and *The Lucky Spot*" (*CPII* vii). With this history of composition clarified, the evolution that Henley stresses in the second introduction appears all the more persuasive as an evolution in which *The Lucky Spot* proves a pivotal work if for no other reason than it marks the systematic distancing of Henley from self-conscious southernness. In fact, in light of this record of composition, a certain symmetry emerges about these six early plays, with the two Louisiana settings bracketing the Mississippi ones and perhaps suggesting that, after an apprentice's attempt at a flamboyant and yet foreign New Orleans locale, Henley smartly turned to the environment that produced her and that she therefore implicitly and intimately knew before venturing beyond it once again.

Henley also encodes in her introduction to the later plays this deliberate evolution toward postsouthernness through her cited literary influences and parallels. Her opening paragraph conspicuously ends with the decision to "nick a term from Tennessee Williams" (vi) and characterize her early drama as "memory plays" (vi), thus alluding to *The Glass Menagerie* and Williams's efforts there to temper prevailing mid-twentieth-century demands for realism on the stage. "The scene is memory," he insists in the opening stage directions, "and is therefore nonrealistic" (21), echoing his comments in the production notes.[6] While Henley's "nicking" of Williams's phrase and all its connotations sheds considerable light on her understanding of these plays of the 1980s, the citation also testifies to Williams's influence on Henley, one that indeed here provides for her the very language of self-analysis.

But Williams's identity as a theorist of modern drama is, of course, overshadowed by his identity as a specifically southern playwright. No writer, in fact, has become more emblematic of expressly southern dramatic production than he. Indeed, as one of Williams's biographers Lyle Leverich, among others, argues, with Thomas Lanier Williams's act of self-naming, he became a literal embodiment of southern geography, with all the entailed benefits and detriments.[7] But even more than his name, Williams's drama justifies Jacob Adler's claim that Williams "has done perhaps more than any other single writer to make the world aware of the South" (439). Thus, when Henley cites Williams early on in this introduction, she is self-consciously positioning herself within a particular regional literary production and linking herself to the most central of its figures.

Williams is not, however, the only influence or literary presence that Henley identifies in this introduction. About two-thirds of the way through it, she muses on the genesis of *L-Play*, one of the most difficult of her recent works because of its intended absolute lack of cohesion beyond the symbolism of the letter L:

> I finally got the idea for the play when I realized I had no idea. I felt fragmented, decentralized, clueless. I had become confused over who was more truthful, more enlightened: Sophocles, the Three Stooges, Edgar Allan Poe, Elvis, Nero?? There were so many worldviews, endless realities, tones, messages. I decided to go with it—the mosaic of life. I wrote a variety of different scenes in different styles and different characters. The only unifying element would be that the title of each scene would begin with an L. An L is half a box. It is a letter that is searching to connect, to link. (*CPII* xii)

This passage bears quoting in full, I think, because it so forcefully expresses Henley's O'Connoresque concern with reductive paradigms and her anxious embrace of multiplicity and polyvocality. Despite having this time nicked a term from E. M. Forster in his modernist appeal to connect, Henley exposes herself as thoroughly postmodern, awash in "so many worldviews, endless realities, tones, messages." Because, as she states earlier in the introduction, "Nothing is central, all is fragmented and a mess because there are just too many styles, times, characters, and chaos to choose from" (vii), a specifically southern regional identity that, so important in the early plays, now becomes merely one of many. And once again Henley replicates the evolution beyond southernness that manifests so dramatically in her larger body of work. Of the dozen rapid-fire scenes of *L-Play*, only the first setting is overtly designated as southern, the rest spiraling away from this ostensibly stable starting point in a maddening frenzy.

Caught up in this dizzying swirl of images and investments is, perhaps unsurprisingly, the same codified southern literary production that Henley reifies in her earlier fond citation of Williams. Now, however, southern literariness, like southern identity at large, loses any distinction or separateness. In Henley's characterization, Edgar Allan Poe, among the most canonical figures associated with southern literature and arguably the instigator of the southern gothic tradition, finds himself positioned between those media-generated icons of twentieth-century popular culture, the Three Stooges and Elvis Presley. Moreover, Henley dares to imply that the identities these persons and their performances project are potentially as relevant and culturally significant as those of Poe and his literary production. But even Henley's choice of Poe here is an intriguing one that contributes to an acknowledgment of destabilized, potentially contradictory identities embodied in a solitary individual. For all of his links to the South, Poe is a figure in American literary history with competing associations that are not necessarily contingent upon a regional identity: American Renaissance writer, father of detective fiction, formalist poet, editor, theorist, drunkard.[8] That is, because of a century and a half of wide-ranging critical explorations and constructions of the man and his writing, Poe's complexity—his own rival "worldviews, endless realities, tones, messages"—has been granted, a concession that Henley seemingly envies. At any rate, however, with the citation of Poe at this point in her introduction, the importance of southern literariness has waned sharply and indeed soon disappears altogether.

Henley closes her telling introduction with a discussion of *Impossible Marriage*, providing insights into its composition and production, just as she does with the other plays. With *Impossible Marriage* she returns to a southern setting (Savannah, Georgia) and thereby violates her emphatically self-characterized trajectory away from the South. Yet here she does not foreground this locale; instead, she underscores her intentional citations of the Irish Oscar Wilde, who now replaces any lingering shadows of Williams, much less the destabilized Poe.[9] Henley confesses here as elsewhere that she had agreed to write a "happy play":

> I'd certainly never tried it. Something effortlessly brilliant with keen, incisive wit. Something like *The Importance of Being Earnest*, except by me.
> For the first time I read all of Wilde's plays. What a good time that was. I started looking at drawings by Aubrey Beardsley: sensual, formal, and forbiddenly erotic. (*CPII* xiv)[10]

And indeed *Impossible Marriage* has a distinctly Wildean air, although, one fears, without quite the brilliant flashes of wit. Nevertheless, Wilde's distinctly nonsouthern presence is incontrovertible, and Henley's successful evolution toward postsouthernness emerges yet again through these cited literary presences, progressing from Williams to Poe to Wilde. In at least four narratives, therefore, does Henley emphasize this trajectory that originates with the South but ultimately moves beyond it: in her own lived experience, in the geographic shifts in the settings of her plays over time, in the scenes of *L-Play*, and, finally, in the allusions to literary influences in this introduction.

Although the repetition no doubt attests to how strongly Henley feels about establishing this trajectory, she is, however, too sophisticated a writer only to repeat it with the slight nuances detailed above. Instead, she also seems to deploy another, more complicated strategy among her recent plays to negotiate southernness and southern literariness: parody. Particularly in the wildly comic *Control Freaks*, her 1992 play significantly preoccupied with modes of resisting influence and control, she simultaneously pays homage to previous southern literature through her citation of texts by Tennessee Williams and Eudora Welty *and* upends this literature with her brilliant revisionary spoofing of these texts. In the end, *Control Freaks* does precisely what Linda Hutcheon argues all effective postmodern parody does: "As form of ironic representation, parody is doubly coded in political terms: it both legitimizes and subverts that which it parodies. This kind of authorized transgression is what makes it a ready vehicle for the political contradictions of postmodernism at large" (101). In Henley's treatment, texts by Welty and Williams retain a degree of cultural valorization in the very fact that Henley deems them worthy of citation. Yet, through the outlandishness of her parodic representations, Henley exposes southern literary production as verging on merely an accumulation of spent clichés and tired narratives, ones that, among other things, keep in play problematic assumptions about gender and sexuality.

Henley immediately establishes the preoccupation of *Control Freaks* with clichés and their inescapability with the opening monologue and its echoes. Sister Willard, perhaps the most central of the play's four characters, "has just returned from jury duty" (*CPII* 122) and introduces the play's action with a protracted speech to herself explaining her experience in the courtroom and concentrating on the convicted man:

> He had to sit there in front of everyone wearing handcuffs. The rest of us could raise our arms, but he couldn't. He got a lot of time. We decided to throw the book at him. He had come to no good. That's where chance had taken him and it was too late to change his habits. There was no way to break his patterns. He was a bad egg. A rotten apple in a barrel. You might as well spit at him as look at him. I'm sorry to say this man was less than dirt and we had to put him away for good. It was an easy decision. Like choosing chocolate over vanilla. (113)

Just three pages later Sister again offers to her brother, "Oh, he was a bad man. A rotten apple in a barrel. You wouldn't have liked him, Carl. Not one bit. We socked him away for life. I wanted to watch him fry. But they only let you give him life" (116). Finally, in the play's closing moments, she rages to the dying Carl, "You're a bad egg, a rotten apple in a barrel! I'm sorry to say this man was less than dirt and we had to put him away for good" (146). In each instance, trite phrase piles upon trite phrase—"throw the book at him," "had come to no good," "a bad egg," "a rotten apple," "less than dirt," "socked him away," "watch him fry," "put him away for good," and so on—to the extent that few can question Henley's intentional foregrounding of the clichés, a move that persists throughout the play. Carl and Betty Willard, Sister's brother and sister-in-law, and Paul Casper, the family's guest, speak in language no less deliberately hackneyed than in this opening monologue. Thus Henley's dialogue repeatedly suggests that she has come to hold language as inescapably repetitive, a series of exhausted citations in which humans are even reduced to parroting themselves parroting others.

If, then, readers and viewers are immediately cued to analyze these repetitions at the level of phrase and sentence, it is but a short leap for these same readers and viewers to see other citations functioning more broadly in *Control Freaks*. It is here that Henley begins her subtle references to seminal southern literary texts and their authors, not least of whom is Tennessee Williams, one of the figures she has consistently acknowledged as an influence on her, as established in her introductions to the collected plays and elsewhere. When taken at its broadest, the plot of *Control Freaks* strikingly parallels that of *The Glass Menagerie*: a familial trio riven by pettiness, physical deformity, and misdirected erotic desire adroitly manipulates the attentions of a "gentleman caller," all with disastrous results.[11] Granted, Henley's characters are not exact replicas of Williams's foursome, but enough crucial similarities emerge to mark the citations as deliberate, and the differences are telling insofar as what they highlight about Williams's play and especially in what he will—and will not—allow himself to say.

Consider, for instance, the similarities between the fragile Laura Wingfield of *The Glass Menagerie* and Sister Willard of *Control Freaks*. Both young women have tenuous holds on life, fostered in part by their physical deformities and their perceived unattractiveness, all of which has left them single in a world eddying with erotic currents, and thus each woman arguably elicits the most sympathy in the respective plays. But in Henley's parodic resurrection, Sister's baldness (both physical and verbal), her flamboyant wigs, and near schizophrenia replace Laura's genteel pleurosis and slightly mismatched legs, just as her sexual timidity, that which makes her "like a piece of her own glass collection, too exquisitely fragile to move from the shelf" (Williams 5), disappears with Sister's voracious desire for a man, any man. "Hey, how about the man who's coming for cocktails? Would he be my type?" Sister asks. "Well, maybe you have it figured wrong, my type. See 'cause I like different types. I like all types. With me type doesn't matter" (*CPII* 118). Not surprisingly, therefore, when Paul Casper arrives at the

Willards' house, the scene is by no means the delicately painful one of Laura, Jim O'Connor, the news of his fiancée, and the broken unicorn. Instead, Paul at once proposes marriage to the suicidal Sister, who despite—or, rather, because of—saying "the magic word—'No' " (133), "*starts having spontaneous orgasms all across the yard:*"

SISTER: Oooh! OOOh! OOOOOH! OOOOOOOHH! (*Sister collapses to the ground exhausted and panting.*)
(*Paul produces a giant engagement ring.*)
PAUL: I'm gonna ask you one more time. Sister Willard, will you marry me?
SISTER: I—I—I— (*Convulsing with orgasms all alone on the ground.*) Ooh! OOH! OOOHH!
PAUL: Will you?
SISTER: (*Weakly.*) Yes. (135)

Henley even darkly—but hilariously—revises Laura's menagerie of delicate glass animals as, on the one hand, Sister's raisin-eyed gingerbread men and, on the other, her "two fat cats" (116) abusively crammed into a minuscule cage, all of which, however, come to an ill-fated end. When Sister pulls from the oven the tray of gingerbread men she has fretted over so lovingly, her burned hand drops and shatters the cookies, allowing for the striking image of her "kneeling among the gingerbread men trying to piece the charred crumbs together" (138) and thus almost directly replicating Laura stooping over the shattered unicorn. Similarly, Sister must cope at the play's end with the corpses of the hideous cats poisoned by her "doubling-crossing bitch" (141) sister-in-law.

But what is one to make of these parallels to Williams's play that Henley so carefully constructs and then distorts in *Control Freaks*? Her revisions seem to me to accomplish at least two not unrelated goals: to self-consciously rewrite southern gender roles and, in the particular case of *The Glass Menagerie*, to figuratively kill off the literary forebear with his actual death in the play. Within this context, *Control Freaks* might aptly be subtitled "Laura's Revenge," since in Henley's treatment the abusively egotistical brother does not ultimately dictate the narrative, abandoning the pathetic sister to the dismal fate of spinsterhood, as Tom Wingfield does. Instead, by the end of Henley's play, Sister exorcises her demons through her brutal killing of the shit-covered Carl—"*She lunges in the bushes after him and stabs him over and over and over again*" (*CPII* 146)—and, thanks to a deliberately self-referential deus ex machina, soars over the audience into the future, leaving behind the chaos and abuse of her past: "*She dances across the firmament with her dress*" (146). This ending does not, however, come unexpectedly. As the charted parallels suggest, Henley has deliberately been crafting a female protagonist whose identity is hardly constituted by the passivity of Williams's culturally emblematic Laura. For all her weakness, Sister *is* aggressive, sexual, and willing to acknowledge the gratification that comes with erotic pleasure, and she *does* eventually liberate herself. In short, then, this parody allows Henley to move beyond the clichéd women of canonical southern literary production and offer ones who become active agents in their own lives.

This revision of *The Glass Menagerie* also handily allows Henley to efface Tennessee Williams himself, just as she does in that introduction to the second volume of the collected plays. As suggested, though, in *Control Freaks* a degree of violence marks the effacement, a degree directly proportional to the abuse that Carl heaps upon Sister. If Williams's play ends with Tom's guilty near-confession of his psychological abuse of his sister, Henley's play leaves no such ambiguity. Carl's offenses range from the merely disgusting to the truly horrifying, the most indicative being his manipulation of Sister to clean up the massive shits he leaves each morning in the yard and his protracted incestuous abuses, those that she has repressed: "Yes, I—I sodomized you once when you were sleeping. . . . Occasionally, I'd come in your room in the morning and I'd let you suck me. You'd swallow every drop like feeding milk to a hungry baby" (*CPII* 145). This confession on Carl's part does not, however, like Tom's, end the play, and Carl ultimately lies dead at Sister's hands as a result of his truth telling. Thus, because of the strong autobiographical encoding of Tennessee Williams in Tom Wingfield in *The Glass Menagerie*, Henley, through a chain of associative links, repays the older playwright for whatever intentional or unintentional acts of violence his work has enacted on subsequent regional writers and their abilities to escape his control. And once again Henley puts southern literary production behind her, figuratively killing it off even as she cites its tremendous—but perhaps not always beneficial—early influence.

If one accepts *Control Freaks* as a strategic parody of *The Glass Menagerie*, Henley also manages to point to Williams's own early silence about homosexuality, thus implying that both his depictions of female sexuality and gay desire emerge as problematic in the context of late-twentieth-century erotic practices. It has become commonplace in Williams scholarship to acknowledge that the character Jim O'Connor is an amalgam of Jim Connor, Williams's fraternity brother, and Stanley Kowalski, Williams's coworker at International Shoe Company in St. Louis who was eventually immortalized in *A Streetcar Named Desire*. Both men, it seems, exerted significant erotic pulls on the young Williams, who was then struggling to accept his homosexuality. As one of Williams's biographers Donald Spoto clarifies, "There is no evidence of a realized homosexual affair between Williams and Kowalski, but according to Dakin [Williams's brother] it was clear that Tom had a powerful erotic and romantic attachment to Kowalski:

Kowalski's name was often mentioned by Tom, and to see them together was to see a love-struck hero-worshipper and the idol of his dreams" (44).[12] Thus, for Williams, perhaps the most significant underlying current of eroticism in *The Glass Menagerie* was the relationship between Tom and Jim, and yet Williams carefully deflected this homoeroticism, just as he would continue to do in his early plays.

Henley, on the other hand, makes male homosexuality crucial to *Control Freaks*. She brazenly allows Carl, with all his exaggerated heterosexuality, to indulge in at least the simulation of same-sex interaction with another man when he forces the poisoned Paul to suck the antidote from a dildo: "Let's see you crawl. Get down on your knees. Now crawl. *(Carl extends a lifelike rubber vibrator out to Paul.) (Paul starts crawling to Carl, as Carl stirs the potion with the vibrator.)*" (*CPII* 143). Paul does, in fact, eventually suck the life-giving cock, as Carl continues to croon: "Good dog. He's a good dog. *(Carl takes the vibrator out of Paul's mouth and kicks Paul to the ground.)*" (143). With this, Carl, arguably Williams's textual surrogate, clearly reinforces homophobic discourse even as he raises the specter of gay sexuality himself, not unlike the scenarios that many critics have identified and seen as contingent upon Williams's closetedness in texts such as *The Glass Menagerie*.[13] And yet, according to Henley, what is the final outcome of Carl's enactment of gay sexual practices simply for reasons of sadistic control? His savage murder by Sister for his even queerer acts of heterosexual incest and scat play. Paul, on the other hand, ironically lives because of his willingness to engage in what he and Carl perceive as demeaning gay acts. Male over-investments in heterosexuality, such as those Williams felt himself compelled to enact in his early literary production, thus seem as offensive to Henley and her postmodern sexual sensibilities as do Williams's and others' depictions of female sexuality and sexual autonomy.

These lenses of gender and sexuality are also components in Henley's negotiations of Eudora Welty in *Control Freaks*. Like Williams, she seems to have exerted tremendous influence over Henley, but the images and narratives cardinal to Welty's literary production appear as flawed—or at least as problematically dated or provincial—as Williams's when it comes to more contemporary handlings of gender and sexuality, and it is on precisely these images and narratives that Henley hones in and moves beyond.[14] Her tactic, though, is again the same: to take the stereotype of the disenfranchised, largely passive, single woman of canonical southern literary production, remove her from that regional context, and allow her a gratifying act of revenge. To do so, Henley manages to yoke with Laura Wingfield perhaps her only serious rival as the most famous southern literary spinster: Sister, the narrator of Welty's "Why I Live at the P.O."

If anything, though, the characters who share the same name, which incessantly reduces them to a subordinate role within the traditional patriarchal family, are even more similar than Henley's Sister and Laura. Both broadly comic, the two Sisters struggle even more overtly than Laura with erotic competition within the family and the anxiety of the resulting rejection. For Welty's Sister, this anxiety springs from having lost Mr. Whitaker, the Pose-Yourself photographer, to her own sister's manipulative broadcasting of Sister's physical defects: "Stella-Rondo broke us up. Told him I was one-sided. Bigger on one side than the other, which is a deliberate, calculated falsehood: I'm the same" (Welty 46). Similarly, for Henley's Sister, this anxiety arises from having lost her own brother, whom Sister proclaims "the last of the good catches" (*CPII* 118), to the trick-turning Betty. And, if Welty's Sister must suffer Shirley-T., who appears to be the walking proof and thus constant reminder of Stella-Rondo's sexual activity, Henley's Sister must suffer Betty's perpetual sexual performances: the wearing of the "Carl's little pussy" (120) underwear, the retelling of Paul's demands for infidelity ("Suck me dry. Make me cry like a baby. Like a little baby. I wanna come through your nose" [122]), the clandestine smearing of her vaginal secretions across Paul's face (131), and so on. Even the two Sisters' initial modes of coping are strikingly parallel, since both incessantly talk their way through their resulting anxiety.

It is here, though, that Henley begins to establish the strategic differences necessary for effective parody. If Welty's Sister retreats to the P.O. in an ostensible act of self-determination, she nevertheless remains dependent upon a listener to hear the extended self-justification of her participation within the familial strife. Henley's Sister, although equally garrulous, begins the play having already moved beyond this need for an outsider's consoling presence, since she has, thanks to Henley's parodic exaggeration, a range of voices contained within her, and, in fact, several moments crucial to the play's action revolve around the autonomous debates between Sister, Pinkie, and Spaghetti within Sister's head. Of course, Henley takes this move to autonomy on Sister's part even further when she grimly watches Betty's fatal shooting, licenses Paul's humiliation and exile, and, most significantly, kills her incestuous brother herself. The end result is that the physical space of the family—the kitchen, the yard, the bedroom—becomes Sister's conquered territory, and she may do with it as she pleases. Welty's Sister, on the other hand, for all the activity entailed in confiscating the oscillating fan and transplanting the four-o'clocks, loses the field altogether and finds herself self-exiled to "the next to smallest P.O. in the state of Mississippi" (Welty 47). All Sister's protests of contentment—"Of course, I like it here. It's ideal, as I've been saying. You see, I've got everything cater-cornered, the way I like it" (56)—are hollow performances, so that, despite the rich comic ironies of the story, Welty ultimately leaves readers with a profoundly unsettling image of female dependency and sexual anxiety, that is made all the more poignant when juxtaposed against *Control Freaks*. Tony Earley summarizes the plight of Welty's Sister in stating that she "is horribly alone [and] will spend the rest of her life in a tiny, tiny place, with no chance of escape, unloved and unmarried, dependent upon the charity of her family. Her monologue to us, unbeknownst to her, is at once a comedic tour de force and a heartrending cry in the wilderness" (ix). This is precisely the fate that Henley refuses to allow her revision of Welty's narrator; thus, the younger writer's narrative is equally a comedic tour de force but also ultimately a heartwarming cry of affirmation and female autonomy.

These efforts on Henley's part, whether in the repeated, multilayered narrative delineating a geographic abandonment of the South or in the parodic spoofing of southern literature, its key authors, and its distressing gender politics, seem, however, only to have added to the complexities and anxieties of her regional identity rather than resolved them. Throughout the last decade, a crucial subset of Henley's critics has seemingly refused to grant the importance of this evolution away from southernness and instead has continued to impose that label upon Henley, using it as the consistent entryway into assessment. Almost without fail, she continues to be set up in critical discussions as southern: the foremost writer of "southern-gothic comedies" (Senior 70), the master of the "quirky Southern sensibility" (Pogrebin), "quirky Southern characters" (Churnin), "endearingly eccentric Southern women" (Siegel), and "gothic Southern life" (Stearns), all as epitomized by *Crimes of the Heart*. Some reviewers are even more insistent in their "southern" characterizations. In his review of *Signature*, for instance, Alvin Klein pays special attention to the "Mississippi-born playwright's ever-zany wayward and poetic style, which has been associated with eccentricities of a particular Southern kind," while Edward Karam begins his *Times* (London) review of *Impossible Marriage* by noting that "Beth Henley has a knack for creating endearingly eccentric Southern characters who rebel against convention, most famously in *Crimes of the Heart*." Others, like Benedict Nightingale, are simply excessive: "Beth Henley is one of the few modern dramatists who has persistently managed to create a world recognisably her own. Think of her *Crimes of the Heart* or *Miss Firecracker Contest* [sic], and instantly you can smell the wisteria on the porches and dead dogs rotting in the street, and hear the mad crash of crockery and the coy little expostulations of 'honey child' and 'poppa sweet potato.' " Even the *Collected Plays*, those volumes that perhaps best showcase Henley's range, have met with this reductive treatment, since their value apparently lies in the presentation of "a distinctive voice of the American theater, one that could be described as modern Southern Gothic" (Luddy 91).

By no means, though, do all critics of this ilk see these ostensibly inescapable southern investments as assets for Henley. Geoff Chapman, for example, grouses from Toronto that Henley, that "author from America's deep south ... whose *Crimes of the Heart* won a Pulitzer Prize and was translated into a decent movie," has "merely shifted" the characters of *Abundance* "from her familiar southern fried gothic setting to one you might call toasted western wacko." But other critics seem to valorize the southern-set plays, a move apparently licensed by the Pulitzer for *Crimes*, and hold those efforts of Henley's part to move away from this locale to be inferior. T. H. McCulloh, writing of *Abundance*'s Los Angeles premiere, deems it "a strange play to have come from the author of the very contemporary 'The Miss Firecracker Contest' and the just-as-current Pulitzer Prize–winning 'Crimes of the Heart,' " thus deploying precisely this move and implying a contentment with the tried and true southern Henley. Similarly, Graydon Royce finds the greatest problem of the Minneapolis production of *Impossible Marriage* to be its missing southern setting: "First, this staging has no Southern bearing other than the pedestrian accents. The atmosphere is cool Norway Pine, not steamy Mississippi Magnolia." Again Henley is deemed problematic when she abandons her southernness.

Even in the introduction to the second volume of the collected plays, in which Henley works so diligently to distance herself from a regional identity, the invited comments of actors, translators, and producers often echo the critics and subtly impose a southern identity upon her. For instance, in his brief notes on *Control Freaks* and his performances in it, actor Bill Pullman breezily terms Henley "that Southern Madam of Murder and Mischief" (*CPII* x). Comparably, albeit with a more serious tone, Alfre Woodard reflects on her work in *L-Play* during its Los Angeles run and praises Henley: "Her unselfconscious approach to circumstance and character honors the flesh and blood folk that populate our families, our romances, and the four directions—especially the South" (xiii). Thus, as with Pullman's characterization, Woodard refuses to cede Henley's southernness and instead accentuates it.

For Henley, then, southernness has proved itself the same sticky problem that O'Connor identified. Once pasted on with the likes of *Crimes of the Heart*, it cannot be removed, try as Henley might. This process is, however, a profoundly serious one, since this imposition of regional identity is perhaps the foremost reason that Henley's critical reputation has fallen so dramatically in the last decade. As suggested by the smattering of reviews cited above, the postsouthern plays have not fared well, meeting with mixed responses at best. *Abundance*, for instance, garnered praise from Mimi Kramer, who deemed the play "a real treat" (105), and Nancy Churnin, who identified "a leap in maturation," but these pronouncements were rare. Instead, pans abounded. Potentially working, like Kramer and Churnin, from a gender bias, Robert Brustein complained of *Abundance*, "The play makes no sense at all, and when I look at my notes I can't make sense of them either. I sat through this affair in a vague delirium, keeping awake only by watching two women signing the dialogue for the deaf" (28). He concludes, "I found the plotting so random, the characters so arbitrary, and the theme so cloudy that I couldn't imagine why it was written or performed" (28). John Simon echoed Brustein's sentiments, tellingly beginning his savage review, "As one watches with trepidation the talented Beth Henley making a fool of herself in *Abundance*, one tries to figure out what could have led the worthy author of *Crimes of the Heart* to this malfeasance of the mind" (92). Rounding out the dismal assessments of *Abundance*, Geoff Chapman deemed it "a mess of melodrama and tongue-in-cheek fancy," the mini-review of the *Washington Times* held it to be a play filled with "leaden material," Buzz McClain found in it "little drama to propel the character study," and Benedict Nightingale nastily concluded, "By the end the West seems a pretty shoddy pace but, by the end, who cares?"

Signature and *Control Freaks* fared somewhat better than *Abundance*, but by no means were the raves and accolades of *Crimes of the Heart* forthcoming. Moreover, for all their praise of *Control Freaks*, both Tom Jacobs and Don Shirley found the ending—which I read as so significant in establishing Henley's postsouthern moves—weak and contrived. There were, however, no such tempered concerns with *L-Play*. Ed Siegel, for instance, savaged it in the *Boston Globe*. And yet readers were hardly surprised to find him ultimately dismiss the play as "just another example of bleak chic" in a review parodically entitled "*L-Play* Is a Lifeless Lemon, Largely Lackluster, Leaden." Even the responses to *Impossible Marriage*, Henley's most recent production that marks a return to a southern setting, have been disappointing. With his usual acumen, Ben Brantley offered a solid but mixed review in the *New York Times*, but other critics refused to be as gracious. David Patrick Stearns sniffs that "Everybody's so weird, it's eccentricity of its own sake," while Edward Karam echoes that "the characters drown in quirkiness." Regional productions have spawned even nastier reactions. In his pan of the Minneapolis production, Graydon Royce returns to the valorization of the early southern Henley, asserting, "Too bad the theater [Minneapolis's Theatre in the Round] didn't open its 49th season Friday night with Henley's 'Crimes of the Heart,' which won her the Pulitzer Prize in 1981. Instead, we get her 'Impossible Marriage,' an unmemorable trifle."[15]

When taken as a whole, these critical responses project onto Henley the uncomfortable hint of perhaps not failure but, instead, of futile efforts to fulfill her early promise. And, while there are, no doubt, a range of factors at play in this critical construction, both at the level of individual performances and of the broader trajectory, Henley's southernness seems significant. Even when critics, such as those cited above, do not necessarily address the playwright's regional associations, these persons seem to hold out the implicit southernness of *Crimes of the Heart* and the other early plays as the yardstick by which to measure Henley's contemporary work. And yet these efforts on her part are precisely those that seek to move away from this regionally based mode of determining artistic value. In short, author and critics remain at cross-purposes.

Because of these conflicting cultural and critical investments in regional identity, Beth Henley enters the twenty-first century in an unenviable position and faces what other playwrights associated with the South perhaps do not. Turning to one extreme of an implied spectrum, she cannot remain wholly invested in the region, as, say, Alfred Uhry does. Granted, he seeks in works like *Driving Miss Daisy*, *The Last Night of Ballyhoo*, and *Parade* to complicate southernness as it relates to Jewishness, but Uhry never attempts to deny or displace regional dictates. Indeed, he is, by virtually every criterion, a southern writer. Turning to the other extreme of the spectrum, Henley, with the mixed blessings and burdens of the early southern plays, cannot ignore the region, as, say, Tony Kushner does. Despite his Louisiana childhood, Kushner's *Angels in America* and subsequent work, if anything, noticeably overlook the South in otherwise erstwhile efforts to capture and queer America. Quite simply, for most theatergoers, critics, and readers, Kushner is *not* a southern writer. Because of her particular literary career, in initially embracing and benefiting from southernness only to find it constricting but inescapable, Henley cannot assume either Uhry's position or Kushner's. She remains neither southern fish nor nonsouthern fowl, trying diligently of late to assume the latter identity but haunted by the former. Hers is therefore an anxious position in contemporary drama, and one waits with anticipation to see if Henley, like Sister, will ever be destined to once again dance across the critical firmament.

Notes

1. If *The History of Southern Literature* represents the major late-twentieth-century codification of southern literary production, the sprawling *Encyclopedia of Southern Culture* perhaps represents the parallel codification of southern popular culture. Its 1,634 pages, however, do not mention Henley at all, further testifying, one thinks, to the uneasiness with which she was handled in certain southern contexts of the 1980s.
2. No southern anthology or reader that I know of, for instance, contains Henley's work. Norton's recent *Literature of the American South*, an anthology devoted to the reshaping of southern canons, includes a number of writers tangential to traditional understandings of southern literature, such as Henry Louis Gates, Jr., yet the collection does not include Henley. There are, of course, a number of political factors at work in this particular case, as discussed below.
3. The critical success of Henley's early plays is due in part to the ease with which they can be positioned within virtually all these paradigms. Consider, for instance, *Crimes of the Heart*, Henley's most successful work, which has been simultaneously read as a hymn to traditional southern society, a bizarre

collection of gothic freaks (complete with a hanged cat), and an interrogation of interracial sexual mores.
4. I do not want, however, to imply that O'Connor is free from imposing her own restrictions on the paradigms in which her fiction "appropriately" functions. Indeed, much O'Connor scholarship has had to counter her implicit dictates that her work be read as religious and, more specifically, Catholic writing.
5. See also Henley, Interview 255–256 for a similar articulation.
6. See Williams 7–10 for his now famous theorization of "memory plays."
7. See Leverich 274–275.
8. The intersections of Poe's biography and geography also destabilize an enduring southern identity, if indeed any such thing ever exists.
9. Critics and reviewers have also persuasively suggested the influence of William Shakespeare, Richard Brinsley Sheridan, and Anton Chekhov on *Impossible Marriage*, an argument that only further underscores a shift away from deliberately southern literary models. See Brantley; Karam; Pogrebin.
10. Henley's comments are even more direct elsewhere: "I was very dedicated to the idea of ripping off Oscar Wilde" (Senior 70). See also Brantley.
11. Reviewer Don Shirley briefly notes the same parallel: "Paul is somewhat like a twisted parody of the gentleman caller in *The Glass Menagerie* (a play cited by Henley, in a recent interview, as one that her mother had acted in). In fact, an alternate title for Henley's own play could be 'The Crass Menagerie'" (F1). Shirley probably refers here to Henley's 15 December 1993 interview with Mary Dellasega. See Henley, Inteview 252.
12. See also Leverich 113, 130, 149.
13. See, for instance, Clum.
14. For an insightful discussion of the problems of Welty's broader influences, see Earley.
15. Pogrebin also offers an overview of Henley's critical reception.

Works Cited

Adler, Jacob H. "Modern Southern Drama." *The History of Southern Literature*. Eds. Louis D. Rubin, Jr., et al. Baton Rouge and London: Louisiana State University Press, 1985. 436–442.

Andrews, William L., et al., eds. *The Literature of the American South*. New York and London: Norton, 1998.

Brantley, Ben. "Fairies Adrift in Love's Garden." Review of *Impossible Marriage*, by Beth Henley. *New York Times,* 16 October 1998, E1, final late edition.

Brustein, Robert. "She-Plays, American Style." Review of *Machinal*, by Sophie Treadwell, and *Abundance*, by Beth Henley. *New Republic,* 17 December 1990, 27–29.

Chapman, Geoff. "Abundance of Western Wacko." Review of *Abundance*, by Beth Henley. *Toronto Star,* 15 July 1993, D10, final edition.

Churnin, Linda. "'Abundance' of Riches by Blackfriars." Review of *Abundance*, by Beth Henley. *Los Angeles Times,* 1 October 1991, F1, San Diego County edition.

Clum, John M. " 'Something Cloudy, Something Clear': Homophobic Discourse in Tennessee Williams." *Displacing Homophobia: Gay Male Perspectives in Literature and Culture*. Eds. Ronald R. Butters, John M. Clum, and Michael Moon. Durham and London: Duke University Press, 1989. 149–167.

Dellasega, Mary. "Beth Henley." *Speaking on Stage: Interviews with Contemporary American Playwrights*. Eds. Philip C. Kolin and Colby H. Kullman. Tuscaloosa and London: University of Alabama Press, 1996. 250–259.

Earley, Tony. "Preface: Letter from Sister—What We Learned at the P.O." *New Stories from the South: The Year's Best, 1999*. Ed. Shannon Ravenel. Chapel Hill, N.C.: Algonquin Books, 1999. vii–xi.

Heilman, Robert B. "The Southern Temper." *Southern Renascence: The Literature of the Modern South*. Eds. Louis D. Rubin, Jr., and Robert D. Jacobs. Baltimore: The Johns Hopkins University Press, 1966. 3–13.

Hutcheon, Linda. *The Politics of Postmodernism*. London and New York: Routledge, 1989.

Jacobs, Tom. Review of *Control Freaks*, by Beth Henley. *Daily Variety*, 21 July 1993.

Karam, Edward. "Verdict Misadventure." Review of *Impossible Marriage*, by Beth Henley. *Times* (London), 4 November 1998.

Klein, Alvin. "Hooray for Hollywood? More Like 'Horrors!' " Review of *Signature*, by Beth Henley. *New York Times*, 12 May 1996, B12, national edition.

Kramer, Mimi. "Picturing Abundance." Review of *Abundance*, by Beth Henley. *New Yorker*, 12 November 1990, 105–106.

Leverich, Lyle. *Tom: The Unknown Tennessee Williams*. New York and London: Norton, 1995.

Luddy, Thomas E. Review of *Collected Plays, 1980–1989* and *Collected Plays, 1990–1999*, by Beth Henley. *Library Journal*, July 2000, 91.

McClain, Buzz. " 'Abundance' Has Plenty in Intriguing, Taxing Way." Review of *Abundance*, by Beth Henley. *Washington Times*, 29 March 1994, C22, final edition.

McCulloh, T. H. "Scattered Staging Depletes Camino Payhouse's 'Abundance.' " Review of *Abundance*, by Beth Henley. *Los Angeles Times*, 15 September 1993, F2, Orange County edition.

Nightingale, Benedict. "Way Out West Leads Nowhere Fast." Review of *Abundance*, by Beth Henley. *Times* (London), 3 November 1995.

Noble, Donald R. "The Future of Southern Writing." *The History of Southern Literature*. Eds. Louis D. Rubin, Jr., et al. Baton Rouge and London: Louisiana State University Press, 1985. 578–588.

O'Connor, Flannery. "The Fiction Writer and His Country." *Mystery and Manners*. Eds. Sally Fitzgerald and Robert Fitzgerald. New York: Farrar, Straus and Giroux, 1961. 25–35.

———. "The Regional Writer." *Mystery and Manners*. Eds. Sally Fitzgerald and Robert Fitzgerald. New York: Farrar, Straus and Giroux, 1961. 51–59.

———. "Some Aspects of the Grotesque in Southern Fiction." *Mystery and Manners*. Eds. Sally Fitzgerald and Robert Fitzgerald. New York: Farrar, Straus and Giroux, 1961. 36–50.

Pogrebin, Robin. "Sharing a History as Well as a Play." *New York Times*, 11 October 1998, Sec. 25: 5, final late edition.

Ravenel, Shannon. Preface. *New Stories from the South: The Year's Best, 1989.* Ed. Shannon Ravenel. Chapel Hill, N.C.: Algonquin Books, 1989. vii–ix.
Royce, Graydon. "Flat Script and Cast Hinder 'Marriage.' " Review of *Impossible Marriage*, by Beth Henley. Minneapolis *Star Tribune,* 13 July 2000, 4B, metro edition.
Senior, Jennifer. "A Marriage of Convenience." *New York,* 14 September 1998: 70–71.
Shirley, Don. " 'Freaks' Slips at End but It's a Fun Ride." Review of *Control Freaks*, by Beth Henley. *Los Angeles Times,* 19 July 1993, F1, home edition.
Siegel, Ed. "*L-Play* Is a Lifeless Lemon, Largely Lackluster, Leaden." Review of *L-Play*, by Beth Henley. *Boston Globe,* 28 August 1996, C5, city edition.
Simon, John. "Yo, Kay!" Review of *Oh, Kay!*, by George and Ira Gershwin, and *Abundance*, by Beth Henley. *New York,* 12 November 1990, 92–93.
Spoto, Donald. *The Kindness of Strangers: The Life of Tennessee Williams.* New York: Da Capo, 1997.
Stearns, David Patrick. "Star Power Can't Save Henley's Troubled 'Impossible Marriage.' " Review of *Impossible Marriage*, by Beth Henley. *USA Today,* 20 October 1998, 4D, final edition.
Welty, Eudora. "Why I Live at the P.O." *The Collected Stories of Eudora Welty.* San Diego, New York, and London: Harcourt Brace Jovanovich, 1980. 46–56.
Williams, Tennessee. *The Glass Menagerie.* New York: New Directions, 1970.
Wilson, Charles Reagan, and William Ferris, eds. *Encyclopedia of Southern Culture.* Chapel Hill and London: University of North Carolina Press, 1989.

4
The Lucky Spot as Immanent Critique
REBECCA KING

Critics of Beth Henley's plays often focus on her representations of families, which she tends to portray as highly dysfunctional according to normative accounts of the modern nuclear family. Feminist analyses particularly attend to whether Henley provides alternatives to patriarchal family relations, with conflicting conclusions.[1] While the gendered nuclear family is an important focus of feminist critique, however, modern political and philosophical discourse has employed family relations as models of social relations in general since at least the late seventeenth century, when capitalism and its supporting ideology of middle-class liberalism began their conquests of aristocratic political, social, and economic values and practices.

Gendered subjects figure as foundational concepts in early liberal discourse, to be sure. However, these discussions also provide versions of the subject and of sociality that ground a broad array of assumptions basic to liberalism and liberal capitalism. Liberal representations of the individual and family originate in part in seventeenth- and eighteenth-century political and philosophical arguments that examine the legitimacy of state power and power relations in general, the nature of the individual, the family, and economic and social relations at large. In these discussions can be traced the development of what C. B. Macpherson calls "possessive individualism" against the backdrop of change from a feudal, agrarian culture to an industrial, commercial one.[2] Early liberal and capitalist arguments, specifically those by Hobbes and Locke, Locke's pupil the Third Earl of Shaftesbury, Francis Hutcheson and his pupil Adam Smith, make claims for individual political, economic, and moral autonomy, for natural rights to life, liberty, private property, and for a free market where self-interested pursuit of individual interests in an organic world also furthers public interests.[3] These debates construct a private, domestic sphere characterized by altruistic individuals related by affective bonds, the sphere of the family, where women and children are subject to the father's governance, and protected from intrusion by the state. Opposed to the private sphere is the public sphere of politics and economics, characterized by autonomous, self-interested individuals whose relationships are structured by the exigencies of contract and the market.[4] The family serves in these accounts as the foundation of social existence, as the site where children are born and educated to become productive citizens and, according to gender, to take their places in the domestic or economic spheres.

From this perspective, it is possible to trace in Henley's plays an immanent critique of modern Western culture in general, and of liberalism and capitalism more specifically. *The Lucky Spot*, which premiered in New York in April 1987, is particularly suited to analysis in this context since it is tightly organized by its critique, which Henley mounts through the play's temporal and geographic settings, its place and character names, and through the stories of the characters who appear in the play and of those who don't—parents and siblings of the major characters. In functioning as immanent critique, *The Lucky Spot* adopts as its own the norms constructed by capitalist and liberal ideologies, which the play reveals to be unreachable and indeed causative of forms of oppression and suffering that capitalism and liberalism aimed at overcoming as they sought to replace aristocratic economic, political, and social systems with less restrictive values and practices.

In particular, *The Lucky Spot* is iconoclastic in its treatment of an American dream predicated on a liberal meritocracy, revealing that, despite their liberatory potential for some, capitalism and liberal meritocracy often result in social and economic dislocations, in homelessness and unemployment. In this play, life itself is a risk, as is any capitalist venture, and those with little to lose can easily lose everything. Henley's play also explodes the myth of the traditional family, portraying the nuclear family central to liberal ideology as fragile, potentially destructive, and, for some, entirely elusive. Ultimately, the play portrays as fundamentally destructive the pervasive effects of the selfish forms of individualism constructed through contract and market relations that are necessary for survival in a free-market world of liberal capitalism.

The play concerns the dilemmas of seven characters who are variously associated with the Lucky Spot Dance Hall and its new owner, Reed Hooker. The play's setting—a nineteenth-century southern plantation home converted to a commercial dance hall—represents the transformation of feudal aristocracy to a free-market capitalist economy, from a world organized around kinship relations to one in which individuals are supposedly free to construct their own lives and to achieve material success according to their merits. The temporal setting of the play, Christmas Eve of 1934, foregrounds the effects of the Great Depression, the immediate result of overspeculation on the stock market, and of long-standing laissez-faire economic policies that ultimately widened the ground between rich and poor and gave way in subsequent years to Keynesian policies that instituted restrictions on free trade, providing social programs intended to enable the disadvantaged to participate in and benefit from the economic system. While Henley's play is set in 1934, however, its perspective is that of the late 1980s, which saw the emergence of new versions of laissez-faire economics during the Thatcher and Reagan eras of government deregulation and promotion of competition.

Furthermore, the play's Christmas setting allows Henley to critique Protestant ideology, which provides the moral and ethical contexts for liberalism and capitalism, by dramatizing its failure to provide for caring and solidarity in a secular society grounded in self-interest and competitive individualism. Christmas, of course, marks and celebrates the birth of Christianity, the founding moment in which love and charity replace Mosaic law as the fount of justice. At the end of Henley's play, however, the new owner of the Lucky Spot and its staff are homeless and unemployed as a result of gambling and deceit, practices that Henley represents as necessary forms of selfish individualism constructed by capitalism and liberal meritocracy, rather than as social or individual moral failures. Thus, the play functions as a cautionary tale, pointing out deficiencies of liberal and capitalist ideologies, and reminding its audience of the consequences of practices based thereon.

In Henley's play, gambling and prostitution serve as pervasive tropes that function as paradigms for free-market capitalism and its construction of the selfish forms of individualism necessary for survival and thriving. The names of the main character and the play's setting take their meanings from the domains of gambling and prostitution, providing humor, but also making clear the tenuous, predatory nature of existence in such a world. The Lucky Spot is located in the small village of Pigeon, Louisiana, sixty miles west of New Orleans. The village is aptly named since its new owner, Reed Hooker, owes his fortune, including the Lucky Spot property, to the "pigeons" he has duped or bested in gambling and speculation. A rumrunner during Prohibition, Hooker is a latter-day Rhett Butler, an opportunistic speculator. He has also been the "pigeon." As the play opens, he has lost his fortune in a card game, retaining only his title to the Lucky Spot, which he had won earlier in "a five-day card game down on the Gulf Coast" (*CPI* 215). We learn, furthermore, that he is the pigeon in this transaction as well, since the former owner has used the property as collateral for a $350.00 loan to his cousin. The village's name also reflects Hooker's attitude toward its male citizens, "simple country folks," pigeons to be lured in by promises to satisfy what Hooker assumes to be their desires for the "glamour, magic and music of the city sporting life" unrequited by their ordinary lives (216). Hooker's name reflects his function of procuring women to satisfy the locals' desires, while the name of his business venture hopefully announces the basis of any success it might enjoy—luck. The Lucky Spot's name, its history, and its function thus call attention to the risks involved in any capitalist enterprise, as well as to the commodification of desire necessary for its success.

Prostitution, of course, represents a commodification of sex and sexual desire. While sexuality encompasses its own complex history, simply put, Christian and liberal ideologies value sexuality in terms of the production of families, indeed as the source of the family and as such the founding impulse of social relations in general. Prostitution thus represents serious moral and social perversion of fundamental values and practices. Henley's play, on the other hand, indicts such views as naive, while she also represents sexual oppression as a perversion of social relations into economic relations.

In *The Lucky Spot*, prostitution is the outcome of unequal power relations and dire need. Perhaps the most sobering account of prostitution is Sue Jack Hooker's prison narrative. Sue Jack is Reed Hooker's wife, and she has spent three years in Angola Prison after attacking Caroline Carmichael, Hooker's lover. After her release from prison, Sue Jack arrives at the Lucky Spot, and tells Hooker of her fight to survive in a world in which prisoners are controlled by guards who use their power to procure sex. She explains to him how "many nights there were just t'survive in that prison" (*CPI* 257), of the days she would "do three prison guards for a cup of dirty water," or the time she was "on [her] knees" just "for a pair of shoes."[5] Ironically, she tells Hooker about these experiences to minimize his objection to her intention to become the lover of Whitt Carmichael, the lien holder for the Lucky Spot, so Hooker can retain his investment.

Her account, however, also functions critically in a number of ways. The prison refers to the actual Louisiana State Penitentiary at Angola, Louisiana, a village named for the African colony, settled initially by exiled Portuguese criminals, which provided slave labor for the eighteenth- and nineteenth-century South, and which in the 1980s was the site of civil warfare between groups allied to the USSR, the United States, and South Africa, all interested in exploiting Angola's diamonds and petroleum. In Henley's play, slavery and imprisonment, each the converse of liberty, are thus closely related, calling into question the relevance of Christian and liberal notions of equality, individual worth, and sexuality in a world of unequal power relations and material and cultural poverty. In fact, the play relies on concepts of freedom articulated by Sue Jack to call into question the meaning of freedom in a world where survival necessitates selfish individualism. From prison, she reenters a world in which she initially finds herself alone and unemployed—"free t'be a globe-trotter once again. T'live by my wits" (*CPI* 239). Freedom for Sue Jack at this point in her life means freedom from love, connection, and the hope she had held that her husband still loved her. Freedom, then, comes to mean freedom to roam geographically and socially, possibly but not necessarily to experience upward social and economic mobility.

Her experiences in prison also mark the extremes of corrupt social relations, differing only in degree from the experiences of the other characters in the play. Here, Henley calls into question the relationship between liberal ideals of freedom and autonomy and actual lived experience under these ideals. In Henley's play, freedom and autonomy have not resulted in individual well-being. Rather, survival and success in the free-market world of the play has often necessitated selfishness rather than cooperation or benevolence. Social relations between Henley's supposedly free individuals, no less than those between Sue Jack and the prison guards, are often determined by the exigencies of survival and by contingency. In both cases, a Hobbesian world pertains, in which selfishness motivates behavior, and, as in twentieth-century Angola, life becomes a war of each against all, with the powerful dominating and exploiting the weak and needy.

Sue Jack and Reed Hooker represent the weak and needy relative to the powerful Whitt Carmichael, who represents monied interests and those who have succeeded by their wits. Carmichael exploits Hooker by calling in the loan for which the property serves as collateral and by forcing Hooker, who cannot pay off the loan, to sell him the property so he can begin drilling by New Year's Day, telling the inhabitants that "those high finance matters don't really concern" them as "poor people," implying that he knows of mineral wealth on the property that is unknown to Hooker (*CPI* 258). Exploitation of poverty and powerlessness ironically recalls Locke's injunction against exploitation, which accompanies his justification of private property:

> As *Justice* gives every Man a Title to the product of his honest Industry, and the fair Acquisitions of his Ancestors descended to him; so *Charity* gives every Man a Title to so much out of another's Plenty, as will keep him from extream want where he has no means to subsist otherwise; and a Man can no more justly make use of another's necessity, to force him to become his Vassal, by with-holding that Relief, God requires him to afford to the wants of his Brother, than he that has more strength can seize upon a weaker, master him to his Obedience, and with a Dagger at his Throat offer him Death or Slavery.[6]

Locke, of course, assumed that the poor and needy would be provided for within traditions of Christian charity and ancient republican concepts of civic duty. In twentieth-century America, however, such assumptions are not uniformly reliable.

Henley's characters, in fact, are entirely secular in their orientation, and uneducated in both Christian and civic traditions. Even though Henley sets the play's action on Christmas Eve, references to "Christ" and "God" occur only as profane utterances. Indeed, one impoverished character, Cassidy, has never seen a tree in a house before Turnip,[7] Hooker's helper, brings in a pine to decorate for Christmas. For the materially and culturally impoverished

The Lucky Spot *as Immanent Critique* 69

inhabitants of the Lucky Spot, Christmas involves rituals that no longer relate even to the pagan tree ceremony, and certainly not to its Christian meaning as a holy day or its significance in ushering in a new ethics of love and compassion. For them, poverty and ignorance and an economic system that rewards selfish acquisition have eroded both Christian and secular charitable traditions, leaving no formal institutions in place to provide for the well-being of the needy.

In addition to employing tropes of gambling and prostitution, Henley furthers her play's critique through its southern setting. With its roots in aristocratic ideology and practice, the South is particularly suited to the play's critique of liberal claims that capitalism and liberalism construct a more humane world than the feudal, aristocratic world they sought to replace. In the New South, middle-class liberalism and capitalism have become hegemonic by 1934, even though the white, upper- and middle-class South continues to cling to aristocratic values, despite the replacement of aristocracy by liberal meritocracy.[8] Residual elements of aristocratic ideology persist in the play, as they do in American culture, in conditions quite cut off from their original contexts. The play's southern setting allows Henley to represent individual lives and social relations under the current system as absurdly anomalous in terms of both aristocratic and liberal ideologies.

For instance, noting Sue Jack Hooker's changed appearance since her imprisonment, Carmichael ask about her "silk hands" (*CPI* 227) and is shocked when she rubs her callused fingertips across her face. Earlier in the play Turnip describes Sue Jack as a "real lady" evidenced by the "fine lace gloves" (210) that she always wore. These statements are obvious references to Scarlett O'Hara, the lead character in Margaret Mitchell's *Gone with the Wind*, which chronicles the demise of southern feudalism and the emergence of the New South. Scarlett had been taught that one could always tell a lady by her soft, white hands, which must never display signs of manual labor. While the postwar Scarlett's workworn hands mark her poverty and signal a decline in her social status, Sue Jack's hands were "great" (217) not because she belonged to a leisured elite class but because she was an expert professional cardplayer, whose tipless gloves allowed her more effectively to handle the cards that provided her livelihood. The luxurious clothes that she wore before her downfall mark her status as a "lady" for Lacey, another impoverished character, who equates signs of wealth with both status and merit.

Turnip's and Lacey's observations take their humor from the categorial dislocation of the aristocratic designation of "lady" to their own understanding of the term, indicating destabilization of aristocratic class-based signifiers by meritocratic ideology and practices. Her designation as a lady reflects confusion between aristocratic associations of status and genealogy with wealth and leisure, and progressive associations of wealth with merit. In fact, Sue Jack is no lady according to either aristocratic or liberal standards, even though she has attempted to style herself as one despite her alcoholism, brawling, and cardsharping, and the fact that her "silk gowns and mink furs" (*CPI* 222) were gifts from men whom she lured with her beauty. Middle-class liberal ideology, grounded in Protestant morality and the domestic ideal of the moral and spiritual superiority of women, does not sanction prostitution, gambling (especially for women), or, until recently, women working outside the home. Turnip's and Lacey's designation of Sue Jack as a lady appear comically absurd in light of these values and their naive understanding of class. Moreover, Sue Jack's situation reflects the limited access to the signs of merit available to the poor, especially poor unmarried women, while it also questions social distinctions between prostitution and marriage, the socially sanctioned means by which women can attain status and wealth—silk gowns, etc.—according to both aristocratic and liberal ideologies.

Setting her play in the South, then, allows Henley to reveal similarities between liberal, capitalist culture and the oppressive aristocratic system it supposedly replaced. The old southern manor house where the action takes place symbolizes this transition. It has passed out of family ownership through a card game, just as Gerald O'Hara obtained Tara in *Gone with the Wind*. Like a Tara that must be transformed in order to survive as the South moved from a feudal plantocracy into a modern industrial/commercial culture, the house has become a commercial ballroom, reenacting the replacement of feudalism and aristocracy with capitalism and meritocracy.

Henley's play, however, makes clear the nature of these changes and the persistence of oppressive power relations, despite the liberatory claims of the modern progressive tradition. The "authentic slave quarters" (*CPI* 220) have been painted "fancy colors" to transform them into "bungalows" that now serve as dormitories for the dance hall girls, effacing their origins by providing them with new colors, just as aristocractic and liberal ideologies efface the exploitative origins of wealth through mystifying descriptions based on claims of genealogical or meritocratic rights to private property and hierarchized power relations. No longer housing slaves, the "bungalows" now house a group of poor southern women, only one of whom—Lacey—we actually meet. Lacey has been sent into the world, like the other poor characters in the play, with legacies of hurt and abandonment only, and, like them, must make her way in a meritocratic world by dint of her own efforts and good fortune. She has gone "broke trying t'crash the movies" (260), one of few progressive narratives available to young women in the early twentieth century that holds out the promise of material wealth, glamour, and romance without requiring marriage. As is the case for most aspirants, however, Lacey has failed to achieve this dream, and now all her "stuff's in pawn," and she doesn't "even have a decent rag on [her] back" (260). The dance hall girls' description of their situation, "dancing on the edge of a cliff" (246), represents the perils of the new order for individuals like Lacey and the other characters in the play who have few marketable skills and are now employed by a gambler who has just lost his fortune in a card game. In fact, Hooker loses the Hall and plunges along with his employees into unemployment and homelessness, a not uncommon fate in a capitalist economy. Furthermore, while the new order has abolished legalized slavery, autonomy is revealed in this play as an illusion for the dance hall girls, and indeed, their employer, whose legacies imprison them in poverty and homelessness, subjecting them to exploitation and oppression. Meritocracy, then, has ushered in no substantive change in social and economic relations; rather, the conditions of individuals now depend on their ability to find or keep a place atop a newly rationalized hierarchy and to exploit those who can't.

The transformed hall also critiques liberal concepts of individual rights, particularly private property rights. Central to liberal concepts of private property is John Locke's articulation of natural rights and a moral basis for private property as essential elements of liberal and capitalist ideologies. Although Locke rationalizes ownership as a function of God's commandment for "Man . . . to labour" (309), claims for a moral basis for private property appear in *The Lucky Spot* as no more natural or moral than arguments that ground aristocratic ideology or slavery. Henley undermines such claims through the history of the Hall. While the plantation originally stayed in the family through inheritance, its most recent ownership has been determined by speculation and gambling. The newest owner of the Hall lives by his wits and the proceeds from his gambling, as did its previous owner. During the play, the house changes hands again through a series of negotiations only thinly disguised as business proposals. Hooker suggests that Carmichael invest in the Lucky Spot since Hooker cannot pay off the loan. Carmichael refuses the offer and ultimately buys the place from Hooker, who is forced to sell due to his poverty, but only after Hooker refuses a poker game proposed by Carmichael. Sue Jack, along with the property, would go to the winner. The Hall's history thus exposes the contingent rather than universal, moral basis of property, home, and heritage, suggesting as well that in a capitalist culture grounded on the sanctity of private property, even private property—and individuals—can become commodities that change hands through speculation and exploitation.

Carrying the gambling trope to its logical extreme, Henley's play represents life itself as a gamble. Turnip articulates this sentiment when Hooker persists in opening the Lucky Spot in hopes of making enough money to retire the loan, even after the townspeople appropriate most of his resources in payment of his debts, and all the dance hall girls except Lacey leave town. Turnip dismisses Hooker's efforts as vain, seeing their work to create a new life as "a low down rutty rotten little game we're all playing" (*CPI* 240). For Turnip, life's game is not "clear-cut" like checkers, in which "somebody wins and somebody loses." Rather, he sees himself and the other inhabitants of the Lucky Spot as "big-time losers; everyone of us. No ringing in the cold deck, no aces up the sleeves, no hold outs. Just stacking up piles and piles of chips, t' give 'em all away. All losers! Everyone of us—Christ, what a racket" (240). Contingency and wealth—not birth or merit—account for life's winners and losers, a situation that Henley's play underscores and that capitalist and liberal ideologies ignore altogether, at least before the social "safety nets," instituted in response to the massive displacements of the Depression, were put into place to catch dancers who fall off the cliff.

Gambling, then, pervades the lives of this play's characters, representing the contingent nature of life, but also depicting laissez-faire capitalism's denial—indeed, its celebration—of exploitation. The wealthy Carmichael represents the kind of exploitation that Locke proscribes but Henley's play represents as fundamental to successful capitalist ventures. He is a gambler and a liar who seeks to extend his wealth by exploiting Hooker's love for Sue Jack and his extensive debts. A philanderer who formerly gambled with Sue Jack and still desires her as a lover, Carmichael is also the brother of the woman Sue Jack had attacked, resulting in her imprisonment. To disguise his motives for wanting the Lucky Spot property, Carmichael tells the Hookers that he wants to buy the Hall to satisfy a promise to his father, who doesn't want Sue Jack to be associated with it in any way. Rather than being motivated by love for and loyalty to his family, or by sympathy for Sue Jack or Hooker and his misfits, Carmichael wants to buy the Lucky Spot before it is auctioned off to settle Hooker's debts, so he can profit from the minerals located on the property. Due to his selfish interests, Carmichael violates principles of family loyalty as well as Christian principles of charity, exploiting and deceiving Hooker, who does not know about the oil that could solve his financial woes and provide employment for him and his dependents.

By representing market and contract relations as forms of gambling that necessarily involve exploitation and often deceit, Henley attacks liberal and capitalist ideologies for their destructive impact on family and social relationships, particularly on relationships in the play that liberal ideology constructs as bonds formed by love, affection, and duty. Specifically, Henley represents the fundamental social relation of liberal ideology, namely, that between husband and wife, in terms of market relations when Sue Jack's love for her husband prompts her to prostitute herself in order to save Hooker's dream. While Sue Jack's actions are motivated by her love for Reed, Carmichael's actions reveal that even love can become the basis for exploitation in the world of Henley's play.

Sue Jack's proposed arrangement with Carmichael serves another critical function by questioning contract theory's reliance on assumptions of equality between contracting parties. Basic to liberalism and capitalism are assumptions of the autonomous individual who is free to engage in contractual relations, guided by principles of self-interest that also further social interests, concepts most notably expressed by Adam Smith's invisible hand metaphor. Market relations, particularly under laissez-faire conditions proposed by Smith as best promoting individual and national well-being, are based on liberal assumptions of individual autonomy and the freedom to enter into voluntary contractual arrangements between equals. However, meritocracy creates inequalities, while capitalism relies on existing or created inequities—a lack, a need, or desire. Inherent in contractual agreements, then, are conditions of inequality and potential oppression, even though the relations constructed through these agreements may appear to be voluntary and beneficial to all parties.

While gambling and prostitution function as critiques of selfish individualism constructed through liberal and capitalist ideologies, Henley's play mounts its harshest critique through the family constellations that the play constructs. Although the nuclear family and its nurturing, educative functions ground liberal and capitalist ideology and practices, for the poor characters in *The Lucky Spot*, the family has not been a stable source of nurturing and preparation for citizenship and material success but a source of rejection, abandonment, and failure resulting for the most part from contingency. The play's seven characters are joined by their absent parents, who haunt the dialogue and lives of the characters we see on stage. We learn a good bit about these families, even though this information is hardly germane to the plot or even necessary for character development, serving rather as immanent critique of liberal norms. Family relationships and circumstances in this play are so extreme in their departures from liberal norms that they often appear as grotesque or absurd aberrations. In fact, they underscore the absurdities of liberal norms and the destructive effects of institutions predicated on ideals that ignore fundamental realities of lived experience.

Early liberal discourse describes the family as the origin of all social relationships, and as the institution that nurtures and trains individuals for citizenship and success in the progressive world.[9] Henley's play, on the other hand, functions as immanent critique of these claims, continually asking its audience through its characters' family experiences to consider how the lives of children, who represent the most dependent and nonautonomous of any culture's citizens, are shaped by incompetent or uncaring parents and family, or by other situations beyond their control, and how these experiences continue to inform their lives. Sue Jack confesses that she never met her "daddy," but if she did, she would "like nothing better than t'spit straight at him" (*CPI* 229). Sue Jack's mother "went insane due to religious troubles" and "shot herself while looking in a full-length mirror." Cassidy lost both parents as a child of five, her father to abandonment, her mother to fatal illness. Lacey, on the other hand, was raised by her mother, who always told her that she was "swivel-hipped" and would "never be anything more than some poor man's pudding" (229). Though they are now estranged, Lacey is desperate to prove her mother wrong. Despite being left once at the altar, Lacey hopes that her job will introduce her to a man who will love and marry her. Although Turnip has not been abandoned by his family, like Lacey, he has been psychologically abused. He tells Lacey that his brothers always told him that he was stupid and that he would never get a girlfriend with a name like his.[10] While we never meet these parents and siblings, they continue to exert power over the lives of these characters, even those who never knew their parents. Furthermore, while the main characters in the play have experienced abandonment and/or poverty, Whitt Carmichael represents the failure of even a materially wealthy family to produce the benevolent, responsible citizens that Locke, Shaftesbury, and Hutcheson envisioned, producing instead a ruthless capitalist incapable of any but selfish motives, in his relations with family no less than with others.

The nuclear family that grounds liberal ideology becomes in Henley's play an institution incapable of bearing its ideological weight. The character in the play who represents perhaps the grossest failures of the family to account for well-being is Cassidy Smith, the fifteen-year-old naive who is pregnant by Reed Hooker, and who expects him to marry her so her child will not "be born out a bastard" on whom "everyone in the world will look down" (*CPI* 221). Cassidy has tried to abort the pregnancy by "rolling herself down the staircase and eating boxes of match heads and banging at her belly with a two-by-four" (213), all to no avail. Her backup plan is to marry Hooker. She has invited Sue Jack, who has been estranged from her husband since the death of their three-year-old son, to join the group at the Lucky Spot on her release from Angola. She expects Sue Jack to divorce Reed so she can marry him, hoping that "she can go away forever" (221). The inauspicious and contingent beginnings of this incipient family give the lie to ideological assumptions that families are the result of rational, caring individuals forming contractual alliances as equals in a joint venture to produce and educate children.

Reed Hooker, in fact, does not intend to marry Cassidy, although he has a sense of what the liberal ideal offers and requires for women. He has suggested to Cassidy that he will marry her so she will quit bothering him; however, he actually intends to "send her off to some respectable school, let 'em teach her how t' cook," so she can "find a nice guy" (*CPI* 213). His intentions toward Cassidy reflect his desire for her happiness, which he defines in terms of liberal ideals that her past has never allowed her to enjoy. He wants to break the cycle of deprivation that Cassidy has known all her life.

Cassidy's situation reveals multiple inadequacies and fallacies of liberal concepts of marriage, family, and community. Cassidy has always known material and cultural poverty, and a community that failed to help her when she was a child. Her father left before she was born, and she was a homeless orphan by age five, when her mother and siblings died from diphtheria, a disease transmitted by fecal contamination, thus associated with poverty and lack of basic hygiene. The only home she had known was burned to prevent the spread of the disease, providing protection for the rest of the community, but not for Cassidy. Although the trope of the orphan in progressive narratives often symbolizes the character's freedom to write her or his own narrative, Cassidy's story provides a counternarrative that reflects realities, ignored by liberal ideals, that govern the lives of dependents—women, children, the poor, and the disabled, like the blind wife of Sam, The Lucky Spot's only paying customer. Read against the progressive narrative of the orphaned female who leaves home poor and virtuous, and makes her way in a naughty world before finding happiness, security, and social standing through marriage, Cassidy's experience becomes an absurd parody.

Through Cassidy's birth family, Henley exposes fault lines in Locke's description of marriage and family, which involves rational adults contracting a marriage in order to create a family bound by affective ties and committed to nurture and educate functional citizens who can then reproduce the family cycle. Fathers can break marriage contracts by leaving. Parents may be unable for many reasons to provide the nurturing and education that enable children to survive as adults. Parents can die, leaving surviving children even more vulnerable to contingency than they are within an impoverished family. In the absence of community commitment to benevolence and duty to those outside the family, children without family protection might be provided with minimal care, at best, or exploited, at worst.

Having exposed the fragile and contingent nature of the liberal family and community through Cassidy's birth family, Henley assigns her to another kind of family. This time, Henley turns to Hobbes's ideas as equally likely as Locke's to account for human nature under conditions of want, and as perhaps more accurate in their portrayal of unequal power relations in a private sphere where legal protection of the weak is by liberal definition unavailable. While Locke's family is bound by affection, Cassidy's new family exposes the exploitative nature of inherently unequal power relations within the family that result from age and gender differences. After killing off Cassidy's birth family, Henley consigns her to Mr. Pete, a trail-driver who reflects the worst of Hobbesian excess, the man who lives in a state of nature, in this case, on the frontier, where law only minimally pertains and where might makes right. Mr. Pete represents Hobbes's claims that we are essentially self-interested and thus in need of a powerful sovereign to limit the effects of our predatory nature. On the lawless frontier, as in the liberal private sphere, he is unconstrained from using Cassidy as a sex slave and domestic worker. Cassidy functions as a wife, fulfilling Mr. Pete's sexual needs, and providing unremunerated domestic labor that furnishes him with material sustenance, allowing him to carry on his business without the expense of paying for assistance. Cassidy's relationship to Mr. Pete thus represents a grotesque Hobbesian family, stripped of Locke's ideals of affection, gender equality, and fulfilled female domestic sainthood.

In this family, unequal power relations pertain within the lawless private domestic sphere, just as they do on the frontier; Mr. Pete can and does exploit his child-woman for selfish gain. In a world where survival necessitates selfishness—the frontier, for instance, and, Henley's play suggests, the world of laissez-faire economics—this arrangement makes logical, if not moral, sense. Cassidy saves Mr. Pete untold emotional, material, and economic expense. In this world, Cassidy's value lies in the surplus value she enables Mr. Pete to accrue, which Henley also equates with her value as a commodity when Mr. Pete loses Cassidy and a car in a card game with Hooker. Cassidy, utterly without power as woman and child, is passed from man to man in absurd parodies of both precapitalist gift-giving rituals and capitalist exchange.

Cassidy, whose name parodically alludes to the cowboy icon that represents American expansionism and the solitary American romantic hero, also parodies the liberal domestic ideals of the valued child and the pure woman. Her childhood is described only in terms of her use value to Mr. Pete, and we learn from her that Mr. Pete used her sexually, beat her, branded her thigh "with his holy cross" (*CPI* 245), and fed her cow feed.[11] Represented through animal imagery, she was Mr. Pete's pack animal, and also the "kitty" in the poker game that places her with Hooker. When Hooker wins the game, he chooses Cassidy and an old Chevy, instead of a chestnut mare, as his poker winnings. Furthermore, her transfer to Hooker recalls the English practice among the lower classes of "wife-sale, by which a husband led his unwanted wife to market by a rope tied around her neck, and sold her to a bidder, probably arranged beforehand, according to the same rules that governed livestock auctions, the last recorded case having been in 1887" (Stone 35). While dehumanizing effects of selfish individualism and commodification of human need lie at the heart of laissez-faire capitalism, Cassidy's experience reveals the vulnerability of women and children within the liberal nuclear family, where they can be exploited to provide labor and/or sexual services, a situation that American civil and criminal laws have only recently begun to recognize.

Cassidy and Hooker make up a third family constellation, representing another family formed by contingency, although Hooker's motives, unlike Mr. Pete's, are represented as altruistic, at least in part. In fact, Henley's characters finally divide along the lines of those whose selfish impulses are redeemed by sympathy and benevolence, and those like Mr. Pete and Carmichael who have no redeeming features. Despite apparent similarities between Mr. Pete and Hooker in their treatment of Cassidy, Henley identifies Hooker with forms of sympathy and benevolence that reflect Shaftesbury's and Hutcheson's visions of innate moral capacities for caring. Henley distinguishes between the two men in terms of their capacities for sympathy and benevolence, while also portraying these qualities as socially valuable but ultimately contingent.

Concepts of sympathy and benevolence grounded eighteenth-century liberal claims for individual moral and political autonomy, providing descriptions of human psychology and social behavior that depart in significant ways from the unrelentingly rational, atomistic, egoistic accounts provided by Hobbes and Locke. John Locke's pupil Anthony Cooper, Third Earl of Shaftesbury, based his arguments for moral autonomy on an innate moral capacity, analogous to the physical senses, that allows each individual to enter into the pleasure and pain of others. For this moral sense to become the basis of durable social relations, however, Shaftesbury argued that parents must cultivate their children's reason so that sympathy would lead to benevolent action. One of Shaftesbury's most important concepts, however, was that of an organic universe in which each individual act impinges on all others, so that omission of good, no less than commission of bad, affects all. Shaftesbury saw the social and civil worlds as reflections of a benevolent diety, and suggested that we innately understand good and bad as a function of an internal spectator that models the deity's benevolence. While Francis Hutcheson relied on concepts of an organic universe, he internalized benevolence as itself a moral sense, an affective quality rather than one depending on cultivated reason. He described a common moral sense of connection that drives us to desire approbation and to avoid acts that arouse censure.

Both thinkers thus saw the social world as continuous with the private, and the individual as ineluctably connected to others, providing significant alternatives to Hobbes's and Locke's accounts, calling into question as well liberal concepts of separate public and private spheres with their different models of sociality. Furthermore, Shaftesbury and Hutcheson provide an alternate understanding of autonomy, describing it in terms of individual capacity to discern and act on moral principles that guide both individual and social well-being, thus defining autonomy in terms of connection rather than separation from others. Their concepts underwrite much of the eighteenth-century's political and philosophical discourse, with the poles of conservative and liberal arguments often marked by concepts of the extent and durability of sympathy and benevolence as social principles, and the corresponding need for a more or less powerful central political authority.[12]

In Henley's play, Hobbes's and Locke's concepts exist alongside those of Shaftesbury and Hutcheson, often within the same character, as is the case with Reed Hooker. In explaining to Turnip why he chose Cassidy instead of a mare as his winnings from Mr. Pete, Hooker reveals his capacities for sympathy and benevolence, even for those outside his immediate family or community. He tells Turnip that he chose Cassidy because she looked so sad and he thought he could make life better for her, though he later voices his regret over this choice since it has complicated his life so much. Nonetheless, his remarks and Cassidy's explanation of her pregnancy reflect Shaftesbury's and Hutcheson's concepts of sympathy and benevolence as the foundation of a just social order, although in the organic universe of Henley's play their expressions appear as grotesque aberrations, as naive, self-destructive lapses in prudent principles of self-interest necessitated by economic survival.

Hooker's treatment of Cassidy allows Henley to contrast the Hobbesian world of competitive self-interest and Locke's world of contract and market relations with a world based on sympathy and benevolence. In contrast to Cassidy's life with Mr. Pete, Reed Hooker has provided a fairly decent, if somewhat unstable, home for her. Furthermore, Hooker's sexual encounters with Cassidy significantly differ from Mr. Pete's abuse. While Sue Jack, in a fit of anger, accuses Hooker of abducting and raping a child, Hooker and Cassidy are both represented as motivated by care and concern for the other, and their sexual encounters occurring as a result of human need and natural sexual desire. In the progressive narrative of upward mobility, pregnancy follows marriage, marking the successful reproduction of a new family. Cassidy's pregnancy represents neither the female progressive narrative nor male dominance of a submissive female. Rather, her pregnancy is the result of her attempts to console Hooker when she would hear him sobbing and crying out in the night, apparently out of sorrow over losing his child to death and his wife to alcoholism and prison. Cassidy knows from her years with Mr. Pete how to make Reed "feel better" (*CPI* 245). Although her sexual knowledge results from criminal abuse by her supposed caretaker, her naive response to Hooker represents an innate sympathy for his suffering, and it stands in sharp if grotesque contrast to the forms of rape and prostitution the play features by way of critiquing social relations in the form of Hobbesian dominance and exploitation.

Hooker, in fact, had not wanted to take advantage of Cassidy, and had been locking her in the attic at night so she could not come to him. Hooker is an ambivalent character—capable alike of gratuitous acts of goodness and egregious moral lapses. He has promised to marry Cassidy, even though he is already married and has no intention of fulfilling his promise. However, his plan to send her to school where she will learn hygiene and domestic skills reflects his concern for her well-being. Furthermore, Hooker intends to keep the baby, possibly to replace the one he mourns, hoping that Cassidy will meet some nice young man and marry, providing her with something like a progressive female narrative of rising in status through marriage. Although we do not learn directly of his motive for wanting to keep the baby, his grief over his lost son and his concern with giving Cassidy a happier life suggest that he wants a child to love and raise in the way that Locke and others suggests family affection and duty operate.[13]

Hooker often acts out of concern for others, even those who are not his family, and even when it means self-sacrifice. We learn more about Hooker's benevolent nature when Cassidy tells Sue Jack that he once helped a "skinny kid" who fell from a tree and "split up his lip real good" (*CPI* 245). Hooker had amused him with a trick, using a nickel that he then gave to the boy. His benevolent actions contrast to the selfishness of Mr. Pete and Carmichael. However, in the world of Henley's play, kindness and generosity seem anomalous, even self-defeating, when individual survival often necessitates others' loss. Henley's play thus dramatizes the fragility of benevolence as a principle of social relations and well-being in a free-market economy organized around contract and market relations.

In addition to dramatizing the inadequacies of the nuclear family to provide for well-being in a capitalist world, Henley also undermines essentialist notions of feminity that ground liberal concepts of family and a domestic private sphere, primarily through Cassidy's lack of domesticity and Sue Jack's maternal failures. Henley represents Sue Jack as a failed mother, one who, furthermore, no longer can bear children since she "got sick in prison" (*CPI* 253). Sue Jack's and Reed's only child, Andy, was hit by a car when he was a toddler, according to her, when he had tried to chase a hummingbird, and had run in front of a car. After his death, she descended into alcoholic and gambling hell, culminating in her attack on Caroline Carmichael and her prison term. In prison, she has picked cotton and raised hogs for three years (227), forms of manual labor common to poor southern women and others, despite ideological silences in this regard.

Despite having worked like a male field hand, Sue Jack also functions as a nurturer, representing feminine qualities associated with the domestic female of liberal ideology. Indeed, like Reed Hooker, Sue Jack is distinguished from the play's characters who act solely from self-interest. Although initially represented as a gambler, drinker, and fighter, she reveals her capacity for empathy and selflessness in her attempts to save the Lucky Spot for Hooker. Furthermore, she brings the Lucky Spot inhabitants Christmas gifts that she has made in prison, and she encourages Hooker to marry Cassidy in order to provide a stable family for them both and the expected child, even though she loves Hooker. In order to convince Reed to marry Cassidy, Sue Jack tells him the truth about their son, Andy: he was hit by a car when she went into a bar for a drink and left him alone outside. While she is capable of selflessness, then, she has failed profoundly as both a mother and a wife, her experiences serving as another commentary on the fallacies of liberal notions of family as an adequate foundation for individual and social well-being.

Indeed, Henley's portrayal of all the female characters in *The Lucky Spot* prominently targets the essentialist views of gender that ground liberal versions of the family and notions of separate domestic and public spheres. At its most basic level, *The Lucky Spot* plays with gender-bending through the names of its women characters. More fundamentally, however, Henley undermines essentialist views of women as innately domestic and naturally destined for motherhood. Cassidy's name alludes to a fully male world of the cowboy, and she is the least "feminine" or domestic of the three women. In addition to her past life as a trail-driver's assistant, her cooking disgusts Hooker, who also complains of her hygiene, noting that she "could plant a vegetable garden underneath those fingernails" (*CPI* 214). She responds that she "ain't got no hairpin" to dig out the dirt, which "gets stuck there" (214–15) when she's working, providing another commentary on hands as class markers. While Cassidy's pregnancy and her concern and care for others mark her capacity for femininity, her ambivalence about motherhood, utter lack of domesticity, poverty, and sexual past disclose the remoteness and irrelevance of liberal gender ideals for Cassidy, even as she and Hooker see her future success in their terms.

Lacey, on the other hand, embodies typical elements of the liberal feminine ideal in her name, values, and behavior. She trips repeatedly, falling to the floor as a result of her "weak ankles" (*CPI* 220), reflecting cultural associations with femininity and physical weakness. Her emotional nature, her belief in "love" (224), and her notions of how women gain the love and respect of men also characterize her as feminine. Lacey's conversations reveal the norms that have shaped her aspirations and actions. She tells Cassidy that the "bloom of youth" will carry her far in attracting men, and that she must avoid crying since she has "only got this one little face t'get by on for your whole life long." She praises Sue Jack's beauty, her "wit," and her ability to "hold a prolonged conversation with a man," an ability that Lacey's "auntie" has told her will gain a man's "admiration and respectability" rather than simply his "grudging physical desire" (222–223). However, Lacey notes that "most girls would be" confused by such conversations, as Cassidy says she would be, since they are "too stupid t'think" of such things (223). Lacey's aunt's maxim, of course, contradicts her culture's attitudes toward feminine intellectual achievement, while Lacey's remarks reflect ambivalence, at best. In other regards, however, Lacey has fully internalized ideological dictates for women, including the imperative to marry a man whom she has won by her beauty and other feminine attractions, even though her actual experiences with men have been devastating. Lacey tells the others that she has been abandoned at the alter, and that she seems to attract men who hit her, including one who "tried t'drowned [her] in the bathtub." Nonetheless, she continues "to believe in love," even though she has "never really known it." Her concern with looking "perky" (224) and beautiful so she can attract a man reveals that she has failed to interrogate the ideology that has constructed her values and experiences, and that simultaneously has led to dependence, abandonment, and poverty rather than to the love, happiness, and emotional fulfillment that represent success.

Sue Jack's name and personality also emphasize Henley's interrogation of a naturalized femininity that grounds the liberal project. Her name combines the feminine and masculine, as do her personality and experience. Her past marks her as independent and aggressive, her experiences as a cardsharp, fighter, and prison inmate signifying her as masculine. On the other hand, she has used her beauty to attract men, and she has married and become a mother, even though neither experience has been successful by liberal ideological standards. By play's end, however, Sue Jack and Hooker are reconciled, having recognized and accepted their love for each other. Cassidy realizes that she does not want to marry without love, and renounces her claim to Hooker. Hooker and Sue Jack passionately kiss and exchange Merry Christmas wishes, as she becomes Hooker's "sweet Sue" (262). While Sue Jack's name shift reflects the relativity of gender signifiers and other liberal constructions of the family, their reunion suggests that their family will survive through their love for each other despite and maybe even because of their failures to conform to liberal norms.

Henley thus affirms love as the basis of family relations and, by extension, for social relations in general, even while her play rejects liberal gender norms and idealized concepts of family. Henley closes her play with an alternate version of family, an arrangement that nonetheless reflects the capacity of love and care to provide fulfillment. Despite being sent into the world with legacies of abandonment and hurt, these misfits form a family of sorts who nurture one another to the extent that they can. Although the Luck Spot fails to attract enough paying customers on Christmas Eve to save them from Carmichael, they gather on Christmas morning to celebrate the day with each other. Sue Jack's grimy gifts make up in part for their disappointment on discovering that the Christmas pig has been stolen by someone to whom Hooker owes money.

This group of eccentrics mirrors the only normal family represented in the play as characterized by love and devotion—that of Sam, the only customer at the Lucky Spot, who comes to them because he misses his deceased wife. Sam's marriage is characterized entirely in terms of sympathy, affection, and benevolence, since Sam's wife is blind and utterly dependent on him. Sam's relationship with his wife represents the converse of Mr. Pete's and Cassidy's, even though both are characterized by profound dependence and the potential for exploitation. Sam tells the Lucky Spot crowd that he took great joy in caring for his wife, even picking seeds out of her watermelon, a gentle act of selflessness that has no economic or self-interested connotation, but rather is directed toward providing pleasure for a loved one.

Despite having enjoyed a loving relationship with his wife, however, Sam is now alone and lonely, another situation that liberal norms of family fail to consider. Nonetheless, his unselfish care for his utterly dependent wife models a form of benevolent social relations that selfish forms of individualism and capitalism cannot account for, and that Henley's play suggests is rare in a world in which survival and material flourishing require us to act selfishly.

The play thus ends with a Christmas morning that commemorates Christian charity and love within an unconventional family. The crowd at the Lucky Spot re-creates Cassidy's first remembered Christmas: Sam brings peppermint candy, and Hooker brings in oranges. This new family is not bound by ties of kinship, but by bonds of affection and sympathy, representing an alternative to the naturalized family of liberal and capitalist ideologies. At the end of the play, Henley has not resolved their problems. They still face eviction and they are still poor.

Although some of Henley's critics claim that her plays re-create patriarchal oppression that her female characters cannot escape, I suggest that *The Lucky Spot* is concerned with forms of patriarchal oppression that transcend gender, and that Henley's refusal to rescue her characters is a function of the play's critical task. Henley's play dramatizes ways in which her characters, like her audience, are constructed by and embedded in modern Western culture, suggesting moreover that substantive change in the lives of individuals must involve wholesale changes in cultural attitudes and practices. The historical context of *The Lucky Spot* suggests that such changes have been for the most part gradual, often involving unintended and unenvisioned consequences that in large degree have not involved changes in the power dynamics that characterize social relations, serving rather to preserve hierarchic economic and social structures. Providing alternatives to oppressive aspects of liberal and capitalist ideologies and practices would limit Henley's ability to portray the complexities of experience and history, and thus of change. Where change is possible, Henley's play implies, it must involve fundamental changes in assumptions about individuals and social relations, and in cultural institutions like the family and the institutions that support and shape economic values and practices. By revealing ideological silences, contradictions, and inadequacies, *The Lucky Spot* points to failures and thus to prospects for change aimed at promoting individual and social flourishing, while leaving open the possibilities.

Finally, to dramatize realistic solutions to her characters' dilemmas would deprive Henley's work of its satiric value. Henley holds up to ridicule those aspects of Western culture that she sees as destructive, exposing logical and practical failures of fundamental liberal assumptions and norms. The formal demands of satire require her to dramatize rather than resolve these failures. To approach her play through the conventions of dramatic realism, as some critics have done with her plays, is to ignore the integrity of its form and critical aims. Indeed, while the play offers no specific political or social solutions to the dilemmas it dramatizes, it makes clear that certain values and practices promote well-being, while others do not, making available these insights alongside the problems that the play exposes within the American liberal tradition. In so doing, her work takes its place within a rich critical tradition.

Notes

1. See Laurin R. Porter, "Women Re-conceived: Changing Perceptions of Women in Contemporary American Drama," *Conference of College Teachers of English Studies* 54 (1989): 53–59. Porter suggests that family configurations featured in Henley's plays represent an escape from patriarchal relations. She notes that although Henley's "women are initially defined in terms of their relationships with men," their actual relationships "are all familial in nature," representing new families formed entirely of women (53). She finds that these women "reinvent the family on their own terms," so that finally they are no longer dependent on men to define themselves (59). Karen L. Laughlin, in "Criminality, Desire, and Community: A Feminist Approach to Beth Henley's *Crimes of the Heart*," also sees positive alternatives to patriarchal domination in Henley's plays. In *Crimes of the Heart*, Laughlin suggests that Henley's characters offer feminine alternatives to self-destruction as well as powerful models of female community as alternatives to patriarchal family relations. Alan Shepard ("Aborted Rage in Beth Henley's Women") qualifies such optimistic readings by noting that Henley's females are not able to flee patriarchal control, but despite their unawareness of the gains of the feminist movement, they nonetheless "grope towards liberty" in their defiance and rejection of social norms (107).

   Other critics claim that Henley fails altogether to provide alternatives to patriarchal oppression. See Jonnie Guerra, "Beth Henley: Female Quest and the Family-Play Tradition," in *Making a Spectacle*, ed. Lynda Hart (Ann Arbor: University of Michigan Press, 1989) 119–130. Guerra suggests that Henley's reliance on realism and conventional dramatic forms precludes her ability to transcend patriarchal structures. Reading Henley's plays as an "attempt to adapt the family play to portray the female quest for autonomy" (119), she notes that in these plays, "there exists no marital happiness, nor is there intimacy or mutual understanding in the marriage bond" (121). Guerra concludes that Henley's female characters' "quests for autonomy" are truncated due to Henley's reliance on realism and the formal conventions of the family play (128). She thus finds that Henley's plays finally "affirm rather than strike out against women's confinement" to a stifling, emotionally bankrupt domestic sphere.

   For a particularly acute treatment of the failures of Henley's plays *vis-à-vis* feminist theory, see Janet V. Haedicke, " 'A Population (and Theater) at Risk': Battered Women in Henley's *Crimes of the Heart* and Shepard's *A Lie of the Mind*," *Modern Drama* 36 (1993): 83–95. Haedicke considers Henley's plays as fully embedded in a patriarchal culture that they can only reproduce but never transcend. She indicts both Henley's plays and modern feminism, suggesting that *Crimes of the Heart*, in particular, is finally regressive in its failure to escape the " 'reactionary foundationalism' of modern feminism, which posits Truth in individualized subjectivity (consciousness raising) and refuses to deconstruct the subject though insisting on gender as a construct" (86). For Haedicke, Henley opposes truth and freedom to silence and power, thus foreclosing critical examination of oppressive power relations by allowing her characters merely the pleasure of self-discovery through confession rather than liberation from the patriarchal conditions that have constructed them. She claims, furthermore, that Henley clings to illusory icons of unity in identity and family, and offers her female characters only Nietzsche's slave morality, or the power of reaction and a politics of *ressentiment*. She finds that Henley's plays provide no "transformative politics to counter violence against women in the family," thus "revalidating individualism and the traditional family" (87). While I find Haedecke's analysis insightful, I conclude that Henley's failure to provide alternatives is central to the critical aim of Henley's plays.

2. C. B. Macpherson, *The Political Theory of Possessive Individualism. Hobbes to Locke* (Oxford: Clarendon, 1962). See also Alan Macfarlane, *The Origins of English Individualism. The Family, Property and Social Transition* (New York: Cambridge University Press, 1978); Thomas E. Heller, et al., eds., *Reconstructing Individualism. Autonomy, Individuality and the Self in Western Thought* (Stanford, Calif.: Stanford University Press, 1986); and Isaac Kramnick, *Republicanism and Bourgeois Radicalism. Political Ideology in Late Eighteenth-Century England and America* (Ithaca, N.Y.: Cornell University Press, 1990).

3. My comments on Locke derive from his *Two Treatises of Government*, ed. Peter Laslett (Cambridge: Cambridge University Press, 1966). Commentary on Hobbes comes from *Leviathan* (Oxford: Oxford University Press, n.d.), and from commentary provided by W. G. Pogson Smith in his introduction of that volume, as well as discussions by other Hobbes scholars, including discussions on individualism in the volumes mentioned above by MacFarlane, MacPherson, Heller, and Kramnick. Discussion of Shaftesbury, Hutcheson, and Smith come from the following: Anthony Cooper, Third Earl of Shaftesbury, *Characteristics of Men, Manners, Opinions, Times, etc.*, 2 vols. (1710, reprint, ed. John M. Robertson, Gloucester, Mass.: Peter Smith, 1963); Francis Hutcheson, *An Essay on the Nature and Conduct of the Passions and Affections*. London: Darby and Browne (1728, reprint, New York: Garland, 1971); Adam Smith. *The Theory of Moral Sentiments* (1759, reprint, Amherst, N.Y.: Pantheon, 2000) and *The Wealth of Nations* (1776, reprint, ed. Edwin Canaan, intro. Robert Reich. New York: Modern Library).

4. In his introduction, Robert Reich reminds readers that *The Wealth of Nations* is primarily a moral treatise, and that economics was for the eighteenth century a moral science. He notes that Smith's treatise "is resolutely about human beings—their capacities and incentives to be productive, their overall well-being, and the connection between productivity and well-being" (xvii).

Smith was convinced that his system would promote general well-being. What we now refer to as classical liberal capitalism refers in general to the practice of investing money in order to make money, involving as well the systems of free trade, industry, and labor that Smith describes as fundamental to his economic system, which sees labor and the production of commodities, rather than gold and silver, as the true measure of a nation's wealth. Reich points out that Smith did not envision "large-scale industrialization and the scandalous conditions of urban poverty, unsafe workplaces, child labor, and pollution that scarred the nineteenth and twentieth centuries," or the use of his ideas by "the rising class of industrialists as theoretical justification for *not* seeking to remedy these and related social ills" (xix).

5. Interestingly, the second part of Sue Jack's explanation does not appear in the *Collected Plays*. Both the Dramatists Play Service edition of *The Lucky Spot* (61) and *Four Plays* (199) contain the following dialogue:

> SUE JACK: Look, this is nothing to me. He's just one guy, one night. Christ, Reed, don't you realize how many men, how many times—
> HOOKER: (*Overlapping.*) Stop it! Don't!
> SUE JACK: (*Running on.*) . . . How many nights there were just t'survive in that prison.
> HOOKER: (*Overlapping.*) No more. Please.
> SUE JACK: (*Running on.*) This?! This is nothing! Nothing!!
> HOOKER: (*Overlapping.*) Shut up. You. Be still.
> SUE JACK: (*Running on.*) Why, there were days I'd do three prison guards for a cup of dirty water. And once for a pair of shoes I was on my knees—I crawled on my knees—

6. Locke, 188. Isaac Kramnick (*Republicanism and Bourgeois Radicalism.*) notes that Locke provided a moral imperative for acquisition (221), as opposed to Hobbes's account of private property as the outcome of human selfishness.

7. Turnip is characterized by his supposed stupidity, having grown up hearing his family tell him how stupid he is (*CPI* 241). His name, given by his parents, suggests that he has fallen off the proverbial truck, although he tells Lacey that it doesn't "stand for" and is not "short for" anything (226). Henley, however, recuperates Turnip's intelligence by having him provide nurture and care, by his skepticism about a system that only produces "losers" (240), and by his rejection of his family's account of his worth.

8. Keep in mind that the Founding Fathers were by no means egalitarian in their views, despite the wording of the Declaration of Independence. Rather, meritocracy represented for them a social and economic hierarchy based on merit rather than birth. Like the ruling classes in England and Europe, they shared in a distrust of the masses (read unpropertied laborers) as a destabilizing element incapable of self-determination.

9. While Hobbes felt that all social relations were based on self-interested alliances, Locke described the family as originating through contract between husband and wife for the purpose of raising a family, although he also describes family bonds as affective rather than simply contractual. Typical of

his rationalist view of human affairs, Locke's marriage contract could provide for divorce once the family responsibilities were concluded. Shaftesbury and Hutcheson elaborate on Locke's description of the family's affective bonds and its function in producing caring, dutiful citizens. For all four thinkers, the family forms the unit of social life, and each describes the father as the head as a result of social convention, thus reinscribing a patriarchal hierarchy. Gender equality for Hobbes is a function of equal ability of husband and wife to kill each other, for Locke, a matter of equal ability to engage in contractual relations and conduct the business of the family.

10. Sue Jack's brief reference alludes to a large body of feminist critique of liberal gender norms. The mirror represents a means by which women internalize cultural norms that value women in terms of their appearance. The self-inflicted gunshot "in front of a full-length mirror" represents the deadliness of liberal culture for women, and others, who cannot thrive or survive within the conditions of their culture. For women, feminist theory suggests, internalizing cultural imperatives necessitates "killing" aspects of the self that do not conform, as well as effacing one's own needs and desires in order to care for others. Lacey's mother's criticism of her daughter reflects her internalization of cultural devaluation of women, while it also implies the cultural ideal of marriage to a rich man. See Carol Gilligan, *In a Different Voice. Psychological Theory and Women's Development* (Cambridge, Mass.: Harvard University Press, 1982), as well as her more recent work on adolescent psychological development of girls and boys. Turnip's remark suggests that Henley sees liberal culture as destructive for men as well.

11. Mr. Pete, Cassidy explains, was "a member of the Church of Innocent Blood" (*CPI* 245) and he calls Cassidy a "godless bag a' stench" (244). Mr. Pete, the most despicable of the characters referred to or actually in the play, is the only one who is described as a Christian. The name of his church and his reference to Cassidy suggest that Henley wants us to consider his beliefs and actions as logically, if not morally, consistent with Christian doctrine.

12. See Adam Smith, *The Theory of Moral Sentiments*, 472 ff., on Hutcheson's arguments that desire for approbation is not motivated by self-love. Eighteenth-century conservative arguments saw benevolence as dissipating beyond family, community, and especially nationality. Liberal arguments claimed that sympathy and benevolence are capable of universal application, if appropriately cultivated. Sympathy and benevolence also became associated with gender and class. For example, see John Mullan, *Sentiment and Sociability: The Language of Feeling in the Eighteenth Century* (Oxford: Clarendon, 1988), and Lucinda Cole's "(Anti)Feminist Sympathies: The Politics of Relationship in Smith, Wollstonecraft, and More," *ELH* 58.1 ([1991]): 107–140. Cole, for instance, notes that Adam Smith described sympathy as more developed in educated, cultured men. Thus, the poor are isolated from the mutual sympathy that binds society, so that they have no fellow feeling with their betters, a situation that for Smith represents a greater source of their discomfort than the material effects of poverty (113). Henley's play rejects these distinctions.

13. Hooker's grief over his lost son provides another allusion to Rhett Butler in Mitchell's *Gone with the Wind*, which functions as a pervasive subtext. Henley essentially rewrites Mitchell's text, critiquing its ongoing influence on southern culture and American culture in general, and parodying the absurdities of romantic southern culture that Mitchell's text addresses through dialogue and the narrator's commentary. Hooker's mourning for his son is not a parody, however, but a parallel to Butler's response to his daughter's death, which marks both Hooker's and Butler's humanization from self-interested speculators to loving, grief-stricken fathers.

Works Cited

Cooper, Anthony, third earl of Shaftesbury. *Characteristics of Men, Manners, Opinions, Times, etc.* 2 vols. 1710. Reprint. Ed. John M. Robertson. Gloucester, Mass.: Peter Smith, 1963.

Guerra, Jonnie. "Beth Henley: Female Quest and the Family-Play Tradition." In *Making a Spectacle*. Ed. Lynda Hart. Ann Arbor: University of Michigan Press, 1989. 119–130.

Haedicke, Janet V. " 'A Population (and Theater) at Risk': Battered Women in Henley's *Crimes of the Heart* and Shepard's *A Lie of the Mind*." *Modern Drama* 36 (1993): 83–95.

Hobbes, Thomas. *Leviathan*. Oxford: Oxford University Press, n.d.

Hutcheson, Francis. *An Essay on the Nature and Conduct of the Pasions and Affections*. London: Darby and Browne. 1728. Reprint. New York: Garland, 1971.

Laughlin, Karen. "Criminality, Desire, and Community: A Feminist Approach to Beth Henley's *Crimes of the Heart*." *Women and Performance* 3.1 (1989): 35–51.

Locke, John. *Two Treatises of Government*. Ed. Peter Laslett. Cambridge: Cambridge University Press, 1966.

Macpherson, C. B. *The Political Theory of Possessive Individualism. Hobbes to Locke*. Oxford: Clarendon, 1962.

Porter, Laurin R. "Women Re-conceived: Changing Perceptions of Women in Contemporary American Drama." *Conference of College Teachers of English Studies* 54 (1989): 53–59.

Shepard, Alan. "Aborted Rage in Beth Henley's Women." *Modern Drama* 36 (1993): 96–108.

Smith, Adam. *The Theory of Moral Sentiments*. 1759. Reprint. Amherst, N.Y.: Pantheon, 2000.

———. *The Wealth of Nations*. 1776. Reprint. Ed. and intro. Robert Reich. New York: Modern Library.

Stone, Lawrence. *The Family, Sex, and Marriage in England 1500–1800*. New York: Harper Torchbooks, 1979.

5
Abundance or Excess?
Beth Henley's Postmodern Romance of the True West

KAREN L. LAUGHLIN

> But nobody's interested in love these days, Austin. Let's face it.
> —SAM SHEPARD, *TRUE WEST* (35)

> ... if real history belongs to men, and women's history is merely the fantasy of historical romance, postmodern cultural analysis of history and the "real" offers a way of revaluing female discourse.
> —DIANE ELAM, *ROMANCING THE POSTMODERN* (3)

In an essay on "Battered Women in Henley and Shepard," Janet Haedicke castigates Beth Henley's *Crimes of the Heart* for being "ultimately regressive compared to Sam Shepard's *A Lie of the Mind*." She also takes exception to feminist uneasiness with Shepard's "macho vision" (83), at least as it relates to this particular Shepard play. Like others who have been critical of Henley's Pulitzer Prize–winning drama, Haedicke finds in *Crimes* at best a "regressive," "modernist feminism," play that "reflects an antipolitical preference for reason over power, truth over politics, security over freedom, discoveries over decisions, and identities over pluralities" (84). Whereas Henley's politics "can only kindle kitchen fires," she argues, Shepard's play "decenters the subject in a political, amoral truth, which reveals the mind's lie" (91).

Rather than challenge directly Haedicke's assessment of *Crimes of the Heart,* or her praise of Shepard's feminist revision in *A Lie of the Mind*, I suggest we rethink this opposition by considering another Henley-Shepard pairing. Henley's 1989 play, *Abundance*, set not in contemporary California but in the "Wild West" of the Wyoming Territory in the late 1860s, revises and extends Shepard's exploration of the myth of the American West in his 1980 family drama, *True West*. In her story of two mail-order brides who come west to seek their fortune, Henley looks at the West through the lens of romance, a romance based largely on women's desires and ambitions. In so doing, she proposes a postmodern feminist reworking of the Western myth.

While there has so far been little scholarly commentary on *Abundance*, Robert Brustein's rather humorless critique, reprinted in his *Reimagining American Theatre,* appears to recognize the play's leanings toward romance, as well as the gendered nature of those leanings. "For Beth Henley," he observes, "the Wild West is mostly a backdrop for intermarital affairs and monosexual friendships. In her cute, eccentric way, she has domesticated a savage episode of American history into a story of broken hearts and damaged hearths, where even the Indian wars are an occasion for discussing relationships" (108). Brustein's comments reflect an attitude toward romance (and its treatment of history) that Diane Elam moves to counter in the book that provides my second epigraph and much of the theoretical framework for this chapter. In setting up the term "postmodern romance," Elam suggests that one thing romance and postmodernism share is a quality of excess. She argues, "Romance's excess over itself, its capacity to appear where least expected, is analogous to postmodernism's paradoxical ability both to precede and to come after itself, to come both before and after modernism" (12). Just as postmodernism exceeds temporal boundaries, so romance exceeds generic boundaries, often turning toward history to do so.[1] In reading "the romance of women's desires as 'postmodern' rather than simply 'unrealistic' or 'foolish,' " Elam revalues romance, and thereby links feminism to postmodernism and its questioning of "the established rules of historical and cultural representation" (2–3).

Commenting on the disputed nature of romance (as well as of postmodernism), Elam asks, "What, for instance, is romance doing in the quintessentially 'realistic' novels of George Eliot?" (12). One might ask a similar question about what many see as the quintessentially macho plays of Sam Shepard. Yet, in linking the typically narrative genre of romance to drama, both plays make a postmodern move, evoking postmodernism's own characteristic blurring of genre boundaries. In addition, Henley's particular blending of history and romance raises useful questions about her commitment to feminist politics and whether that commitment might open itself to seeing the subject in terms of postmodern "pluralities" rather than modernist identities.

Early reviewers of Henley's play picked up on both the historical qualities of *Abundance* and its parallels to Shepard. Calling the play a "Revisionist Western," Frank Rich praised its "disturbing close-ups of the women who lost while the West was won" (167). Linda Winer, in a much less flattering review, recognized "the tried-if-hardly-true tradition of a Sam Shepard personality switch" in Henley's characterization of the emotionally hungry Bess. Rich's review also indirectly suggested a connection between the would-be screenwriters of Shepard's *True West* and the Hollywood screenwriting experience that serves as a backdrop for Henley's own turn to the West. Noting a shift from Henley's typical southern settings to one of Hollywood's favorite locales, Rich described *Abundance* as a "fiercely held parable about the evils that befall women (an author among them) who sell out their identities to men, commerce and celebrity in the golden West" (167). Whether or not Henley's personal choices themselves link her career with Shepard's, her play does share with *True West* a self-reflexive, postmodern awareness of the connections between commercialism and artistic production.[2] The brothers in Shepard's play turn toward the mass market as they learn the difference between a "film" and a "movie." " 'In this business,' " says Lee, citing producer Saul Kimmer, " 'we make movies, American movies. Leave the films to the French' " (30). In Henley's nineteenth-century version of this trend, Bess finds her narrative of Indian captivity transformed into the stuff of a lucrative, but ultimately degrading, lecture tour. In a further, wry twist, Henley notes that the story has garnered the attention of the famous (if unknown to Bess) author of sensationalist melodramas, Dion Boucicault, who wants to turn it into "a hit play" (*CPII* 44).

My comparison of *Abundance* and *True West* is not intended to suggest that the legitimacy of Henley's drama rests on its analogies to Shepard; nor does it seek to assert the superior vision of one play over the other. In focusing on the ways *Abundance* reworks the myth of the American West through the genre of romance, I do want to invite a rethinking of Shepard's highly masculinized version of this myth as presented in *True West*. An intertextual reading of the two plays suggests that, despite its "macho vision," Shepard's play, too, participates in a postmodern Western romance. Such a reading highlights some of the gaps in this version of Shepard's romance of the West and interrogates its potential link to feminist politics. More centrally, though, it argues for the cultural value of Henley's lesser-known play as a means of positioning women within the history of the West while reframing the question of the "truth" of the West as a question of its seductive power.

The most obvious parallel between *Abundance* and *True West* is found in both plays' interrogation of personal and cultural identity, conveyed especially through what Winer calls the "personality switch" (2). In Shepard's version of this reversal, the yuppie would-be screenwriter, Austin, and his scruffy brother, Lee, a self-proclaimed loner and petty thief, have both taken refuge in their mother's home. The moderately successful Austin has temporarily left his wife and children so he can work out a screenplay deal. Lee has apparently come home to plunder Mom's suburban California neighborhood before returning to his independent life in the desert. As the play progresses, it is Lee of course who is closing in on a $300,000 deal for a "Contemporary Western" screenplay, "[b]ased on a true story" (Shepard 18).

Austin, envisioning a burgeoning criminal career, fills the stage with stolen toasters and then makes plans to leave his family and follow Lee's desert life.

Working in a clearly more feminine mode, *Abundance* similarly pairs Macon Hill, a would-be writer "drunk with western fever" (*CPII* 5), with her seeming opposite, Bess Johnson, a romantic who has come west hoping for "a match made in heaven" (7). Although the two women are not related by blood, their shared status as brides-to-be creates a sisterly bond that deepens as they begin their married lives. But, like Shepard's ultramasculine Lee, Henley's ultrafeminine Bess eventually begins to take over the language and desires of her "sister." She is the one who lives out Macon's dreams of adventure as she is captured by Indians, eventually returns to write an account of her adventures, and takes her story on the lyceum lecture circuit. Macon's life, too, begins to resemble Bess's original, domestic dream as Macon becomes increasingly attached to her pioneer home and its material possessions.

In both plays, the apparent theft of character traits works against psychological realism, even as the characters purport to justify the role reversals they experience. After Lee wins over Austin's producer, Austin tries desperately to expose his brother as "a hustler" (Shepard 33). Austin later seems to attribute the brothers' similarities to family resemblance, noting, "we all sound alike when we're sloshed. We just sorta' echo each other" (39), and even before his success with Saul, Lee tells his brother, "I always wondered what'd be like to be you" (26). Yet the very excess of the brothers' transformations, perhaps best embodied in the array of stolen toasters Austin matches against his brother's stolen television set (scene 8) as well as the extreme violence of the play's ending, defies a simple psychological explanation.[3] Similarly, Macon initially suggests that Bess survived the hardships of her captivity by "picturing" her (*CPII* 42). But it soon becomes clear that Bess's transformation has gone much further than simple reliance on lessons learned from her friend as an exasperated Macon tells Bess, "You stole from me. *You stole me.* I showed you how to walk and speak and fight *and dream . . .*" (47, emphasis added). Even Macon's protest that she is "the real thing" and that Bess is "just a watered down milquetoast version. Them Indians stole the wrong woman" (47) only reinforces the instability of personal identity in this play.

In what Fredric Jameson might call a postmodern pastiche, these characters' actions, and especially their desires, are produced by citing—if not stealing from—each other. As their desires shift and transform, each seems to want what the other wants or has. *Abundance* illustrates the nature of this exchange most clearly in Bess's appropriation of Macon's favorite color, blue, and even her suddenly professed love for golden tulips, a flower Bess previously did not even know existed (*CPII* 27, 49). "You thief! Robber—thief! Tulips are mine!" Macon screams. "They belong to me! I seen the picture! You never did!" (49). The very language Bess takes from Macon is itself often focused on desire. Once returned from her capture, Bess adopts, for example, Macon's description of herself as "drunk with western fever" (5) and even claims Macon's strange longing "to see the elephant" (43). Refusing to give Macon the fifty dollars she needs to save her homestead, Bess throws back at Macon her own bold assertion from the play's opening scene: "Honey, I'd rip the wings off an angel if I thought they'd help me fly!" (6, 48).

In both of these plays, then, desire circulates. It is not just the property of the one who voices it.[4] And the often-excessive desires of both Shepard's and Henley's characters—as well as the romantic nature of these desires—highlight the difficulty of attributing private emotion to any single individual. Rather than taking over an identity based in a world given to the characters (and the audience) as "unproblematically real," these characters inhabit what Elam calls "a reality that is *invested by desire*" (156). Theirs is, in other words, the "reality" of romance, and their explorations of what it means to be masculine or feminine within this "reality" suggests plurality—or better yet, instability—rather than identity.[5]

The more overtly feminine frame of *Abundance* makes it easier to see this play's appeal to romance, while illustrating something of the unstable or excessive nature of romance as a genre. The play's first scene evokes several variations on romance and romantic excess. Most familiar, perhaps, is Bess's appeal to the romance of fairy tales or the novels of Sir Walter Scott. She dreams, "I was hoping we'd be in love like people in them stories. The ones about princesses and chimney sweeps and dragon slayers" (*CPII* 7). "Down in the Valley," the folk song that opens the play and becomes a central motif, likewise conveys Bess's large-scale romantic desires. As the play begins, she sings "Build me a castle forty feet high/ So I can see him as he rides by" (5). In contrast to this fairy tale romance, Macon's initial dream evokes the classic romance of the West. Alluding in another way to the abundance of the play's title, her vision is of "the boundlessness of it all" (5). In a much more masculine mode than Bess's, she is eager "to discover gold and be rich . . . to erect an ice palace and kill an Indian with a hot bullet" as well as, more incongruously, "to see the elephant" (5–6). Henley introduces Jack Flan, Bess's eventual husband, as a violent, masculine figure reminiscent of Shepard's more brutal male characters. (Within a minute of his entrance he has knocked both Bess and Macon to the ground.) Yet Henley's introductory description of Jack, as "handsome, with an air of wild danger" (7) seems right out of a twentieth-century romance novel and, true to form, he eventually seduces a principled but lustfully yielding Macon after Bess is taken captive. Finally, Bess's captivity narrative elicits another popular variation on romance, one that a review in the *St. Louis Chronicle* eventually is said to describe as "excessive and outdated like a worn-out melodrama one would read in a dime novel" (50).[6]

Given its combination of Hollywood ambitions and Lee's rough-and-tumble life in the desert, *True West* would seem to be closer generically to the Western than to romance. Of course, the play draws heavily on this more classically masculine genre, most notably in Lee's screenplay scenario and references to his independent desert existence. Yet romance is not so subtly lurking in the background of *True West,* and, as in *Abundance*, the references to romance are multifaceted. Whereas Lee wants to write "the first authentic Western to come along in a decade" (Shepard 30), Austin envisions "just a simple love story" (31), reminding us that Hollywood, too, has an investment in romance. Picking up on Austin's description of the screenplay as "a period piece," Ronald St. Pierre identifies Austin's work as a type of historical romance and suggests that this project reflects "Austin's detachment from the true West" (39). Yet romance of a sort even contaminates the Western genre directly when Lee and Austin evoke their favorite film, *Lonely Are the Brave,* describing it as one in which Kirk Douglas "dies for the love of a horse" (Shepard 18). The brothers' screenplay competition evokes a rather different Hollywood romance, as Austin helps Lee envision what the sale of a screenplay might mean: "A ranch. . . . A whole lot of money" (24–25). Catching the "strike-it rich" fever, Lee envisions himself trading in the cowboy's horse for his own car and "Sittin' around dreamin' stuff up. Gettin' paid to dream. Ridin' back and forth on the freeway just dreamin' my fool head off" (25).[7] Connected to this vision is the brothers' romanticization of the "paradise" of *House Beautiful* properties in Mom's suburban neighborhood, first described by Lee after a robbery reconnaissance mission (12) and echoed by Austin as he sets out for "[c]rimes beyond the imagination!" (39). Lee also introduces a more historical reference in the play's opening scene, when he compares Austin's writing by candlelight (itself, perhaps, a sign of romance) to "what the old guys did . . . The Forefathers. . . . Cabins in the wilderness" (6).[8]

In contrast to Bess's romantic dream of a log cabin idyll with her "true one" (*CPII* 19), Lee's vision here is a masculinized one, with no mention of the pioneer women who likely made the candles in those cabins. In fact, what is most striking about the references to romance in *True West* is that women are absent from virtually all of them. While producer Saul Kimmer hints that all the movies he likes contain a "[g]ood love interest" (Shepard 18), the only love interest in the Hollywood Western the brothers acknowledge is a horse, and the focus of Lee's own Western screenplay is on the two men involved in a heterosexual love triangle. Whereas women tend to play a central role in traditional romance, Shepard all but erases them from his romance of the West.

Instead, Shepard largely internalizes masculine-feminine tensions within Austin and Lee. We see this most clearly in the initial contrast between the rugged, macho Lee, emerging from his desert adventures and the gentrified, almost feminized Austin, writing Hollywood romances in his mother's kitchen. The play's subsequent "personality switches" of course destabilize this dichotomy, and Shepard's exploration of this opposition provides a postmodern reworking of the classic Western clash between the uninhibited masculine violence of the frontier and the emasculating influence of the domesticating woman.[9] Though he does not pursue the gender implications of this contrast, Stephen J. Bottoms sees a self-conscious irony in the play's "dichotomy between civilization and wilderness" (200). Consistent with my own reading of the play as postmodern romance, he suggests that the play's true "American West—whether untamed or wild—is an undifferentiated landscape of frustrated desire" (200).

Nevertheless, femininity in the play is largely subsumed into the male characters, leaving little or no space for women. Even Mom, who makes a brief appearance in the play's final scene, is reduced to little more than a maternal cliché. When she returns from an Alaskan vacation to find all of her beloved plants dead, she simply comments "Oh well, one less thing to take care of I guess" (Shepard 54), apparently abandoning her rather modest caregiving role with relative unconcern. She is likewise ineffectual in her role as disciplinarian as she tries to stop Austin from strangling Lee with a numb "You boys shouldn't fight in the house. Go outside and fight" (56). On the one hand, such clichés might be read as another facet of Shepard's postmodern pastiche, making Mom into more of a performed role than a unified subject. On the other hand, her reminder that the boys have "the whole outdoors to fight in" (57) reinforces a concept of separate spheres that seems remarkably traditional within Shepard's otherwise postmodern frame.

As Raynette Halvorsen Smith points out, "The artificiality of Mom's kitchen is associated with domestication, domestication with feminization, and feminization with emasculation" (279). While Shepard might be testing gender boundaries by placing his western males in their mother's kitchen, the fact that the brothers' violence has virtually destroyed their mother's home at the end of the play suggests that his modern day cowboys have failed the test. Rather than opening up a postmodern space for both men and women, the domestic space of the ravaged kitchen finally resembles "a desert junkyard at high noon" (Shepard 50), and the brothers square off like a pair of gunslingers ready for a shootout. Shepard highlights the masculine quality of this terrain with Mom's final line. When Austin urges, "Stay here, Mom. This is where you live," she can only reply "I don't recognize it at all" (59). There may no longer be a unified, "true West," but even the postmodern fragments of that West are clearly unrecognizable to Mom and appear, at least in Shepard's version, to belong solely to men.

In contrast to this masculine exclusivity, Henley asks what happens when the West is opened up to feminine as well as masculine desire. And, while Shepard's very title poses the question of "truth," both his play and Henley's more insistently romantic vision shift emphasis away from finding the "truth" of the West and toward exploring its ideological power. As Elam suggests in the final chapter of her book, however, romance (at least postmodern romance) allows us to rethink the workings of ideology, seeing it "as a kind of persuasion, as a *rhetorical* activity" (146) understood less in terms of a deceptive, false consciousness than as a form of seductive (and hence gendered) play. *Abundance*, with its more overt turn to romance, lets us see this seductive quality quite clearly while highlighting the perils of that seduction for women in particular.

Initially, in somewhat traditional fashion, the seduction of romance serves as a "form of social control," especially for Bess.[10] Preying on Bess's desire to "do things right" (*CPII* 10) once she is married, her husband, Jack, effectively silences her in the play's early scenes, refusing to let her cry, sing, or even read to him. In a quasi-Brechtian *gestus* prior to the moment of Bess's capture by the Indians, we even see her kneeling at Jack's feet to shine his boots while he barks, "I can't see myself in the toe" (26). Yet even before she is kidnapped by the Indians, Bess has also been seduced by Macon's dream of adventure in a wilder west than she has discovered through her failed pioneer romance. She transfers her love from Jack to Macon and begs her friend to go even farther west with her: "Let's start all over" Bess urges Macon. "I realize now—now that you're brushing my hair, that I love you so much more—so much more than anyone else" (23).

In contrast to Bess, Macon is increasingly captivated by the material comforts of her life as a farmer's wife. This material seduction is most apparent in the many items Macon and her husband, Will, order from the catalogues—from copper pots and scarlet sofa cushions to a hairpiece from Boston. As Bess tallies the goods she has been collecting for their westward journey, Macon puts her off, waiting for her pumpkin patch to mature, her "rainbow-colored petticoat" to arrive in the mail, and her chance to judge the annual baking contest (*CPII* 25). The Christmas scene between Macon and Will highlights Macon's own seductive power, as she uses Will's sexual desire for her as leverage to persuade him to plant wheat as a cash crop (20–21). Henley thus shows her characters taking off and putting on various possibilities, as if desire were a costume like the glass eye Will has ordered in an attempt to make himself more attractive to his wife or Macon's "waterfall curls." This mail-order hairpiece is a doubly seductive emblem of Macon's material desires. Not only does it fulfill her ambition to stay in step with "the latest sensation" (27) but it also makes her increasingly attractive to Jack, who physically seduces her at the end of the scene in which she first tries it on. In addition, it points toward femininity itself as a kind of disguise or masquerade, a constructed identity or performance that, to borrow from Mary Ann Doane, becomes "manipulable, producible, and readable" (54). In Henley's world, though, this can be a dangerous disguise, one over which the wearer does not always have control, as we see again later in the feminine attire imposed on Bess when she returns from captivity.

Another central dimension of Henley's Western romance is its turn to history, where "truth" or "reality" again becomes oddly suspect. The history of the American West is, in some ways, a relatively unspoken backdrop for Henley's play. A little research on the Wyoming Territory in the late 1860s, however, reveals a potentially feminist side to this choice of setting. Nicknamed "the Equality State," Wyoming had an active woman suffrage movement. It was the first territory to extend the franchise to women, doing so in 1869 (about the time when the play begins), shortly after Wyoming was made a territory. In what is generally thought to be an effort to attract settlers to the sparsely populated territory, Wyoming extended other rights to women as well, including the right for married women to own property. Though she does not openly exploit this historical detail, the status of Macon and Bess as mail-order brides hints at the potential intersection between the marriage market and the Wyoming Territory's rather surprising openness to women's rights.[11]

While *Abundance* can be read in the context of a modernist feminist project of historical recovery, the play does much more than retell the history of the West from a woman's point of view. Rather than focus on historical women of the West or the tantalizing details of Wyoming's place in women's history, one of the few historical details to which Henley alludes directly is the presence in Wyoming of the Oglala, a division of the western Sioux. She does so, of course, through Bess's tale of her Indian captivity. Here, too, "reality"—now understood as a grand narrative of verifiable events—is filtered through romance.

It is this filtering that appears to be at issue in Brustein's censure of *Abundance* for what he sees as a senseless addition that uses "even the Indian wars" as "an occasion for discussing 'relationships' " (108). But perhaps this conflation of captivity and domesticity is not so outlandish or politically incorrect. In a review of three recent books on the captivity narrative, Gordon M. Sayre points out a contemporary tendency toward "reexamination of what constitutes captivity" that goes so far as to expand "the very meaning of 'captivity' to include aspects of women's confinement by men" (861).[12] Such narratives, he points out, also incorporate "tropes of racial and cultural prejudice" even as they take their places within the genres of sentimental fiction and romance (860). In making an experience of Indian captivity a part of her picture of the "Wild West," Henley draws significant parallels between Bess's experience and her life with her brutish white husband, even while insistently blending the categories of history and romance.[13] In this sense, she goes beyond merely filling in the "truth" of what was in fact a fairly common occurrence for western settlers. She also seeks to politicize the relationships among and between the men and women who helped settle the West.

We see the blending of history and romance as Bess first returns from what Macon calls "the vale of death," her skin "dark and burnt," her hair "thin and sunbleached," and her chin tattooed (35). Explaining her tattoos to Macon as a sign of her marriage to Oglala chief, Ottawa, Bess seems at first to have transferred her romantic dreams onto her Native husband. "I thought he was true one. He gave me black horse," she says, in dialogue that, like the scars on her face, marks her as a "white Indian" (37).[14] While her only child with Jack died in infancy, Bess also appears to have fulfilled her maternal desires as she bore Ottawa two children. In comparison with the historical sources, Bess's difficulty in returning to her former life does not appear to be much of a stretch. As Gary Ebersole points out, "There is . . . considerable evidence that returning to the white world after living with the Indians was easier said than done. Captives who had spent a considerable period of time with the Indians . . . frequently had taken on an Indian identity. Not only did they dress and talk like Indians, they thought like them, shared many of their values, and . . . even carried their bodies differently. Some of the former captives also carried facial or bodily scars that marked them for life as white Indians" (5).

While there is a definite romantic quality to Bess's version of her life as a "white Indian," Henley also uses this scene to make clear the politics of the white settlers of the West. Macon admonishes Bess to drop her attachment to her Native husband: "No, no. He was bad. He was an Indian. He was bad." Bess reinterprets Macon's ideological lesson as she agrees, "Yes, bad. Sold me. Sold me cheap. Two horses, blanket, beads, bullets. Cheap" (37), referring to the ransom paid by the U.S. Army when they rescued her. There is another note of historical truth in this detail. Although many captives, mostly women, were adopted and acculturated by the tribe, for the most part, the primary motivation for capturing settlers was to achieve a bounty or ransom. But Bess's response to the fact that Ottawa sold her "cheap" also becomes another in a series of betrayals in the play that includes the affair between Macon and Jack as well as Bess's transfer of her love from Jack to Macon.

What is the "true" history here? Bess's felt experience of Ottawa's betrayal, Macon's allusion to the white construction of the "Indians" as brutal savages, and even Bess's ever-romantic hopes for an idyllic wilderness romance are all part of an experience that seems to exceed the boundaries of conventional history. And it is an experience that is shaped as much by economic and political considerations—Bess's "cheap" price, Macon's prejudice, and even the fact that Ottawa was apparently "threatened with a massacre 'fore he'd sell her back" (*CPII* 35)—as it is by personal emotions and desires.

Henley further links these emotions and desires to a wider political stage through Professor Elmore (the analogue to Shepard's Hollywood producer, Saul Kimmer), who entices Bess to write a book with him "that would help prevent others from falling prey to similar atrocities" (*CPII* 40). This aspect of Henley's story also has a clear basis in historical fact, as the composition and publication of many captivity narratives were linked to obvious economic benefits. Like many of the published narratives embellished to serve specific agendas, Bess's tale allowed an opportunity to expound, on behalf of the "land speculator" promoting her lecture tour, "certain philosophical beliefs" concerning "western expansion and the concept of manifest destiny" (45). Once more, Henley personalizes these political details. Despite her apparent attachment to her romantic Indian chief, Bess claims to have "no problem" accepting the contract stipulation that she "demand the immediate extermination of all Indian tribes" (48). By the end of her public speaking career, she proclaims her relief at never again having "to rhapsodize about writing with fish blood and being scantily-clad in a thin bark skirt" (50). And yet, in her final encounter with Macon, which takes place the same day she renounces the lecture circuit, Bess nostalgically describes her adventures in terms right out of Disney's *Pocahontas*: "Yeah, the Oglalas knew such beautiful places. I saw rivers that were so clear you could see every pebble and fish. And the water was any color you could dream: pink and turquoise; gold and white; lime green" (52).

Here, too, romance overlaps with both history and material desires, as Bess's speaking contract proves very lucrative indeed. Bess has apparently earned enough to buy an estate in White Plains, where she plans to retire with the now submissive Jack, who, in another of the play's personality switches, now claims to be Bess's "true one" (*CPII* 51). But rather than emphasizing an alternate "truth" or corrected version of western women's lives—in Indian captivity or in their log cabin homes—Henley reminds us of the constructedness of both that history and women's roles within it. When Bess taunts Macon by urging her to scar her own face and take Bess's place on the lecture tour, *Abundance* asks to what extent the "wild woman" Bess has become in itself a construction (47–48). The shackles earlier placed on Bess to keep her from running away, like the veil she is to put over her scarred face, may be a bit too obvious as symbols of the constraining nature of the "civilization" and western femininity to which she has returned. But Bess's eventual reappearance without veil but carrying a parasol and wearing new shoes underlines the instability of her roles as both white Indian and Western "lady." We again see femininity as masquerade, and it is not at all clear in the play what "truth" might lie behind these masks.

In its elements of romance, its anachronisms, and even the allusion to Bess's performance of her personal history on the lecture circuit, *Abundance* does not prefer "truth over politics" (Haedicke 91) but rather raises politically charged questions about the ways we know history and the very linearity of historical time. Indeed, the very plot of *Abundance* is something of an anachronism, as it blends romance, melodrama, the Western, and other genres in a postmodern pastiche.[15] In her analysis of popular, women-centered fiction, Rosalind Coward argues that nineteenth-century women's novels tended to focus on the heroine's choices concerning marriage. The marriage decision is generally the culminating point of these narratives, and their heroines tend to be intensely silent. In mainstream popular fiction of the late twentieth century, in contrast, Coward notes that women protagonists cannot seem to stop talking about their intimate personal lives, lives which generally exceed the bounds of marriage even as they continue to define women in terms of their sexuality. Viewed from this perspective, *Abundance* appears to be a twentieth-century version of a nineteenth-century tale. Rather than culminating in the marriage of the two 1860s mail-order brides, Henley's play uses this moment as her starting point. Though her heroines are garrulous indeed, Bess, at least, speaks in the public forum of the lecture hall rather than exclusively in intimate confession. And, though anchored in domesticity and romance, Bess's story places concern for female sexuality and desire in the context of a broadly based historical and political critique.

The play's final scene does leave itself open to the more modernist reading implied in Haedicke's analysis of *Crimes of the Heart*. After a fifteen-year separation, Bess and Macon are reunited for a moment of sisterly bonding and discovery reminiscent of the birthday party ending of *Crimes*. In contrast to the carefully framed, violent showdown between the brothers at the end of Shepard's *True West*, Henley here gives us Bess and Macon exchanging whistled tunes and then a sharing laugh that comes "from deep in the bottom of their hearts" (*CPII* 53). The ever romantic Bess has apparently come to see Macon to reminisce and share her sadness at the recent news of Chief Ottawa's death. Macon's references to the pain in her heart recall the "slicing pains" in her chest that Meg, from *Crimes of the Heart*, experienced when reading news from home (*CPI* 13). And Macon's desire for "somebody t'tell" (*CPII* 53) echoes Meg's insistence that talking about one's life (the personal confession of which Coward speaks) "is an important human need" (*CPI* 26).

Perhaps, though, Henley is not merely repeating but rather quoting herself in this scene, in yet another layer of pastiche that questions the notions of authentic desire and the unified subject. Whether self-conscious citation or not, the scene makes clear that fixed notions of identity as well as a clear understanding of linear history and purpose still elude these characters. Even as the characters cite desires to find "true love" or touch the stars (a desire initially attributed not to the women but to Bess's dead fiancé, Mike), Macon comments, "You know, when I was younger, I never knew who I was, what I wanted, where I was going or how to get there. Now that I'm older, I don't know none of that either" (*CPII* 53). Is this said with modernist nostalgia? Or with a postmodern awareness of the seductiveness of desire, even if it is a desire for that modernist, unified self? Does Henley leave us in a world of romance defined in terms of largely personal desires or does this ending, too, open out onto power and politics?

The setting of the play's final scene provides a clue to Henley's more political orientation. In contrast to the kitchen settings of both Henley's *Crimes of the Heart* and Shepard's *True West,* Henley situates Bess and Macon in the marketplace—not the marriage market but the carnival atmosphere of an 1890s tent show. It seems an almost classic location for the sometimes grotesque characters we recognize as so characteristic of Henley's writing.[16] But this location also suggests that both Bess and Macon have in a sense sold, even prostituted themselves—as evidenced as much by the commercialization of Bess's captivity tale as by the syphilitic sores on Macon's face. This suggestion in turn brings us back to both Henley and Shepard themselves, for whom Bess and Macon might also serve as doubles. In evoking the tried-if-not-true Hollywood terrain of the West, both playwrights invite reflection on the politics and economics of their own writing and on the perennial problem of commercialization or "selling-out" faced by anyone who writes for a mass audience—on stage or screen. Again, there is no definitive "truth" that will solve this problem. All we can do, it seems, is share a laugh, face each other down in a competitive shootout, or perhaps dream of other possibilities opened up by the world of romance.

Notes

1. This comment on the temporal excess of postmodernism points, for example, to Jean-François Lyotard's notion of postmodernism as modernism's "nascent state" rather than simply as its historical successor (79).
2. See especially Fredric Jameson's interrogation of the links between postmodernism and late industrial capitalism, especially as developed in his essay on "Postmodernism and Consumer Society." In describing Shepard as a "reluctant postmodernist," Stephen J. Bottoms notes the way Shepard's writing has gravitated toward an awareness "of its own colonization by a flashy, violent, and spiritually bankrupt society" (9). I would argue that *Abundance* shows a similar awareness on Henley's part.
3. Arguing against any simple contrast of Lee and Austin, Ronald St. Pierre notes that the two characters become one another "because of their fraternity, but also because of their mutual envy" (43–44). Bottoms's reading of *True West* takes this analysis several steps further, recognizing a tension between the postmodern instability of Shepard's two main characters and a more realistic motivation for their shifting roles. "Both men's personae" he notes, "prove to be highly unstable compositions of shifting, conflicting desires, devoid of any reliable sense of self and thus capable of extreme volatility.

Paradoxically, though, a more essentialist reading of the situation exists alongside this contingent one: there are clear traces of the concern with biological heredity which had dominated the previous family plays, and to some extent Austin's climactic violence reads as another image of an inherited blood curse" (195).
4. This argument draws on Elam's intertextual reading of Kathy Acker's *In Memoriam to Identity* and Jacques Derrida's *The Post Card* in the final chapter of *Romancing the Postmodern*. Both *Abundance* and *True West* work toward the dispersal of unified subjectivity theorized in the two works Elam discusses, though in ways that are arguably less extreme than Elam's examples.
5. I am of course returning to Haedicke's terms here, though the postmodern frame of my essay suggests that it may be more productive to think of identity in a less binary fashion than Haedicke does. The characters in these plays do at times seem to construct a kind of ready-made identity from their fellow character's desires. But the very fact of their shifting desires implies an instability of identity that exceeds not only the bounds of psychological realism but also the either/or dichotomy of identity and plurality.
6. Acknowledging that he and Bess have come to the end of their popularity, Professor Elmore remarks, "People are no longer interested in hearing about the untamed savages. Times have changed. Indians today are beloved circus performers" (50). These references to both the "dime novels" and the Wild West Shows that were so popular toward the end of the nineteenth century place Bess's lectures on her Indian captivity in a sequence of public entertainments that anticipate the Hollywood Western and its own version of the western romance.
7. Lee's vision here has its analogues in *Abundance* in the get-rich-quick schemes of Bess's husband, Jack, and perhaps also the machinations of the entrepreneurial Macon as she directs her husband's management of their farm.
8. Though she argues for an eventual deconstruction of gender myths in *True West*, Raynette Halvorsen-Smith sees Austin's candlelight writing as a way of displaying his "romantic bent" (280). Megan Williams, in contrast, emphasizes the contrast between the candlelight and hanging plants and the clearly artificial "synthetic grass" that carpets the set. In a reading that is also indebted to Jameson's "Postmodernism and Consumer Society," Williams suggests that Lee's references to the "Forefathers" in fact highlights the "basic artificiality and falseness at the root of an American history of origin. . . . [I]f Austin's candlelight and the 'wilderness' are in fact similar, then we as a culture have taken our national and individual identities from a past that never existed" (Williams 62–63). As I will argue below, *Abundance* shares with *True West* this postmodern sense of the constructedness of the past.
9. See Bassan, Halvorsen-Smith, and St. Pierre for contrasting, but in many ways complementary, discussions of Shepard's handling of this dichotomy.
10. The latter phrasing is taken from Elam's reading of George Eliot's novels and their interweaving of realism and romance (126).

11. An illustration in the April 1916 issue of *The Woman Voter* highlights Wyoming in what it labels "The First Suffrage Map 1869." It describes the map as having been "Drawn by Hamilton Wilcox in 1869" and anachronistically identifies the "state" (Wyoming was not admitted to the Union until 1890) as "The Woman Suffrage State" where there is "No Crime. No Pauperism. No Drunkenness. No Social Evil. No Wrongs Against Women." According to Larsen's *History of Wyoming*, the territory's legislators "showed much interest in women's rights" and accorded rights to women that were not generally given to women at that time in other parts of the country. These included an "act to protect married Women in their separate property, and the enjoyment of the fruits of their labor," a school law that barred pay discrimination against women teachers, and another law reserving seats in the gallery of the House of Representatives for women interested in observing the proceedings of that body (78). Larsen's study cites a range of possible reasons for the suffrage decision—from a sense of justice on the part of legislators, to a desire for favorable publicity, to the possibility that the voting rights act was the result of a joke that went awry and became law. In any case, as Larsen points out, "With only one woman in Wyoming over twenty-one years of age for every six men over twenty-one . . . adoption of woman suffrage was less revolutionary than it would have been in a state or territory where there were as many women as men" (80).

12. Sayre is here referring to Castiglia's *Bound and Determined* and Burnham's *Captured by Sentiment*. His review essay also comments on Ebersole's *Captured by Texts*.

13. Noting three distinct phases of the Indian captivity narrative, Kathryn Zabelle Derounian-Stodola divides the published literature into "authentic religious accounts in the seventeenth century, propagandist and stylistically embellished texts in the eighteenth century, and outright works of fiction in the late eighteenth and into the nineteenth centuries" (xii). *Abundance* seemingly adopts the characteristics of the latter, but Bess's story does owe much to historical fact. Henley may have relied on several captivity narratives in crafting her play. Like Bess's chronicle, Sara Wakefield's autobiography *Six Weeks in the Sioux Tepees* (1864) and the heroine of James Seaver's *A Narrative of the Life of Mrs. Mary Jemison* (1824) praise and defend their captors. Although Wakefield was released after six weeks, Jemison, like Bess, married a warrior and had children. (Jemison actually willingly remained with the tribe for over fifty years.) But many of the details of Bess's Indian experiences can be found in the story of Olive Oatman, who was captured by Mojaves, along with her sister, as her family tried to travel across the New Mexico Territory. Oatman was only a girl of fourteen at the time of her capture in 1850, but Richard Dillon's 1981 account of her five-year captivity reports that she dressed in the bark skirts of the Indian women, was marked with the tribe's chin tattoo, and reportedly became the wife of the Mojave chief's son, to whom she bore two children. It is also worth noting Dillon's emphasis on the ways Oatman's story shocked Victorian sensibilities, though her lecture tour was apparently designed to raise funds for churches as well as to promote Reverend Royal B. Stratton's biography of the Oatman family. Further details

of Oatman's story (including pictures of the tattooed woman) can be found in Dillon's 1995 follow-up essay. There is an additional reproduction of a portrait of Olive Oatman with chin tattoos much like Bess's in Ebersole's *Captured by Texts* (4). Oatman has what appear to be four or five lines running vertically from her lower lip down her chin. There are two additional lines, looking rather like elongated arrows, extending perpendicularly from each outer vertical line, running along each lower jaw. I wish to thank my research assistant, Carl Duke Curtis, for his assistance in finding and compiling this material.

14. The Ottawa, of course, were an entirely different tribe who lived in what became the northeastern United States and Canada. The name of Bess's Indian husband appears to be a conscious incongruity or anachronism on Henley's part.

15. In addition to the reference to Boucicault, Henley leans heavily on the formulas of melodrama when she introduces Macon's failed bid to save her homestead toward the end of the play. Like Shepard's appeal to the model of the western male hero threatened by the emasculating feminine, however, this detail smacks as much of contemporary Hollywood film versions of this struggle as it does of nineteenth-century analogues, offering another example of Henley's own version of postmodern pastiche.

16. In what may be another self-citation, this fairground scene recalls the end of Henley's 1984 play, *The Miss Firecracker Contest*, set on the carnival grounds in Brookhaven, Mississippi.

Works Cited

Bassan, Maurice. "The 'True West' of Sam Shepard and Stephen Crane." *American Literary Realism* 28.2 (1996): 11–17.

Bottoms, Stephen J. *The Theatre of Sam Shepard: States of Crisis*. Cambridge: Cambridge University Press, 1968.

Brustein, Robert. "She-Plays, American Style. Review of *Machinal, Abundance. Reimagining American Theatre*. New York: Hill and Wang, 1991. 104–108.

Burnham, Michelle. *Captivity and Sentiment: Cultural Exchange in American Literature, 1682–1861*. Hanover, N.H.: University Press of New England, 1997.

Castiglia, Christopher. *Bound and Determined: Captivity, Culture-Crossing and White Womanhood from Mary Rowlandson to Patty Hearst*. Chicago: University of Chicago Press, 1996.

Coward, Rosalind. "The True Story of How I Became My Own Person." *Female Desires: How They Are Sought, Bought, and Packaged*. New York: Grove, 1985.

Derounian-Stodola, Kathryn Zabelle. *Women's Indian Captivity Narratives*. New York: Penguin, 1998.

Dillon, Richard H. "The Ordeal of Olive Oatman." *American History* 30.4 (1995): 30–32, 70, 72.

———. "Tragedy at Oatman Flat: Massacre, Captivity, Mystery." *American West* 18.2 (1981): 46–54, 59.

Doane, Mary Ann. "Film and the Masquerade—Theorizing the Female Spectator." *Screen* 23 (September–October 1982). Rpt. In Patricia Erens. *Issues in Feminist Film Criticism*. Bloomington: Indiana University Press, 1990.

Ebersole, Gary. *Captured by Texts: Puritan to Post-modern Images of Indian Captivity*. Charlottesville: University Press of Virginia, 1995.

Elan, Diane. *Romancing the Postmodern*. London: Routledge, 1992.

Haedicke, Janet V. "Battered Women in Henley's *Crime of the Heart* and Shepard's *A Lie of the Mind*." *Modern Drama* 36 (1993): 83–95.

Jameson, Fredric. "Postmodernism and Consumer Society." *The Anti-Aesthetic*. Ed. Hal Foster. Port Townsend, Wash.: 1983. 111–125.

Larsen, T. A. *History of Wyoming*. Lincoln: University of Nebraska Press, 1965.

Lyotard, Jean-François. "Answering the Question: What Is Postmodernism?" *The Postmodern Condition: A Report on Knowledge*. Trans. Regis Durand. Minneapolis: University of Minnesota Press, 1984. 71–82.

Rich, Frank. " 'Abundance,' Beth Henley's Revisionist Western." *New York Times*, 31 October 1990. Rpt. in *New York Theatre Critics Reviews*. 166–167.

Sayre, Gordon M. "Captivity Canons." *American Quarterly* 50 (1998): 860–867.

Shepard, Sam. "True West." *Seven Plays*. New York: Bantam, 1984. 2–59.

Smith, Raynette Halvorsen. "*'night Mother* and *True West*: Mirror Images of Violence and Gender." *Violence in Drama*. Ed. James Redmond. Cambridge: Cambridge University Press, 1991. 277–289.

St. Pierre, Ronald. " 'True-to-Life Stuff': Versions of the West in Shepard's *True West*." *American Literary Realism* 28.3 (1996): 37–50.

Williams, Megan. "Nowhere Man and the Twentieth-Century Cowboy: Images of Identity and American History in Sam Shepard's *True West*." *Modern Drama* 40 (1997): 57–73.

Winer, Linda. "Beth Henley's 'Abundance' in a Bizarre Old West." *New York Newsday*, 31 October 1990, 2. Rpt. In *New York Theatre Critics Reviews*. 168–169.

The Woman Voter. April 1916.

6
Existential Despair and the Modern Neurosis
Beth Henley's *Crimes of the Heart*

GENE A. PLUNKA

In *Civilization and Its Discontents* (1930), Freud argued that modern society is largely responsible for the creation of misery, in direct contrast to the psyche's id, which seeks pleasure. In Freudian psychoanalytical theory, the ego (the self or "I" that is in contact with the external world through perception) and the superego (the component of our personalities that forms our ethical and moral judgments) are established through social structures. However, the id, which relates primarily to sex and aggression—the primitive bodily instincts that are established in humans at birth—is oblivious to the external world or the norms and values of society's institutions. The push and pull of the conscious socialization felt directly on the ego and superego diminish or mask our unconscious libidinal desires represented by the id, and thus we become conflicted or anxious. Freud characterized the *angoisse* or angst as neurotic: "It was discovered that a person becomes neurotic because he cannot tolerate the amount of frustration which society imposes on him in the service of its cultural ideals, and it was inferred from this that the abolition or reduction of those demands would result in a return to possibilities of happiness" (Freud 21:87). In the early stages of development during the formative years when the child is being nurtured by the mother, the satisfaction of happiness is the major goal; however, once the individual is socialized and integrated into community norms and values, cultural restrictions are formed. Thus, the libidinal urge toward human happiness eventually conflicts with the purpose of civilization, which is to create a unity out of individual human beings. Freud wrote, "If more is demanded of a man, a revolt will be produced in him or a neurosis, or he will be made unhappy" (21:143). Freud understood the neurosis to be endemic to modern society, a universal condition among civilized nations: "If the development of civilization has such a far-reaching similarity to the development of the individual and if it employs the same methods, may we not be justified in reaching the diagnosis that, under the influence of cultural urges, some civilizations, or some epochs of civilization—possibly the whole of mankind—have become 'neurotic'?" (21:144). The reaction to this dichotomy between individual happiness and the socializing norms of civilization has been a deeply rooted existential despair manifested in *angoisse*, depression, alienation, isolation, and even narcissism. The neurotic condition and humanity's desperate attempts to combat it are clearly revealed in Beth Henley's Pulitzer Prize–winning play, *Crimes of the Heart*.[1]

On the whole, critics and theater reviewers have not depicted the plight of the Magrath sisters as the result of the anomie and *angoisse* that Freud notes is the neurotic impulse of modern society. Instead, critics such as Karen L. Laughlin see the play as a feminist vision of female assertiveness and bonding as an alternative to crimes that are self-destructive (35-51). Jonnie Guerra agrees with Laughlin's view of the play as a feminist statement but one that reacts specifically against the patriarchy instead of emotional crises that are personal: "But the images of women the audience confronts in Henley's plays are predominantly negative ones of suffering, self-destructive females whose lives and identities have been shaped by male family members and the sexist values of the small southern towns in which they reside" (120–121). Helene Keyssar argues that the patriarchal forces are so omnipresent that the Magrath sisters cannot bond effectively since their subservience to norms and values defined by the patriarchy reduces them to caricatures and objects of derision (158–159). Janet V. Haedicke further delineates the play as the domesticity of kitchen-sink drama, which ultimately becomes a sociological treatise on battered women, with Babe's attempted homicide as the focal point for Henley's statement about violence to women in the family (83-95). Critics who see the drama as reflective of contemporary sociology are also supported by Alan Clarke Shepard's view that the play "studies the origins and effects of domestic abuse," depicts culturally sanctioned violence against women, exposes the link between sexism and racism, and suggests the grave consequences of women who begin to realize themselves "as wholly volitional beings" (102–103). Yet these feminist interpretations often seem inadequate because the play's supposed message of power in female bonding in the denouement coincides with the fact that the patriarchal values are still in place; moreover, one could argue that the patriarchy is hardly even recognized by the Magrath sisters. Alan Woods astutely notes that although the play may ostensibly celebrate the power of the individual over a repressive society, the problems are at best only temporarily resolved: Babe still must await court action (through a male-dominated system of justice), Meg is far from finding happiness despite her realization that Old Granddaddy's wish for her singing career was misguided, and Lenny's joy is clearly in the hands of a male suitor, Charlie Hill (261). Thus, Laurin Porter seems to be correct when she argues that *Crimes of the Heart* may initially focus on women's narratives in the context of patriarchal assumptions of womanhood, yet Henley never seriously examines the sociological institutions that shape modern society. Porter concludes, "Ultimately, however, the play fails to challenge patriarchal structures or even acknowledge that they have been the root of the problem" (198). Porter's views coincide with Henley's response to Mary Dellasega, who asked Henley to assess her plays as feminist statements: "I just try to look at people more than at just the sexes and hope that it'll be more a human point of view rather than having some sort of agenda to show that women are better, because I don't actually think they are" (257).

Instead of viewing the play from a feminist perspective, I want to argue that *Crimes of the Heart* represents Freud's notion of the modern neurosis, and the denouement effectively provides a response to the *angoisse* and alienation that permeates society and which typically prevents human beings from achieving happiness. Barbara Kachur's analysis of the play is particularly informative, asserting that the focus is mainly ontological and that rather than being concerned with patriarchal conditioning, female rivalry, domestic confinement, or women's issues, *Crimes of the Heart* is about spiritual bankruptcy and individual isolation (19–20). Kachur notes that the Magrath sisters are striving to find meaning for their unfulfilled lives in a world of existential madness underscored by pain, disappointment, and death (19). This approach seems to concur with the way Henley views the neurotic modern world. When asked to assess political theater in the United States, Henley asserted that the political/sociological perspective was moot: "The problems of just being here are more pressing and exciting to me than politics. Politics generally deal [*sic*] with the facades of our more desperate problems. I don't really feel like changing the world, I want to look at the world. . . . What is amazing to me is the existential madness that we—everyone—are born into" (Betsko and Koenig 221).

What is unusual about Henley's essentially Freudian notion of the search for happiness deterred by the demands of modern civilization producing the ubiquitous neurosis is that the tradition is rarely represented in modern American drama, except perhaps in the dramas of O'Neill and the early plays of Edward Albee. This existential despair and modern angst have been mainly represented in European drama, beginning with Chekhov, extending through the philosophical ideas of Camus and Sartre, and eventually culminating in the anomie and alienation felt in the theater of Beckett, Ionesco, Genet, and Pinter. Although Henley has often been compared with the southern gothic tradition of Eudora Welty, Flannery O'Connor, and Tennessee Williams,[2] and also has much in common with the storytelling narrative tradition of the South,[3] her plays (in terms of content, not form) are actually more closely associated with the tragicomedies of the modern absurdist theater. Ayne Cantrell Durham explains this dichotomy between Henley as southern playwright and her roots in the European tradition of the absurd: "Her plays realistically capture the Southern vernacular and take place in authentic Southern settings, yet they also exaggerate the recognizable and push the bizarre to extremes to reveal the underlying absurdity of the human condition. Whereas Henley's characters are rooted in her Southern heritage, the meaning of their experiences is not limited to time and place" (192). Critics may be confused about Henley's intentions because the setting of *Crimes of the Heart*—a middle-class kitchen—is unlike the bare stage usually associated with absurdist dramas or their precursors (witness the bare nursery in *The Cherry Orchard*, for example). However, William W. Demastes puts Henley in perspective with regard to the setting she employs: "As such, her work escapes the intellectual detachment of the French absurdists and existentialists, and because it takes the horrors of life out of the lecture halls and puts them in a kitchen, it argues that the absurd has an immediacy and relevance to daily existence that other works can't claim to argue" (138–139).

Particularly apropos in relating Henley's theater to the existential tradition that has led to an examination of the modern *angoisse* is the comparison between *Crimes of the Heart* and Chekhov's plays, especially since Henley has stated that Chekhov influenced her more than any other dramatist (Jones 182). Henley also has stated, "When I wrote *Crimes*, I was thinking mainly of Chekhov and *The Three Sisters*. I always thought both plays should be done in repertory" (Smith 12). Jean Gagen and Joanne B. Karpinski have each written detailed analyses exploring the relationships between *Crimes of the Heart* and *Three Sisters*.[4] Karpinski hints at the neurotic condition that both playwrights seem to understand almost intuitively: "Both plays raise the Lamarckian question of whether acquired characteristics (a culture, a psychosis) determine the behavior of the next generation" (236). Just as important, however, is Gagen's comment that both playwrights incorporate bizarre humor into essentially dramas of frustration, alienation, and sorrow (124). Thus, Henley's black humor can be compared to the tragicomedy of Chekhov in which both playwrights use comedy to assuage the guilt, loneliness, and despair of the essentially neurotic modern condition resulting from cultural expectations that negate the natural drive for human happiness. As Matthew C. Roudané has noted, "Indeed, laughter becomes the key to her [Henley's] characters' very survival, a laughter filled with compassion, one that keeps at bay the loneliness, frailty, and loss that otherwise would destroy these offbeat creations" (140). Like Chekhov, who demonstrated compassion for all of his characters despite their frailties, Henley views her protagonists as part of one big family whose offbeat comic pathos helps them to maintain a sense of dignity in a neurotic, absurd universe. Henley has acknowledged that her sense of humor is similar to Chekhov's tragicomic vision: "All these things that I feel inside are desperate and dark and unhappy. Or not *unhappy*, but searching. Then they come out funny. The way my family dealt with hardships was to see the humor or the ironic point of view in the midst of tragedy. And that's just how *my* mind works" (Betsko and Koenig 216). Understanding Henley's comingling of the grotesquely comic with the mundane, as well as her Chekhovian perspective in reducing serious issues to trivialities and concomitantly providing undue importance to the minutiae of daily life, helps us to see how her tragicomedy serves to mitigate, and perhaps to make us more aware of, the modern *angoisse*. Critics who fail to see Henley as part of the European tradition associated with the existential despair often confuse her plays with sick, rather than black, humor. For example, Leo Sauvage, in his review of the Broadway production of *Crimes of the Heart*, found nothing enthralling in what he deemed the badly adjusted, if not mentally retarded, Magrath sisters (19–20), while Anthony Masters, commenting on the 1983 London staging, noted that only someone with a sick sense of humor could relate to the play (15). Several critics were appalled when the Magrath sisters laughed at the news that their grandfather was in a coma, and even a few noted wryly that Lenny reacted more shockingly to the death of her horse than to the patriarch lying comatose. Again, what is overlooked is the way Chekhov, Henley's mentor, uses tragicomedy—often bizarre yet incisive—to understand humans who are searching for dignity in a neurotic world that denies the individual happiness at every turn. Henley sees the bizarre, the grotesque, the pathos of human existence as everyday reality. She states, "If you just watch the evening news, odd things are happening all the time. And if you ever sit down and talk very specifically to people about their lives or their families' lives, it's always incredibly, unbelievably odd, scary and bizarre" (Isenberg 80). Henley uses tragicomedy as a means of understanding humanity's search for dignity in a bizarre, absurd, neurotic universe. Moreover, setting the plays in the South represents not merely the environment she knows best but also the perfect microcosm for lost souls, who, in an almost comically pathetic way, are trying to establish dignity in an absurd universe. Henley acknowledges, "I think Southerners, in a sense, being from the only part of the United States that's been defeated in war, have a certain resiliency and desire to survive defeat and remain dignified in the face of it. Also, in the South it's considered very bad manners to take yourself too seriously or melodramatically. You always have to find the comic side" (Rafferty 67).

Henley stacks the cards against her protagonists from the very beginning of *Crimes of the Heart*, suggesting that the neurosis that Freud described in *Civilization and Its Discontents* imbues modern society with odds that are perceived as virtually insurmountable for contact among individuals. Henley remarked, "I think there are all aspects of human connections that I try to show in my plays. But I do very much believe that men and women have a hard row to hoe, connecting with each other, as do women and women and men and men" (Dellasega 257). Many of Henley's plays occur during a time of turmoil or crisis, usually during a holiday, a ceremony, or celebration of some sort, exacerbating the modern neurosis.[5] Henley's starting point for the play was a crisis: her grandfather, lost for three days, was eventually found walking in the woods in Copiah County, Mississippi, after paratroopers had been called out to help with the search. Henley realized, "So I thought that would be a good idea for a play: a family crisis bringing everybody back home" (Jones 176). The setting of the play, five years after Hurricane Camille, reinforces the notion that nature mirrors society: crises are not to be forgotten, even in normally sedate Hazlehurst, Mississippi. Civilization rears its ugly head to keep us from happiness as one crisis blends into another. We learn that Lenny's horse Billy Boy was killed the previous evening—struck by lightning. Babe, the youngest sister, has just shot her husband Zackery and is now facing a jail sentence; this crisis is the event that brings Meg home from California. Moreover, Lenny is facing a terribly tense situation as she virtually regards her thirtieth birthday as an important rite, albeit not one of celebration since she has no one with whom to share the event. As the play wears on, the crises are exacerbated. Old Granddaddy has a stroke and lies in a coma in the hospital. Zackery has come up with sexually explicit photos of Babe and Willie Jay that appear so incriminating as to send his wife to jail for a long time or at best to an insane asylum, virtually negating Barnette Lloyd's legal work on her behalf and driving her to attempt suicide. Even when the Magrath sisters hear the news that Zackery's liver has been saved, there is only momentary consolation, followed by the announcement that Peekay and Buck, Jr., have just eaten paint. Babe, upon hearing of the death of Billy Boy, sums up the neurotic condition: "Life sure can be miserable" (*CPI* 50). Babe's "insanity" is not atypical, for the modern neurosis cuts across all socioeconomic levels of the culture, as Meg assures her sister, "Why, you're just as perfectly sane as anyone walking the streets of Hazlehurst, Mississippi" (*CPI* 61).

Henley depicts the Magrath sisters as icons for the modern neurosis. Freud stated that the modern neurosis resulted when the happiness of oral gratification under the nurturance of the mother is replaced by the sanctioned behavior patterns of social institutions and their representatives. The father of the Magrath sisters abandoned them at an early age. At first, the mother turned to oral gratification to assuage the despair and loneliness: she sat smoking cigarettes on the back porch, slinging ashes on the insects below. As a result of the deep sense of loss and grief that the matriarch of the family experienced after her husband left her, she hanged herself in the fruit cellar of her home, along with the family cat, when her daughters were young and in need of guidance—Lenny was fourteen; Meg, eleven; and Babe only eight. Alan Clarke Shepard writes that the mother's suicide "is a curse as particular as any in Ibsen, Tennessee Williams, or Sam Shepard, and as general as post-classical Western culture itself . . ." (103). The mother's suicide suggests the modern existential condition, for she killed herself out of loneliness, despair, desperation in the void, and face to face with the anomie and *angoisse* of modern civilization that condemns a life of isolation as meaningless. Exploring the nature of suicide in the play, Lana A. Whited astutely explains how the curse is related to the neurotic condition:

> Because for a woman the family is almost always the primary community, any woman's decision to commit suicide is, ultimately, also a statement about her perception of that community's value in her life. To continue to live is, then, to affirm one's life and relationship within the community. To commit suicide is to reject them, and to insist that we are fundamentally all alone. (72)

The absent father and the death of the mother have created a void in the lives of the Magrath sisters; seemingly, a curse, a significant absence resulting in loneliness and despair, has been passed from one generation to another. Billy J. Harbin notes that the mother's ties with her children were largely unemotional, having provided only shelter for her offspring but not offering nurturing, especially since her suicide has been perceived by the Magrath sisters as a sort of psychological abandonment (84). Deserted by their father and mother, the Magrath sisters are alienated and isolated, divorced from familial nurturance. Babe muses that her mother had affections only for her old cat (19). Although Harbin relates this spiritual bankruptcy to lost American ideals in the tradition of Eugene O'Neill and Sam Shepard, who have lamented the shift from the stability of rural self-reliance and moral certitude to a sterile society and transient instability (83), the problem seems, as Freud suggests, to be more universally widespread in modern society.

In any event, the curse of the existential despair has been passed down through the House of Magrath. The sense of loss and abandonment by the mother and father is now transmitted to the offspring in the form of "crimes of the heart." When asked to explain the title of the play, Henley confirmed, "I guess a lot of it is them [the Magrath sisters] coming to terms with their crimes and trying to unshackle themselves from the past" (Wimmer-Moul 118). The emotional "crimes" thus relate to the way these scarred sisters, cursed by the deeply rooted existential despair, end up hurting themselves, as well as other family members.

Exacerbating the modern neurosis are Chick and Old Granddaddy, who, as female and male, respectively, represent not so much the role that gender plays in the existential despair shared by the Magrath sisters but rather the cultural inhibitions posed by social restraint regardless of gender. After their father's abandonment, the Magrath sisters were torn from their Vicksburg home to live with their grandparents in Hazlehurst. Living in the shadows of the absent male and a mother who withdrew into her solitude, flicking ashes off her back porch while ignoring her offspring, the Magrath sisters were virtually raised by Old Granddaddy. The parental detachment is finalized four years after the move to Hazlehurst when the mother hanged herself and her cat. Old Granddaddy then began to script the lives of the Magrath sisters according to cultural norms; however, the happiness formerly attained through early nurturance by the mother is lost. The oral needs of the child are displaced once the mother dies, and Old Granddaddy's remedy for providing happiness was to stuff the three sisters with banana splits—the food source being a poor substitute for the nurturing the sisters needed. Meg remarks, "The thing about Old Granddaddy is he keeps trying to make us happy and we end up getting stomachaches and turning green and throwing up in the flower arrangements" (*CPI* 39).

Rather than provide happiness that Freud depicts is the goal of humanity, Old Granddaddy becomes the agent for cultural assimilation. Billy J. Harbin notes, "Self-indulgence and the pursuit of material success were his primary means of combating aches of the heart and soul; he offered them to the sisters as substitutes for the familial nurturing" (85). As an icon who reinforces the superficial yet permanently established cultural notion of the American Dream, Old Granddaddy equates success or solidarity in society with money and fame. Babe was exhorted by the patriarch to marry Zackery Botrelle, for he was the richest and most powerful man in Hazlehurst. Lenny recalls, "He remarked how Babe was gonna skyrocket right to the heights of Hazlehurst society. And how Zackery was just the right man for her whether she knew it now or not" (*CPI* 14). Meg, the middle sibling, was, at least in Lenny's view, Old Granddaddy's personal favorite of the three sisters: "She's the one who got singing and dancing lessons; and a store-bought dress to wear to her senior prom" (35). Meg was also allowed to wear twelve jingle bells on her petticoats, while Lenny and Babe were confined to only three. Meg is urged by Old Granddaddy to leave her siblings and pursue a singing career in Hollywood, which would inevitably yield fame and fortune; Hollywood will give Meg "exposure" (15), a chance of "getting [her] foot put in one of those blocks of cement they've got out there" (15). Meg winds up living a life of lies and illusions, even suggesting to Old Granddaddy that her career has reached its zenith with her soon-to-be appearance on the *Johnny Carson Show*. With regard to the lies Meg has been feeding Old Granddaddy, she admits, "All I wanted was to see him smiling and happy" (37). On the other hand, we feel the divisive nature of Meg's neurosis since she is conflicted about her feelings for Old Granddaddy: "I hate myself when I lie for that old man. I do. I feel so weak. And then I have to go and do at least three or four things that I know he'd despise just to get even with that miserable, old, bossy man!" (37). Lenny, the eldest sister, has probably been the one who was most affected by Old Granddaddy's tutelage and influence. While Babe and Meg have at least broken free from the household in favor of marriage and a career, respectively, Lenny has stayed at home to act as a surrogate mother cum wife for Old Granddaddy. After her grandmother's death, Lenny moved to a cot in the kitchen to be closer to Old Granddaddy and attend to his whims and needs. In other words, she has become completely acculturated according to Old Granddaddy's norms and values. As Babe notes, "She's turning into Old Grandmama" (20). As the voice of socialization, Old Granddaddy makes Lenny feel unworthy because her shrunken ovary is unacceptable in a culture where the female is judged by her ability to produce offspring. Insisting that no man would marry a woman with a deformed ovary, Old Granddaddy forced Lenny to become overly self-conscious about her condition. After meeting Charlie Hill through a dating service, Lenny introduced him to Old Granddaddy. Lenny mistakenly assumes that Charlie will refuse to marry her because of her shrunken ovary, which we later learn is nonsense because Charlie tells Lenny he does not like children and certainly wants none of his own. When Lenny laments that she will never be happy, Meg agrees: "Well, not if you keep living your life as Old Granddaddy's nursemaid—" (42). In short, as Freud suggests, the assimilation process ascribed to modern civilization is depicted by Henley as creating a neurosis that interferes with happiness.

Unfortunately, the acculturation process as ascribed through Old Granddaddy's norms and values has gone awry, replaced by the modern neurosis. Meg's singing career that was supposed to be the ticket to a glamorous life has fizzled out; instead, she is working in the most unglamorous role as a clerk for a dog food company. Babe's chance to skyrocket to the top of Hazlehurst society has brought her to the abyss—she will acquire notoriety only as Hazlehurst's illustrious female criminal, infamously etched in the minds of this closely knit community. Finally, Lenny has lost her sense of self-worth to become a pathetic figure depressed and devoid of love. In short, Old Granddaddy leads the Magrath sisters to the void of existential despair; he is best represented by his absence in the play.

Chick Boyle, the Magrath sisters' first cousin, is the other agent of acculturation or voice of public opinion. Looking like the stereotypical blonde Southern matron with rosy red lips, the type of social-climbing former debutante who might have sought to reign supreme as the town's Carnival Queen, Chick, as her name implies, informs the Magrath sisters how to act properly as females residing in a southern community. Chick is overly concerned about her image, refusing to take the chance of being seen in town with holes in her stockings (*CPl* 5) or with her hair pooching out in the back (7). As the committee head of the Ladies' Social League, and consequently a major voice for the transmittal of acculturating norms and values in the community, Chick, who also has familial and social ties with the Magrath sisters as their cousin and next-door neighbor, assumes responsibility for keeping the Magraths within social boundaries. Harbin correctly notes, "The ideal tradition of the charitable 'good neighbor,' or of the social organization devoted to the cultural enlightenment and well being of the village, finds no expression in the character of Chick. Her petty bitchery, ugly manners and gossip-laden harassment of the MaGrath [sic] sisters personify the spiritual bleakness of the community" (89). Chick despises the Magrath sisters chiefly because they do not conform to cultural expectations. She tells Lenny, "Why, I've had just about my fill of you trashy Magraths and your trashy ways; hanging yourselves in cellars; carrying on with married men; shooting your own husbands!" (*CPI* 57). Chick has had to endure the Magrath mother's suicide—a violation of community norms and values. Rather than trying to maintain a sense of happiness for the Magrath sisters, Chick, as the voice of the acculturation process, exacerbates their neurotic condition. Chick has little concern for Babe's welfare but instead seems only interested in the negative publicity that Babe's crime has brought on Chick's social circles, lamenting to Lenny, "How I'm gonna continue holding my head up high in this community, I do not know" (5). Meg, however, the most rebellious of the three sisters and therefore the one least likely to accept social sanctions, most frequently incurs Chick's wrath. Meg, with her loose reputation in high school, was known in Copiah County as "cheap Christmas trash" (6). Meg's insistence that Doc Porter remain with her during Hurricane Camille, which left him a cripple, did not enhance her status in the community, a fact that Chick consistently conveys to Lenny. When Chick sanctions Meg for smoking, which may lead to cancer, Meg responds, "That's what I like about it, Chick—taking a drag off of death" (17). Meg then takes a long, deep puff of the cigarette and exclaims, "Mmm! Gives me a sense of controlling my own destiny" (17). Meg almost seems to be aware that Chick, the voice of civilization and public opinion, increases the sense of loneliness and despair while concomitantly reducing the subliminal desire for happiness. Meg calls Chick "Little Chicken," comparing her to Chicken Little, the alarmist of the Mother Goose story. Fairy tales provide an important means for the culture to be passed on from generation to generation, but Meg seems to be implying that the world will not fall if she fails to live up to Chick's expectations and her notions of acculturation. Interestingly enough, Lenny, who has the most contact with Chick, chases her with a broom at the end of the play, in effect, exorcising the voice of community so as to relieve the source of the neurosis interfering with human happiness.

Meg's reaction to the modern neurosis has resulted in a narcissistic personality disorder. Freud characterized narcissism as libido withdrawn from the external world and directed to the ego (Freud 14: 75). Freud noted that narcissists seek to be loved rather than to love others; not being loved, insofar as it involves longing and deprivation, increases their self-regard (14: 98).

In *The Culture of Narcissism: American Life in an Age of Diminishing Expectations*, Christopher Lasch has expanded on Freud's study of narcissism. Lasch claims that emerging pathological disorders and neurotic behaviors in modern society clearly have their origins in cultural developments, including changing patterns of socialization, the cult of consumption, and delusions of grandeur that make us yearn for celebrity status or for fame and wealth while fearing old age and death (8, 32–33). Narcissism becomes a means for coping with the tensions and anxieties of modern life that produce feelings of emptiness and disturbances in self-esteem. Lasch defines this culture of narcissism as consisting of individuals who seek to remain at the center of attention, their self-interest negating any regard for others in their quest for immediate gratification. Lasch views the narcissistic personality as characterized by "dependence on the various warmth provided by others combined with a fear of dependence, a sense of inner emptiness, boundless repressed rage, and unsatisfied oral cravings" (33). Emotional titillation without involvement and dependence often makes narcissists sexually promiscuous as well. Plagued by a sense of anxiety and guilt, the narcissist is forever restless, constantly searching for the elusive meaning of life. Expanding on the work of clinical psychologists and psychiatrists who have studied narcissism, including Havelock Ellis, Freud, Heinz Kohut, Otto F. Kernberg, and Lasch, the American Psychiatric Association in 1994 posed diagnostic criteria for Narcissistic Personality Disorder. Narcissism can be designated by having five or more of the following personality traits: a grandiose sense of self-importance, a preoccupation with fantasies of success, belief in being unique with a sense of entitlement, the need for excessive admiration, exploitive of others, lack of empathy for others, envious of others, and arrogant or haughty behavior or attitudes (APA 661). In short, narcissists have a pervasive pattern of grandiosity, self-importance, and a need for admiration but lack empathy for others. Their self-esteem is very fragile, and thus criticism may leave them feeling humiliated or deflated. The American Psychiatric Association also concludes that narcissists "tend to form friendships or romantic relationships only if the other person seems likely to advance their purposes or otherwise enhance their self-esteem" (APA 659).

At age eleven, Meg discovered her mother's suicide, obviously a traumatic experience for an adolescent. This sense of loss and guilt may have contributed to her narcissism, for Meg's life is a continuous failure to get close to anyone. In this early stage of narcissism, Meg seemed to believe that she was special, a unique person with a sense of entitlement who often showed arrogant behavior. Wanting to be accepted by others, Meg was promiscuous in high school, and her loose reputation was well known throughout Copiah County. Meg seemed to have her own agenda, with the result being that she was the center of attention without taking responsibility for her adolescent life. Lenny recalls, "Why, Meg's always run wild—she started smoking and drinking when she was fourteen years old, she never made good grades—never made her own bed! But somehow she always seemed to get what she wanted" (*CPI* 35). Meg was the favored offspring of her grandparents, the only one to get singing and dancing lessons and have the dubious status of wearing twelve jingle bells instead of three on her petticoats. Meg spent time reading *Diseases of the Skin* in the library and hour after hour would stare at a poster of crippled children; instead of giving her dime for the disabled, Meg would spend it on ice cream. Her behavior is the classic case of the narcissist refusing to show empathy for others; rather than donate the money for a noble cause, Meg spends it on herself, recalling Old Granddaddy's desire to eradicate the problems in the Magrath household through instant gratification or happiness by serving the sisters banana splits (in which, of course, ice cream is the chief ingredient). Meg disguises the lack of empathy for others by postulating that spending the dime on ice cream has hardened her to avoid being a weak person. Karen L. Laughlin remarks, "Although initially we might be tempted to characterize part of the particular image Meg has cultivated as 'masculine' (at several points in the play we hear of her attempts to avoid showing signs of weakness), this quest for strength really amounts to a refusal to care, a numbing rejection of her own powerful emotions; it is another dimension of the silencing of her own desires and inner being rather than a movement toward self-reliance" (42). By trying to block out the pain and *angoisse* of the trauma of discovering her mother's body, Meg has become unable to identify with anyone else's pain or suffering. As Thomas P. Adler suggests, "Meg had found their mother hanging in the basement, and her defense against the trauma was to hide behind a defiant humor and harden herself to the misery of others, since to vent her feelings would have signaled weakness rather than strength" (45). This behavior helps to explain her abandonment of Doc Porter during Hurricane Camille, five years earlier. When the roof caved in and crushed Doc's leg, Meg, although in love with him, lacked empathy, and, like most narcissists, thought of herself first and foremost. Henley views this reaction as Meg's main "crime of the heart": "Meg's crime was being so afraid of Doc she left him with his broken leg saying she would marry him and went off to Hollywood" (Wimmer-Moul 118). Meg's guilt is thus exacerbated because her refusal to identify with Doc's feelings left him emotionally, and obviously physically, crippled. When Doc asks Meg why she left, she initially responds, "It was my fault to leave you. I was crazy. I thought I was choking" (*CPI* 44) but then reveals, "I don't know why . . . 'Cause I didn't want to care" (44).

Under the auspices of Old Granddaddy's tutelage, Meg went to Hollywood to pursue celebrity status through her potentially rewarding singing career. Like most narcissists, Meg had exaggerated her talents in a preoccupation with fantasies of fame and fortune. Believing that she is unique and special in Hollywood's fantasyland, Meg isolates herself from others, turning the narcissistic gaze upon herself. She takes the telephone off the hook and refuses to read mail from former acquaintances in the small-town Hazlehurst society that she left. Instead of immersing herself into blocks of cement for eternity (the perfect dream of any narcissist), Meg ironically winds up as a small-time clerk working for a dog food company. Her nightclub career as a singer cum femme fatale has long since been abandoned. During Christmas, Meg remained remorseful, staying inside her apartment. She recalls what degenerated into a mental breakdown due to her neurotic condition: "All I could do was sit around in chairs, chewing on my fingers. Then one afternoon I ran screaming out of the apartment with all my money and jewelry and valuables and tried to stuff it all into one of those March of Dimes collection boxes" (*CPI* 50–51). Meg was then confined to the psychiatric ward at Los Angeles County Hospital. As Nancy D. Hargrove realizes, Meg's mental breakdown has much to do with the guilt of someone who has become emotionally and geographically isolated from others, while hiding under the guise of refusing love because of the need to avoid being vulnerable or weak (59, 61). Moreover, as Lisa J. McDonnell notes, Meg's neurotic behavior helps to link her childhood trauma with her sense of loss and her unwillingness to get close to another human being despite the fact that she desperately stuffs the collection box as some sort of therapy for her deeply rooted alienation (97).

Upon her return from California, Meg shows the effects of her neurotic behavior. She has "*sad, magic eyes*" and carries "*a worn-out suitcase*" (*CPI* 11), which only serves to reinforce her dishevelment. Lenny views Meg as lacking empathy, a true narcissist concerned only with a sense of her own entitlement: "I don't know; it's—it's—You have no respect for other people's property! You just take whatever you want. You just take it!" (41). Ganga Viswanath and Christine Gomez note that Meg's failure in Hollywood now results in a deep sense of guilt that she tries to hide under the guise of indifference (Viswanath and Gomez 5). These feelings of guilt force her to lie to Old Granddaddy about her career, making Meg feel even more insecure.

Lasch noted that narcissists, although often sexually promiscuous, "avoid close involvements, which might release intense feelings of rage. Their personalities consist largely of defenses against this rage and against feelings of oral deprivation that originate in the pre-Oedipal stage of psychic development" (37). To assuage their deep feelings of anxiety and despair due to a world in which they seek admiration through celebrity status that has replaced the happiness of the formative years, narcissists seek to regain the happiness of the nurturing lost in the "pre-Oedipal stage of psychic development" through oral cravings.[6] In writing about orality and identity in the play, Laura Morrow states, "Oral activities also reflect the need for or response to nurturing; an insatiable desire for sweets, for example, may indicate one is symbolically seeking food from a loving mother" (23). Meg's response to distress has been self-destructive behavior; during this family reunion, Meg eats, smokes, and drinks to drown out the modern neurosis, reduce her narcissistic lack of empathy for others, and return to a happier state of oral satisfaction that she had before her mother committed suicide.

The first example of Meg's lack of empathy for others through oral satisfaction is when Lenny tells her of Babe's shooting of Zackery, and Meg's response is to get a soda. When Lenny mentions that Billy Boy was struck by lightning, Meg lights a cigarette. The news of Old Granddaddy's three-month hospital stay has Meg reaching for the bourbon, and when she learns there is none, she settles for a Coke and Empirin, the latter to kill the pain of hearing news she would rather not have learned. We should recall that using food to avoid problems is a staple of the Magrath household ever since Old Granddaddy took the siblings out for banana splits to avoid familial grief. Thus, when Lenny reminds Meg of her potential as a singer and the hopes that Old Granddaddy had for her if she only received the requisite exposure, Meg grabs for the pecans, all the while reminding her sister that her ambitions have been repressed through her daily toil in the dog food company. Chick's entrance and her comment, "We keep looking for your picture in the movie magazines" (*CPI* 17), sends Meg for another cigarette. Chick admonishes Meg for smoking, but the latter responds that it gives her a sense of controlling her own destiny. Instead, as Laura Morrow informs us, Meg's smoking "unconsciously replicates her mother's repression of pain and anger" (32), since it reminds us of her self-destructive behavior of withdrawing from life as she sat on the back porch flinging her ashes at the ants and insects. As the discussion centers around Lenny's loneliness because of her shrunken ovary, Meg bites into an apple and suggests that Lenny's desolation on her birthday can be best addressed if they order a birthday cake. When Meg begins to learn more than she needs to know about Babe's affair with Willie Jay, "that little kid we used to pay a nickel to, to run down to the drugstore and bring us back a cherry Coke" (*CPI* 27), she reaches for Lenny's box of candy and requests cold water to wash it down. Comments about Charlie Hill force Lenny to weep, but Meg's reaction is merely to down another drink and grab a cigarette. All of this oral activity is put into context when we recall that Meg's sole reaction to crippled children depicted in the March of Dimes posters was for her to eat another double scoop ice cream cone. In short, Meg, like her sisters, feeds her stomach when actually it is the heart that is empty.

Lenny's response to the modern neurosis is what clinicians would call Depressive Personality Disorder, known to laymen as depression. The *Diagnostic and Statistical Manual of Mental Disorders* describes depression as behavior indicated by the following: moods of dejection, gloominess, and unhappiness; low self-esteem; brooding and worry; pessimism; and feelings of guilt or remorse (APA 733). The play opens with Lenny pathetically trying to stick a candle into a crumbling cookie she has substituted for a cake. Lenny is celebrating her thirtieth birthday alone, which is significant because she is terribly unhappy about growing old without a spouse to love and support her. Unlike Meg who has fled the nest to seek her fortune in Hollywood and Babe who has married, Lenny has stayed close to home with the result that she now has no one there to ease her pain and suffering. The birthday celebration, carefully orchestrated to include a solo rendition of "Happy Birthday," seems to mark Lenny as a martyr who chooses to suffer alone. When Doc enters and tells her of Billy Boy's death, Lenny, apparently crushed by Babe's plight and Old Granddaddy's deteriorating physical condition, begins to cry. Later in the play, when Lenny learns of Old Granddaddy's stroke, she becomes more gloomy and depressed, worrying that if Old Granddaddy dies, "I'm afraid of being here all by myself. All alone" (*CPI* 52). Although Old Granddaddy certainly contributed to Lenny's isolation, having favored Meg (the most talented) and Babe (the most beautiful) over her (the eldest, with a shrunken ovary), she certainly stood by him, virtually becoming a nursemaid for the old patriarch. Instead of living a life of her own, she became a surrogate for her grandmother (she even wears her grandmother's torn sunhat and lime-green gloves when gardening), and, after several years, as Meg reminds her sister, she wound up "living . . . life as Old Granddaddy's nursemaid—" (42). Laura Morrow's observation about Lenny is particularly appropriate: "Despairing of any chance for appreciation as a woman because of her inability to bear children, she defeminizes her name, Lenora, to the masculine Lenny and resigns herself to tending the garden and Old Granddaddy" (35).

Lenny's guilt about her shrunken ovary and her low self-esteem because Old Granddaddy has made her feel conscious of her inadequacies has made her depressed. Babe admits that after Old Granddaddy's second stay in the hospital, "Lenny was really in a state of deep depression" (*CPI* 21). Rather than brood all day and remain dejected and unhappy, Lenny turned to a dating service, aptly named Lonely Hearts of the South. Her only response was from Charlie Hill of Memphis. Babe suspects that Charlie's one trip to Hazlehurst resulted in the only time Lenny had ever had a sexual encounter. However, Lenny's loneliness and *angoisse* was only exacerbated after Charlie met Old Granddaddy, who promptly refused to sanction the love relationship because Lenny's deformed ovary precludes any chance of her having children. Meg, who has been in California while Lenny's guilt has been increasing and her depression has been getting worse, accurately assesses her sister's mental condition: "Poor Lenny. She needs some love in her life. All she does is work out at that brick yard and take care of Old Granddaddy" (20). Lenny has latched on to Old Granddaddy because she believes, "He doesn't want to see me rejected and humiliated" (42). Lenny has become overly self-critical and guilty about her shortcomings, refusing to seek love because she may be rejected, thus turning to her grandfather because he is the only person to provide what she believes is solace and comfort. Lenny says to Meg, "But I have this underdeveloped ovary and I can't have children and my hair is falling out in the comb—so what man can love me?" (42). Lenny also reveals that the real reason she could not establish a relationship with Charlie was because her feelings of inadequacy and low self-esteem put a damper on her passion before it could get ignited: "Because I just didn't want him not to want me—" (42). Thus, Lenny's crime of the heart is self-destructive guilt and remorse that forces her to abandon a possible relationship in favor of unhappiness and existential despair.

To assuage the depression attributed to the modern neurosis and redeem the happiness of the formative years, Lenny also turns to oral cravings. The play takes place in her living quarters—the kitchen—and opens with Lenny trying to celebrate over one of her favorite foods (the cookie) and closes with a food celebration (the birthday cake). Chick refers to Lenny as a "sweet potato" who has " a sweet tooth," and Doc calls her "Jello Face" (*CPI* 7, 10). Lenny uses food, particularly sweets, to fill the void in her life, mistakenly assuming that the hunger of the stomach can substitute for hunger of the heart. Food becomes for her a temporary means of relieving the depression and spiritual emptiness of her daily existence. Like many depressed people, Lenny consumes food, not for nourishment, but for its value as a palliative for the pain of her loneliness. Billy J. Harbin explains how Lenny's oral cravings function as an opiate in her life: "Food is devoured not for sustenance, but as compensation for grievances of the heart; it has no relationship to the ideal tradition of family gatherings, a sharing with others or mealtime communion" (85). Lenny is particularly in need of oral satisfaction when her guilt and remorse are brought to the surface around other people. When Doc enters, Lenny has to have coffee (*CPI* 8); during conversation with Babe, Lenny reaches for her birthday candy (34), and while Meg poisons herself with bourbon and cigarettes, Lenny sips more coffee (36). Meg probably forces Lenny's guilt and depression to the surface more so than any other character in the play. Consequently, as Lou Thompson observes, when Lenny gets upset over Meg's biting into the box of assorted cremes given to her as a birthday gift, Lenny is expressing her grief at Meg's leaving the game of Hearts (with popcorn and hot chocolate) to be with Doc (100). Lenny's overly hostile reaction to Meg's violation of her sister's oral satisfaction obviously reflects a more deeply rooted resentment of the fact that Meg has been successful with men and was favored by the grandparents while Lenny is left alone and was always made to feel inadequate. Lenny's oral cravings must be fairly well known, for her friends bring her food offerings, such as candy (from Chick) and pecans (from Doc), which certainly must have pleased her in the past.

Babe also represents the anxiety and *angoisse* that results from the deeply rooted existential despair of the modern neurosis. We know very little about Babe's life before her marriage to Zackery except that she among her sisters talks the most about her mother's suicide and tries to ponder its meaning. Babe's alienation and isolation seem to have increased since she married Zackery; there is no evidence that they ever loved each other. Instead, the marriage seems to have been sanctioned and arranged by Old Granddaddy, who, impressed with Zackery's credentials as a lawyer, saw him as Babe's ticket to skyrocket to the heights of Hazlehurst society. Babe thus entered into a marriage that, because of the nature of modern civilization, removed her from happiness. The void that Zackery created in Babe's life is imminently discernible by his absence in the play, much like the absent father, mother, and grandfather. Zackery abused her physically and mentally, which led Babe to enter into a relationship with Willie Jay, a fifteen-year-old African-American male. Thus, the battered female, alone and trying to find a response to her despair, bonded with what seemed to her to be another outcast. When Meg questions the efficacy of Babe's relationship with a black youth deep in the South, the younger sister responds, "I was just lonely! I was so lonely" (*CPI* 28). When Zackery struck Willie Jay after learning about Babe's tryst with the young man, Babe attempted to shoot herself, imitating her mother, who had committed suicide years before. Babe's first reaction to the modern neurosis is therefore self-destructive, a trait that seems endemic to the Magrath household. Babe, however, cannot quite reconcile herself with her mother's suicide, so she rationalizes that the wiser decision would be to turn the gun on Zackery. Babe's shooting of Zackery because of his beating of the innocent boy is her "crime of the heart."

Babe's attempted murder of Zackery and her imminent jail sentence due to the callousness of her crime (making lemonade instead of calling the authorities) forces Lenny to question Babe's mental stability, deeming her sister "ill. I mean in-her-head-ill" (*CPI* 12). Babe's illness is due to suffering from existential despair, admitting, "Why, I feel so all alone" (31). Babe's neurosis increases when her support system vanishes—Willie Jay is sent north to be out of the way, Meg and Lenny are sufficiently preoccupied with their own neuroses, Chick taunts her about the crime, and Zackery has discovered revealing photos of Babe's affair with the black youth, thus making it difficult for Barnette, Babe's only hope for justice, to defend her. Babe also fears that confinement to a mental institution would permanently isolate her from family and friends. Babe, whom we have seen has already been prone to suicide, then tries to commit it twice, first by hanging herself and then by sticking her head in the oven. These suicide attempts gone awry bring Babe face to face with the modern neurosis, helping her to understand the existential despair that lies at the root of her loneliness. Although Babe acknowledges that Meg was the one who found their mother's dead body, Babe seems to be the sibling who is most affected by the mother's suicide, constantly brings up the subject, and seems to be the only daughter haunted by its repercussions. Babe's failed suicide attempts force her to understand why her mother hanged the cat with her: "It's 'cause she was afraid of dying all alone" (60). Babe begins to understand the effects of the modern neurosis. Assuming that angels would be present at the time of one's suicide, Babe realizes, "You'd be afraid to meet 'em all alone. So it wasn't like what people were saying about her hating that cat. Fact is, she loved that cat. She needed him with her 'cause she felt so all alone" (60–61).

Like Meg and Lenny, Babe's oral cravings help her mitigate the modern neurosis that prevents human happiness. After her mother's suicide, Babe fell under Old Granddaddy's influence as his "Dancing Sugar Plum" (*CPI* 14), assuaging periods of loneliness with banana splits. Food and drink substituted for Babe's lack of bonding with others. Barnette recalls that he met Babe at a Christmas bazaar where she was selling cakes, cookies, and candy; Barnette trusted her wares, buying a pound cake from her. Babe trusts Barnette because she associates him with the pound cake, much in the same way that she associates Willie Jay, albeit subconsciously, as the person who brought her cherry cokes from the drugstore. Babe is also the one who insists that ordering the largest cake the bakery has will cure Lenny of her loneliness on her birthday. This infatuation with food and drink as a substitute for happiness explains why Babe's marriage fell apart at the dinner table where, as Laura Morrow asserts, Babe's attempts to nurture her husband through feeding failed miserably (33). In particular, Zackery complained about the food served, and thus Babe's response was to ignore the man who refused the sustenance that Babe thought substituted for happiness: "I'd fall asleep just listening to him at the dinner table. He'd say, 'Hand me some of that gravy!' Or, 'This roast beef is too damn bloody.' And suddenly I'd be out cold like a light" (*CPI* 26). The marriage obviously was an inadequate substitute for Babe's oral gratification and probably never should have taken place, for Babe's only recollection of the wedding is viewed in relationship to orality: "Well, I was drunk on champagne punch. I remember that!" (38). Nevertheless, Babe tries to make amends for a loveless marriage by shooting Zackery in the heart, where the source of happiness is supposed to be located, but instead hitting him in the stomach. Henley is perhaps suggesting that Babe has missed the mark, much like her sisters who, as Lou Thomson observes, feed their stomachs when in reality it is their hearts that have been deprived (99).

During intense periods of distress throughout the play, Babe seeks oral gratification either through eating, drinking, or playing the saxophone. When Babe complains that Chick, the voice of the community, blames the Magrath mother's suicide as a blight on the quiet town of Hazlehurst, she insists on having some lemonade. During the most intense moment of her life, her shooting of Zackery, Babe's response was to make herself a pitcher of lemonade and drink three glasses of it. When she is forced to recount the attempted murder to her lawyer, Babe relies on a bowl of oatmeal to get her through the ordeal. Moreover, Babe's new saxophone, another oral stimulus, is, as Henley herself admits, "more of a freeing image" for the youngest sibling (Betsko and Koenig 217). Finally, when life becomes too stressful, Babe retreats to the sources of her oral cravings: rather than have Meg call her attorney, Babe puts the telephone in the refrigerator, and rather than face a jail sentence, Babe puts her head in the oven.

The anomie, existential despair, and *angoisse* produced by the spiritual bankruptcy of modern civilization can be tempered only by bonding through love. As the Magrath sisters prepare for Hearts, Lenny reminds them of how to play the game: "Hearts are bad, but the Black Sister is the worst of all—" (*CPI* 39). Sniping and quibbling with each other throughout the play and failing to come to terms with their past, the Magrath sisters have committed crimes of the heart, each of them more or less taking turns acting like the Black Sister. In response to a question about why she writes, Henley remarked, "I try to understand that ugliness is in everybody. I'm constantly in awe of the fact that we still seek love and kindness even though we are filled with dark, bloody, primitive urges and desires" (Betsko and Koenig 215). In essence, *Crimes of the Heart* demonstrates the transition that the Black Sisters make, weighed down by the neuroticism of the modern age, as they search for happiness or love lost after the formative years.

Replacing the lost mother and the absent father, who represent the displacement resulting from the neuroticism induced through modern civilization, the Black Sisters stop harassing each other to share in mutual nurturance, allowing them to get through those really bad days. Bonding through love and community (having a heart) produces happiness that we long for but ultimately have difficulty in obtaining under the burden of daily community norms and values. The bonding sustained by the Magrath sisters allows them each to experience their epiphanies. With the help of her sisters, Meg has found the capacity to respond to the needs of others, which, as a narcissist, she has been unable to do. Previously abandoning Doc and her singing career, Meg now develops a new sense of happiness and self-worth as a result of the bonding she has received while confessing the sins of her past to her sisters. Meg tells Babe that mutual confession is fundamental: "To talk about our lives. It's an important human need" (*CPI* 26). After spending the evening with Doc, she acknowledges, "I'm happy. I realized I could care about someone. I could want someone. And I sang! I sang all night long!" (50). Babe, haunted by her mother's death and faced with a possible lengthy jail sentence, rejects suicide as a solution to the modern neurosis because she now realizes that she has two sisters who care deeply about her feelings. Babe, lighting the birthday candles for Lenny and sharing with her sisters in this communal celebration, begins to understand how bonding with others prevents the alienation and isolation precluding one's happiness in modern civilization. Babe realizes, "And I'm not like Mama. I'm not so all alone," while Meg asserts, "You're not" (62). Finally, Lenny's epiphany comes when she chases Chick out of her house, effectively exorcising the voice of community, and supported and encouraged by her sisters, simultaneously pursues Charlie Hill, in essence ignoring Old Granddaddy's advice that her shrunken ovary was the obstacle to her happiness. Lenny learns to come to terms with her depression as she begins to understand that happiness derives from love and sharing through communal support and that the voice of public opinion instead has produced for her nothing but worthlessness.

The last image in the play in which the Magrath sisters share in a communal celebration is in stark contrast to the opening scene in which Lenny, depressed and alone, is ineptly trying to celebrate her birthday by sticking a lone candle into a stale cookie that crumbles; then she begins to cry when Doc enters. At the end of the play, the communal sharing and outpouring of love produces a dramatically different effect. The overjoyed Lenny is no longer alone and even makes a birthday wish while blowing out the candles, now successfully mounted on the cake instead of falling off of the cookie. Lenny wishes that the moment of bonding will last, for she realizes that communal sharing is the key to happiness. The play ends in celebration with two oral images—the eating of the birthday cake and the notes of the saxophone—reminding us that alternatives to true happiness will always exist, but that the freeze frame moment of bonding in "*magical, golden, sparkling glimmer*" (*CPI* 63) offers the only fleeting joy of unity that can assuage the loneliness and despair of the otherwise modern neurosis.

Notes

1. Henley wrote the play, originally titled *Crimes of Passion*, in West Hollywood during 1978. Inspired by her friend, playwright Frederick Bailey, Henley entered the play, then titled *Crimes of the Heart*, in Louisville's Great American Playwriting Competition. *Crimes of the Heart* had its world premiere on 1 February 1979 at the Actors' Theater of Louisville, directed by Jon Jory, where it went on to co-win the contest in besting over four thousand competitors. The play was next performed on 26 April 1979 by the California Actors' Theater at Los Gatos, California, under direction by J. Ranelli. Subsequent productions were at the Loretto-Hilton Theater in St. Louis (October 1979), at Baltimore's Center Stage (18 April 1980), and for thirty-five performances off-Broadway at the Manhattan Theater Club's Upstage Theater (9 December 1980). Melvin Bernhardt, who directed the off-Broadway production, went on to win the Obie Award for Best Direction in 1980–1981. In April 1981, *Crimes of the Heart* was awarded the Pulitzer Prize for Best Play—a very unusual acknowledgment for one so young (age twenty-nine) and writing her first full-length play, particularly a drama that had not yet graced Broadway. After receiving the New York Drama Critics Circle Award for the best American play of the season, *Crimes of the Heart* made its Broadway debut on 4 November 1981 at the John Golden Theater. Under direction by Melvin Bernhardt, the play ran for 535 performances, closing on 13 Feb-

ruary 1983. Productions were later staged in Los Angeles, France, Israel, Australia, Turkey, Peru, Japan, and London (where it was the first runner-up for the Susan Smith Blackburn Prize for Playwriting). Henley also wrote the screenplay for the 1986 film version of the play, which was directed by Bruce Beresford and starred Diane Keaton, Jessica Lange, Sissy Spacek, and Sam Shepard. The film garnered three Academy Award nominations: Best Actress (Sissy Spacek), Bess Supporting Actress (Tess Harper), and Best Screenplay.

2. John Simon started the trend in his review of *Crimes* in which he stated that Babe was a character out of Flannery O'Connor and Meg was from Tennessee Williams. However, he also noted that touches of Chekhov could be seen in Lenny's character (Simon 42).

3. Unfortunately, the play is often incorrectly interpreted as a regional drama rather than as a more universal statement about the modern neurosis. For example, in his review of the play for *Village Voice*, Michael Feingold interpreted the tragicomedy that even he realized was inspired by Chekhov's *Three Sisters* as nothing more than gossip indigenous to small-town life in the South. Refusing to assess the play as a serious examination of the existential condition, Feingold's analysis was colored by Henley's geography: "Perhaps the play supplies a kind of sordid nostalgia for southerners who, behind the facade of their new double-knit suits and nonunion textile factories, like to think they are still pea-pickin', backy-chawin', inbreedin', illiterate cretins at heart—Snopeses who have been taught, painstakingly, to sign their names and clip coupons." See Michael Feingold, "Dry Roll," *Village Voice*, 18 November 1981, 104, 106.

4. See Jean Gagen, " 'Most Resembling Unlikeness, and Most Unlike Resemblance': Beth Henley's *Crimes of the Heart* and Chekhov's *Three Sisters*," *Studies in American Drama, 1945–Present* 4 (1989): 119–128, and Joanne B. Karpinski, "The Ghosts of Chekhov's *Three Sisters* Haunt Beth Henley's *Crimes of the Heart*," in *Modern American Drama: The Female Canon*, ed. June Schlueter (Madison, N.J.: Fairleigh Dickinson University Press, 1990), 229–245.

5. For example, *The Wake of Jamey Foster* occurs before a funeral, *The Miss Firecracker Contest* unfolds during the annual carnival—Brookhaven's highly anticipated event—held on the Fourth of July, *The Lucky Spot* and scene 1 of *L-Play* take place on Christmas Eve (a terrible time for lonely people), *The Debutante Ball* is set amidst the atmosphere of Hattiesburg's most significant coming-out party, and *Impossible Marriage* happens on the day and evening before a wedding.

6. For details about orality in the play, see Laura Morrow, "Orality and Identity in *'night, Mother* and *Crimes of the Heart*," *Studies in American Drama, 1945–Present* 3 (1988): 23–39, and Lou Thompson, "Feeding the Hungry Heart: Food in Beth Henley's *Crimes of the Heart*," *Southern Quarterly* 30, nos. 2–3 (1992): 99–102.

Works Cited

Adler, Thomas P. *Mirror on the Stage: The Pulitzer Plays as an Approach to American Drama*. West Lafayette, Ind.: Purdue University Press, 1987.

American Psychiatric Association. *Diagnostic and Statistical Manual of Mental Disorders*, 4th ed. Washington, D.C.: APA, 1994.
Betsko, Kathleen, and Rachel Koenig. "Beth Henley." *Interviews with Contemporary Women Playwrights*. New York: Beech Tree Books, 1987. 211–222.
Dellasega, Mary. "Beth Henley." *Speaking on Stage: Interviews with Contemporary American Playwrights*. Eds. Philip C. Kolin and Colby H. Kullman. Tuscaloosa and London: University of Alabama Press, 1996.
Demastes, William W. *Beyond Naturalism: A New Realism in American Theatre*. Contributions in Drama and Theatre Studies 27. New York and Westport, Conn.: Greenwood, 1988.
Durham, Ayne C. "Beth Henley." *Critical Survey of Drama: Supplement*. Ed. Frank N. Magill. Pasadena: Salem Press, 1987. 192–197.
Freud, Sigmund. *The Standard Edition of the Complete Psychological Works of Sigmund Freud*. Gen. ed. and trans. James Strachey. 24 vols. London: Hogarth, 1953–74.
Guerra, Jonnie. "Beth Henley: Female Quest and the Family-Play Tradition." *Making a Spectacle: Feminist Essays on Contemporary Women's Theatre*. Ed. Lynda Hart. Ann Arbor: University of Michigan Press, 1989. 118–130.
Haedicke, Janet V. " 'A Population (and Theater) at Risk': Battered Women in Henley's *Crimes of the Heart* and Shepard's *A Lie of the Mind*." *Modern Drama* 36 (1993): 83–95.
Harbin, Billie J. "Familial Bonds in the Plays of Beth Henley." *Southern Quarterly* 25. 3 (1987): 81–94.
Hargrove, Nancy D. "The Tragicomic Vision of Beth Henley's Drama." *Southern Quarterly* 22.4 (1984): 54–70.
Isenberg, Barbara. "She'd Rather Do It Herself." *Los Angeles Times*, 11 July 1993, Calendar: 5+, home edition.
Jones, John Griffin, ed. "Beth Henley." *Mississippi Writers Talking*. Jackson: University Press of Mississippi, 1982. 169–190.
Kachur, Barbara. "Women Playwrights on Broadway: Henley, Howe, Norman and Wasserstein." *Contemporary American Theatre*. Ed. Bruce King. Basingstoke and London: Macmillan, 1991. 15–39.
Keyssar, Helene. *Feminist Theatre: An Introduction to Plays of Contemporary British and American Women*. Basingstoke and London: Macmillan, 1984.
Lasch, Christopher. *The Culture of Narcissism: American Life in an Age of Diminishing Expectations*. New York: Norton, 1979.
Laughlin, Karen L. "Criminality, Desire, and Community: A Feminist Approach to Beth Henley's *Crimes of the Heart*." *Women and Performance: A Journal of Feminist Theory* 3.1 (1986): 35–51.
McDonnell, Lisa J. "Diverse Similitude: Beth Henley and Marsha Norman." *Southern Quarterly* 25.3 (1987): 95–104.
Masters, Anthony. *"Crimes of the Heart."* *Time*, 19 May 1983, 15.
Porter, Laurin. "Contemporary Playwrights/Traditional Forms." *The Cambridge Companion to American Women Playwrights*. Ed. Brenda Murphy. Cambridge: Cambridge University Press, 195–212.
Rafferty, Terrence. "Nobody's Fool." *Savvy*, 8 January 1987, 67.

Roudané, Matthew C. *American Drama Since 1960: A Critical History.* New York: Twayne, 1997.
Sauvage, Leo. "Reaching for Laughter." *New Leader*, 30 November 1981, 19–20.
Shepard, Alan Clarke. "Aborted Rage in Beth Henley's Women." *Modern Drama* 36 (1993): 96–108.
Simon, John. "Sisterhood Is Beautiful." *New York*, 12 January 1981, 42.
Smith, Sid. "Playwright's Progress." *Chicago Tribune*, 20 September 1992, sec. 13, 12.
Viswanath, Ganga and Christine Gomez. "Woman's Quest for Identity in Beth Henley's *Crimes of the Heart.*" *Indian Scholar* 8.1–2 (1986): 1–10.
Whited, Lana A. "Suicide in Beth Henley's *Crimes of the Heart* and Marsha Norman's *'night, Mother.*" *Southern Quarterly* 36.1 (1997): 65–74.
Wimmer-Moul, Cynthia. "Beth Henley." *The Playwright's Art: Conversations with Contemporary American Dramatists.* Ed. Jackson R. Bryer. New Brunswick, N.J.: Rutgers University Press, 1995. 102–122.
Woods, Alan. "Consuming the Past: American Theatre in the Reagan Era." *The American Stage.* Eds. Ron Engle and Tice L. Miller. New York and Cambridge: Cambridge University Press, 1993. 252–266.

7
Southern Firecrackers and "Real Bad Days"
Film Adaptations of Beth Henley's *Crimes of the Heart* and *The Miss Firecracker Contest*

LINDA ROHRER PAIGE

BABE: Gosh, sometimes I wonder. . . . Why she did it. Why mama hung herself.

MEG: I don't know. She had a bad day. A real bad day. You know how it feels on a real bad day. (*CPI* 19)

When students read Franz Kafka's *Metamorphosis*, they astonishingly discover that Gregor Samsa woke up one morning and found himself transformed into a giant beetle. Not sure whether to laugh, cry, or both, students often appear dazed, as if shell-shocked. Perhaps for the first time in their lives, they feel unsure how to interpret or how to react to a piece of literature. Running a gambit of emotions, from sprinkled giggles to despondent sighs, my world literature students, when first acquainted with Gregor and his plight, become baffled by the strange dichotomy of Kafka's comic and fantastic laced with realism. Audience members appear similarly incredulous when they first attend a performance of almost any Beth Henley play or film. Does Henley mean to spoof the South with her quirky characters and their weird situations, or does she intend us to consider her characters as real people with real dilemmas? The playwright and screenwriter declares that she does not "believe in a message," that "it would be disastrous if you could say what the message of *Hamlet* was . . ." (Toscan), yet her films reinforce major themes that surface repeatedly in her plays, issues and concerns sometimes very serious. Though denying the importance of messages, Henley's themes, exponents of her personal values, become easily discernible in her scripts:

Playwrights don't often think consciously about their Themes as they write. Their personal values are integrated enough into how they live their lives and these themes flow into the play as the dialogues goes on the page. That's why the same themes often show up in a writer's work from one play to the next. (Toscan)

Although Henley's impetus is toward entertainment, her plays and films subtly convey themes.

Crimes of the Heart and *Miss Firecracker* encapsulate the major themes of Henley's oeuvre: woman's search for identity, quest for autonomy, and transformation. Frequently, this writer infuses southern traditions and values with gender and racial politics to reinforce her themes and diversify action. Importantly, her female protagonists crave autonomy, but in order to attain it, they must first undergo heated family battles and confront their own despair and self-doubt. Only then will they be capable of transformation and only then do their indomitable spirits prevail. Acknowledging the insistence of Henley's protagonists to control their own lives, Jonnie Guerra notes that "Henley turns a spotlight into the shadow and gives central importance to the dilemmas of women, to their conflicts and suffering within the family and to their questions about personal identity and the meaning of life" (119).

Just as one begins to recognize that Gregor's transformation has not occurred overnight, that the tiny white spot, that "slight pain," manifested itself all along, theatergoers must approach Beth Henley's plays with equal watchfulness, tracing semiotic signs of internal conflict. Too often, play and film reviewers dismiss Henley's work as intellectually light, viewing her characters as mere caricatures. Similar to Gregor, Henley's protagonists appear in chaos, unaware of having been used, of being repressed or oppressed. Also like Gregor's, their chaos stems from personal problems. Ultimately, students recognize that Samsa's transformation to a lesser creature, a sort of regressive metamorphosis, finds its genesis from deep inside Gregor. Though not exactly what one might term psychosomatic, Gregor's illness seems, in part, self-induced, self-imposed. Though some of the ailments of Henley's characters may be psychosomatic, Meg's loss of voice in *Crimes of the Heart*, for instance, they emanate from the recesses of the characters' hearts and minds and from how others treat them. Remember too that Gregor Samsa, like Meg, loses his voice, his ability even to sound human. Bombarded by disease and death, Henley's characters face the task of transforming themselves from fragmented human beings into whole selves. As with Kafka, Henley's technique involves leaving audiences clues to her characters' unusual transformations. Detective-like, we must ferret out the meaning behind the transformations, exposing the roots, the causes that precipitate change.

As perverse an image as is Gregor's, a man trapped inside a beetle's body, Henley's images equally seem contradictory, divided, and sometimes gruesome. Characteristics and situations not ordinarily thought to work on any level together, paradoxically, become allies: festering boils attached to love, liver diseases associated with success, scraped-up dead dogs and romantic heroes, wives shooting husbands and drinking lemonade, women hearing with their eyes or seeing through their voices. This world peopled by Henley marries the fairy tale to the perverse, the monster to the beauty. Emerging from their cocoons, Henley's characters undergo psychological and sometimes physical change, exhibiting a quality of endurance that surpasses beauty. Their trials seem tests of survival and courage, and their obstacles, though often self-induced, arise from their fear of failure. Both films, *Crimes of the Heart* and *Miss Firecracker*, involve tests of courage and survival as well as transformations of character. All three sisters in *Crimes* metamorphose, gaining strength and striving toward autonomy, as do major characters in *Miss Firecracker*, such as Carnelle, Delmount, and Popeye, who gain some state of "eternal grace" (*CPI* 202) and vision. By freeing themselves from bonds that stymie human growth and realization of potential, Henley's protagonists redeem themselves and each other.

Crimes of the Heart makes the transition from the stage to screen successfully, but to varying degrees, as the film lacks much of the original play's ambiguity, of both character and plot. Though delightful, *Crimes of the Heart* appears less interesting as a film and less complex as a work of art because Henley frequents her screen with many absent characters from the original play. Though more successful in its transition from play script to screenplay, *Miss Firecracker* retains most of its verve and beauty, with the added spectacle of prancing contestants in the Miss Firecracker contest, ordinary hopefuls praying for extraordinary luck. Still, on many levels, it too sacrifices complexity of character and theme for entertainment value.

Questioned if her plays "have suffered" in their transition to the screen, Henley avows not. She appreciates both art forms:

> No, I think I've been extremely lucky. I don't feel like there has been a definitive version of any of my plays that I've seen. I think I've seen what I feel to be definitive performances by actors, but it's never all come together in this one wholly perfect experience. I think that's okay because it's still alive, and maybe it'll be perfect somewhere somehow years from now or maybe not, but that's why I don't expect the film to be perfect either. In the movie versions of *Crimes of the Heart* and *Miss Firecracker* there are really great lines and really creative moments. It's exciting for me to see how those two directors saw the works, and I felt like they were both sincere to the spirits of the pieces on different levels. (Wimmer-Moul 113)

Though some critics may fault *Crimes of the Heart* for its southern stereotypes and black humor, this comic and quotesque mixture appeals to most moviegoers.[1] Indeed, audiences greeted the film with enthusiasm, with box office receipts totaling over twenty-two million dollars. Still appealing to video audiences today, *Crimes* may be rented at almost any video store in the country. Audiences revel in the empathetic portraits of southern quirkiness, the Magrath sisters, and enjoy the film's humorous dialogue. Claiming that *Crimes* "exists somewhere between parody and melodrama, between the tragic and the goofy," and is a movie unsure of its direction, Roger Ebert, nonetheless, favorably reviews the film, concluding that he prefers not "know[ing] where it's going, for the path of 'uncertainty' heightens the 'delightful, weird surprise' at the end of a Henley work" (Ebert).

Confused and seemingly erratic, Henley's characters speak to audiences on a universal level, despite their seeming impetuosity and peculiarities. From precarious positions, where at any moment they become subject to fate's whimsy, Henley's protagonists arrive at perilous crossroads: ready to lose or to love, to commit suicide or to celebrate their lives. Importantly, they persist, allowing themselves to love and to recognize their own worth. Indeed, their greatest obstacle seems to be themselves. Because they exhibit basic human insecurities, Henley's characters strike audiences as real. Like us, they appear vulnerable to disease, disappointment, sudden death and suicide, and just plain bad luck. Similar to their creator, they share an affinity for, and an intrigue with, death:

> Oh, yes. I always think about death. I can't get through a day without thinking about it because it's my fate. When I'm working on a play, that's what helps drive me to finish it. Before I completed my new play, *The Debutante Ball*, I was going nuts because I had to go to the Hartford Stage Company for *The Wake of Jamey Foster* [January 1982], and I was working on the *Crimes of the Heart* screenplay. These responsibilities were taking me away from working on *The Debutante Ball*. I kept thinking, if I can at *least* get through these notes for the play, then maybe someone could finish it if I die. (Betsko and Koenig 215)

Rather than detract from the impact of her films, Henley's grotesque elements, straight from the gothic crypt of her imagination, ironically, warm and entertain audiences. Her flare for "split images,"[2] characters notably wrathful but sweet, beautiful but corpse-like, angelic but mean, both startle and electrify audiences. Henley admits, "I know I've always had a fascination with darker images because they frighten me so much":

> I think I'm always confronting myself with them. . . . I think it's sort of the complexities of life that I find most real. If you get things that are just Disneyland, it doesn't seem real to me. The six o'clock news is real, and that's got a lot more grotesque things in it than my plays" (Wimmer-Moul 116).

Vacillating between trepidation and exhilaration, Henley tackled the screenplay for *Crimes of the Heart*, intent upon making her characters seem real. Still proclaiming theater her first love, she nonetheless basked in the unlimited space that film offered: "A screenplay, I think, is much easier to write, because you can virtually have as many characters as you like and go so many places compared to the stage" (Wimmer-Moul 114). Filming on location in Southpoint, North Carolina, the producers of *Crimes* attempted to re-create the play's original setting of Hazelhurst, Mississippi. Directed by Bruce Beresford, the movie ironically landed big name stars to portray Henley's small-town nobody eccentrics, the Magrath sisters. Starring as Lenny, forlornly celebrating her thirtieth birthday by jabbing a wax candle into a crumbling cookie, Diane Keaton gives an outstanding performance. Jessica Lange plays Meg, the twenty-seven-year-old would-be singer/actor turned clerk at a Los Angeles dog food company, and Sissy Spacek portrays Babe, at twenty-four, the youngest Magrath, whose attempt to murder her husband occasions the reunion of the three.

This reunion in the film *Crimes of the Heart* centers in the Magrath house; however, nothing about the house appears rumpled, dirtied, or even out of place—hardly what one would expect given the eccentric sisters residing there. One would expect, further, to find rumpled magazines, clothes, and other paraphernalia stashed in hallway corners and hanging on doorknobs, an oversight directors of the original play rarely make. Indeed, though filmmakers select an ancient-looking two-story house, replete with porticos and verandas, they fail in setting up the insides to look authentic. Even the kitchen lacks a sense of having been used, a problem later exacerbated when klutzy Babe bangs her head against the oven in her partial attempt at suicide, managing only to knock herself out. Though the camera lens peers at a faltering Babe from the opposite end of the oven, a vantage point impossible in the play, the new insides of the oven remind audiences that this indeed is a prop, a Hollywood interpretation of southern reality. Certainly, no Magrath woman would be caught dead in a tinsel-clean oven like that!

Crassly twisting and pummeling her way into a pair of pantyhose, right in the middle of the Magrath's kitchen, Chick offers viewers their first glimpse of herself, the social climbing Magrath cousin. She probably wheedled her way into Hazelhurst high society, despite objections, in a fashion similar to her encasement into the pair of pantyhose. Concerned with the family's reputation because of the Magrath mother's suicide, and other skeletons in the Magrath's closets, cousin Chick worries about her good name: "Well, his mother was going to keep *me* out of the Ladies' Social League because of it," she blubbers (*CPI* 6). A crude make over of a southern belle, Chick, played by Tess Harper in the film, repels audiences by her smug rigidity and self-centeredness. A controller, Chick complains about the Magrath sisters and insists on monitoring their behaviors. Harper's performance in the role succeeds in suggesting that her character has the moral acumen of a scalawag or profiteer, dealing in other people's pain. Blaming the Magraths for family humiliations, Chick admonishes them even for their good deeds.

In one revealing scene in the film *Crimes*, she delights in making Lenny feel cheap for having purchased an inexpensive polka dot dress for PeeKay, Chick's daughter. "The first time I put it in the washing machine, I mean the very first time, it fell all to pieces. Those little dots just dropped right off in the water," Chick impatiently blurts (*CPI* 7–8).

In their struggles to get through their "real bad days" (*CPI* 19) and to gain control of their own lives, Henley's protagonists battle not only the darker sides of their own natures, but also those of Old Granddaddy and Chick. Kafka's *Metamorphosis,* likewise, features Gregor vying against the dark force of the elder Mr. Samsa, as he, inadvertently, wages war to replace his father as head of the house. Artfully interweaving family patriarchs and their agents, the play version of *Crimes* indicates Chick functions as an extension of Old Granddaddy, a mouthpiece of doom and voice of disapproval. Indeed, Henley also insinuates Chick's bond to patriarchy, in both play and film, when this Magrath cousin presents Lenny with a gift of assorted cremes. Chick reads from the card, "Happy Birthday to Lenny, from the Buck Boyles" (*CPI* 7). Rather than sign her name, Chick defers to her husband, the family patriarch, believing, as do many southern women, that a woman is defined by her marital status. Despite quality acting, the movie, unlike the play, fails to integrate its villains into one powerful presence, one that clearly articulates Henley's message that patriarchy squelches female autonomy.

Old Granddaddy in *Crimes*, the film, appears drained of power, merely a watered-down version of the play's most influential absent character. From the near bowels of death, Hurd Hatfield resurrects on-screen a healthy looking grandfather, whose appearance directly contrasts with his description in the play, in which he, in the middle of his third stroke, remains ominous and powerful despite enduring feeding tubes and popping blood vessels. As an actor, Hatfield fails to capture the essence of the play's larger-than-life absent persona and primary antagonist, though in fairness, the problem lies less, perhaps, with acting than with staging. Absent characters often impact other characters and plots more than do characters realized on the stage or screen. Henley's materializing of the family patriarch in the film, indeed, seems a mistake. In one film sequence, Old Granddaddy lies comatose in his hospital bed, Lenny and Babe attending him, while the camera casts pictures across the screen of a younger Hatfield, poised, solid, and handsome. These assorted poses of Old Granddaddy fail to hint at the complexity, or the severity, of the relationship with the three granddaughters. In the play, the old man looms Wizard of Oz–like in the background, his imagined voice permeating the Magrath corridors. Not demanding a broom, as does the Wizard, this Magrath patriarch requires something more impossible for the sisters to earn his approval.

Just as Gregor Samsa could not win approval from his father, Old Granddaddy's granddaughters cannot content him with either marriages or careers. In the play more so than in the film version of *Crimes*, Henley subtly suggests that the old man sugars his love to the point of stickiness, immobilizing the Magrath girls. In one of the film's flashbacks, in particular, the camera follows Old Granddaddy taking the girls, as children, on a breakfast excursion to eat ice cream the day of their mother's funeral. "And plenty of syrup," the grandfather orders, "Just go on and bring a big king-size bowl of syrup." Lenny, Meg, and Babe have yet to digest the fact of their mother's suicide when Old Granddaddy cajoles them into gobbling down as many banana splits as they can eat. Babe reminds her sisters that, after five banana splits, she got sick and vomited. "The thing about Old Granddaddy is he keeps trying to make us happy and we keep getting stomachaches and turning green and throwing up in the flower arrangements," Meg charges. Thus, the Magrath family patriarch sugarcoats even death as a substitute for dealing with the heart. Rather than closeness, consoling the girls in their grief, Old Granddaddy offers but a kind of artificial sweetner.

Henley's play irrefutably delivers an important message: Old Granddaddy's love incapacitates. A typical omission of *Crimes*, the movie, illustrates this point well. In one sisterly exchange in the play, the Magrath women reminisce about how Old Granddaddy used to call Babe his "Dancing Sugar Plum" (*CPI* 14) and how he ardently wished for Meg Hollywood stardom, a fame, Henley intimates, that would entrap this Magrath:

LENNY: Like Old Granddaddy says, "With your talent all you need is exposure. Then you can make your own breaks!" Did you hear his suggestion about getting your foot put in one of those blocks of cement they've got out there? He thinks that's real important.
MEG: Yeah. I think I've heard that. And I'll probably hear it again when I go to visit him at the hospital tonight, so let's just drop it. Okay? (*CPI* 15)

Indeed, Henley's play symbolically suggests that adherence to Old Granddaddy's prescriptions will immobilize Meg, her "foot" and her fate "cement[ed]," hardened in a defined "block"—one of Old Granddaddy's choosing. The grandfather's prescriptions further prove ineffectual when he demands sacrifice of his granddaughters. Babe contends that Lenny, metaphorically, has transformed into Old Grandmama, now wearing the dead woman's gardening hat and gloves. A dutiful kind of surrogate-wife, Lenny sleeps on a kitchen cot in order to attend expediently to the old man's needs. Her behavior typifies what Harriet Goldhor Lerner in *The Dance of Anger* terms "de-selfing," "betray[ing] and sacrific[ing] the self in order to preserve harmony with others . . ." (Lerner 11). Repeatedly, the eldest Magrath defends Old Granddaddy, maintaining that her sisters should feel gratitude because their grandfather gave them a home when their mother died. More so than in the film, the play version of *Crimes* underscores this difference between *should* and *do*: what the granddaughters *should* feel contrasts with what they *do* feel; yet, they dare not rely on their feelings or their own judgments. At one point, Lenny swears that Old Granddaddy saved her from the humiliation of her shrunken ovary, enjoining her to break off the relationship with the man from the Lonely Hearts Club of the South. Decidedly then, the grandfather's manipulation of the three sisters instills in them a lack of self-confidence, fueling Lenny's fears of infertility, weakening guilt-ridden Meg, and encouraging Babe's marriage to a man later identified as abusive. Omitted from the film, the following play scene points to Old Granddaddy's involvement in facilitating Babe's marriage to Zackery Botrelle, a match that becomes for Babe the beginning of a nightmare:

LENNY: He remarked how Babe was gonna skyrocket right to the heights of Hazlehurst society. And how Zackery was the right man for her whether she knew it now or not. (*CPI* 14)

Even though Meg on the surface seemingly has escaped Old Granddaddy's hold by moving to California, she nonetheless is incapacitated by her anger toward him. Lerner's book on anger maintains that, "We know our greatest anger, as well as our deepest love, in our roles as daughters, sisters, loves, wives, and mothers. Family relationships are the most influential in our lives, and the most difficult . . . [i]ssues that go unaddressed with members of our first family only fuel our fires in other relationships (Lerner 11). Meg wards off the pain of having disappointed her grandfather by lying to him and to herself, unable to acknowledge her own anger toward a loved one. Again, the film only partially intimates that Meg's anger has ties to patriarchy and to her lack of autonomy, whereas the play drops endless clues suggesting this. At one point in the film version of *Crimes*, Meg returns from a hospital visit, having told Old Granddaddy a story that she has won a role in an upcoming film, only to be met with uncomfortable silence from Babe, and especially, Lenny:

MEG: All right—I lied! I couldn't help it. . . . When I saw how sick and tired Old Granddaddy'd gotten, those stories—they just flew out! All I wanted was to see him smiling and happy.
LENNY: But still you shouldn't have lied! It just was wrong for you to tell such lies—
MEG: Well, I know that! Don't you think I know that? God, I hate it when I lie for that old man. I do. I feel so weak. And then I gotta go and do at least three or four things that I know he'd despise just to get even with that miserable, old, bossy man!

Indeed, Meg's admission indicates an ongoing warfare, or vendetta, against her grandfather, one whose object is to "get even," but importantly, she further discloses that her lies are "for that . . . old . . . man," not for herself. Her compulsion to package herself to Old Granddaddy as what he wants indicates her fear of rejection. Already frustrating his ambitions for her by losing her singing voice—a self-imposed silencing that prohibits stardom—Meg appears not unlike her mother who misdirected her anger and permanently silenced herself. Mimicking her mother's behavior, the middle Magrath sister directs both anger and pain on herself, denying herself a voice, another "crime of the heart." Though perhaps "get[ting] even" with her grandfather, Meg damages herself more than she affects him. Lerner explains:

> Most of us have received little help in learning to use our anger to clarify and strengthen ourselves and our relationships. Instead, our lessons have encouraged us to fear anger excessively, to deny it entirely, to displace it onto inappropriate targets, or to turn it against ourselves. We learn to deny that there is any cause for anger, to close our eyes to its true sources, or to vent anger ineffectively, in a manner that only maintains rather than challenges, the status quo. (Lerner 10)

Though sidestepping somewhat issues of patriarchal control and of autonomy, *Crimes*, the film, does suggest that another absent patriarch, the father who deserted the family, contributed to the mother's suicide. In scenes occurring in both play and film, the three sisters peruse Babe's old photograph album, whereupon they discover a photo of their mother beside the "old yellow cat" that she hanged along side herself.

BABE: And that old yellow cat. It was sad about that old cat.
MEG: Yeah.
BABE: I bet if Daddy hadn't of left us, they'd still be alive.
MEG: Oh, I don't know.
. . .
MEG: Yeah. Well, I'm glad he left.
BABE: That old yellow cat'd stay back there with her.
MEG: God, he was a bastard.
BABE: I thought if she felt something for anyone it woulda been that old cat. Guess I musta been mistaken.
MEG: Really, with his white teeth, Daddy was such a bastard.
BABE: Was he? I don't remember.
(Meg blows out a mouthful of smoke. After a moment, uneasily.)
BABE: I think I'm gonna make some lemonade. You want some? (*CPI* 19)

Though originally discussing their mother and the cat—a scene enhanced by pronoun ambiguity—the three sisters, unknowingly, establish links binding the father also to the cat, referred to here as if a person, an anyone, and ultimately, to Old Granddaddy. Thus, on some level, they indict their father for complicity in their mother's death. Audiences may further note that Babe's last invitation to drink some lemonade occurred when she shot her husband, Zackery, another bastard. Later, the three Magrath women again will remark about the whiteness of their father's teeth, but by alternating statements concerning "Mama and the cat" with those about the father, Henley comically entwines Daddy, "the bastard," to the old yellow cat. Repeatedly in *Crimes*, the sisters emphasize "old" when referring to Old Granddaddy or the old yellow cat, seemingly according great importance to the agedness of each. Meg establishes another parallel, referring to Old Granddaddy as a "fool" (*CPI* 21), a word which the audience earlier associates with the father. By offering more dialogue, and hence, more materials with which to associate characterizations, the play reinforces this connectedness of family patriarchs—the father, the grandfather, and the cat, and on some level, even Babe's husband—whereas the film limits these relational intricacies. Thus, given the comic juxtapositions and ambiguous pronouncements of the Magrath sisters in both versions of *Crimes*, Henley implies that patriarchy debilitates.

No matter how bleak the situation, Henley, nonetheless, draws humor from unlikely venues, even portraits of death. She expertly does this in a scene created just for the film. In the midst of their rumination about their mother and the cat, the sisters come across a tabloid clipping of the crime scene (at the suicide) in an article from *The Star Confidential*. Laid out beside one another, dead bodies might ordinarily strike audiences as gruesome; however, by blending the fantastic with the macabre, Henley evokes laughter from audiences with this spectacle. With one large and one small sheet covering the corpse of the dead mother and the dead cat, respectively, the photo shows a tiny tail dangling ever so slightly from under the border of the smaller cloth.

Too often critics discount Henley as a talented playwright and screenwriter, assuming that she has no message to give or lesson to teach, no goal beyond the next laugh. Always beneath the surface quirkiness of her characters and her bizarre situations, Henley embeds meaning. At the heart of her stories, this playwright and screenwriter introduces audiences to serious concerns: family secrets, rebellion, racism, autonomy, and even domestic violence. With the film, however, Henley seems less certain about the degree to which she will allow these issues to unfold. Only in the play does she make unequivocally clear Old Granddaddy's negative effect on the Magrath sisters. Even Babe's shooting of Zackery may relate to Old Granddaddy, indirectly, functioning as a kind of retaliatory act, a sort of exorcizing of patriarchal power. Considering that the mother hanged the cat, which, on some level, she equated with the father, also a patriarchal figure, then one might conclude that by killing the cat, the mother vicariously kills her husband, his surrogate. Thus, the Magrath mother very likely had a motive for killing her beloved pet—one of revenge.

Not every critic, however, believes that Henley conveys a serious message about patriarchy, autonomy, or domestic violence. Janet V. Haedicke in " 'A Population and Theater at Risk': Battered Women in Henley's *Crimes of the Heart* and Shepard's *A Lie of the Mind*," notes that most critics totally disregard Babe as a victim of domestic violence:

> The wife battering is the crime behind the crime here, aligning Babe's attempted homicide with that "nearly three-fourths of the violence perpetrated by women [which] is committed in self defense." So cursory, however, is Henley's treatment of this motive, to which the play never again even alludes, that its significance is occluded. Indeed, most critics seem oblivious to the fact that Babe is a battered woman, concentrating instead on the self-destructive violence of the sisters' behavior. . . . (85)

Undoubtedly, the serious issue of wife battering contributes to Babe's motive for trying to shoot Zackery in the heart. Just because she "didn't like his stinking looks" (*CPI* 17), as Babe proclaims, such an attitude hardly seems motive enough for attempted homicide, nor does getting back at Zackery for his cruelty to Willie Jay, as Colby H. Kullman supposes in "Beth Henley's Marginalized Heroines" (23). Appropriately, Henley's abused wife ends up shooting her husband in the stomach, closer to the seat of his bile, than his heart. Henley's treatment of domestic violence, in both play and film, seems accurate and realistic. In both play and film, Babe hides her abuse even from her sisters, despite their obvious concern and support of her. In real life, abused women follow a path similar to Babe's. Indeed, Henley's vision involves truth telling and realism. Rather than "occlude" the "significance" of domestic violence, as Haedicke posits in her essay, Henley accentuates it, paradoxically, by skillfully placing it at the play's margins, the background of the action, not unlike the way society in real life treats domestic violence. An unacceptable topic of conversation, in small- or in large-town America, domestic violence lurks in the corners of our lives. Henley's audiences, therefore, amidst their laughter, must pause to consider this insidious canker that causes a woman as beloved as Babe to remain silent, then to erupt into violence.

Another serious issue Henley addresses in *Crimes* involves family secrets and ongoing feuds. Henley stirs these fires until they crackle and spark. Complaining repeatedly of the scandal brought on the family, Chick obviously underscores the issue of southern family honor. When she crudely threatens that Babe will go to jail or to an asylum, where they will "throw away the key" (*CPI* 17), Meg rallies to her sister's defense, prepared to drive all traitors from the house! A small-scale battle ensues, not unlike the War between the States, pitting cousin against cousin. Further, when Chick magnanimously lectures Meg on the hazards of smoking, she fires, "You know you shouldn't smoke. It causes cancer. Cancer of the lungs. They say each cigarette is just a little stick of cancer. A little death stick." Meg, of course, retaliates in one of the film's most memorable squabbles, a word battle.

MEG: That's what I like about it, Chick—taking a drag off of death *(lovingly inhaling a deep whiff of the cigarette)* Mmm! What power! What exhilaration! Want a drag?

In watching this same scene in the play *Crimes,* theater audiences will hear a difference of one line:

MEG: That's what I like about it, Chick—taking a drag off of death *(Meg takes a long, deep drag)* Mmm! Gives me a sense of controlling my own destiny. What power! What exhilaration! Want a drag? (*CPI* 17)

This line, "Gives me a sense of controlling my own destiny," seems representative of the type of omissions from the screen versions of *Crimes.* Thus, the issue of controlling one's "destiny" is one of autonomy. Unlike Gregor Samsa, who refuses to be autonomous, letting his life be determined by outside forces, Meg identifies and points out her need for autonomy. Though film audiences may glean its significance, still, Henley's play punctuates autonomy as an issue for all to contemplate.

Warfare continues when later Lenny (and Meg in the film version), clucks like a chicken at her cousin and calls her "Chick-the-Stick," an appellation Babe disparagingly used earlier (*CPI* 17, 18, 58). Film, as well as theater audiences, might figuratively associate Chick, another kind of "stick," with poison and disease. Chick, the walking stick, spews her cancerous poisons, her criticisms, in the air. Again, Henley adeptly marries the comic to the gruesome, but underlying this technique, she embeds a motive. Exercising power, even by "taking a drag off of death," Meg indulges in negative behaviors, flirting with death, but paradoxically, her behavior also links to something positive, her need for autonomy. When later in the film Lenny declares that the sisters should be grateful to Old Granddaddy for making a home for them, Meg retorts, "Well . . . but sometimes I wonder what we wanted."

With sister pitted against sister, and cousin against cousin, Henley's film seems almost a parody of the Civil War, which capitalizes on the discrepancy between the reality of the South's Lost Cause versus the Magrath sisters' unabashed refusal to admit defeat. The front has become a plane of mostly verbal retaliation and psychological combat, a miniaturized civil war. Indeed, the sisters not only fight each other but also they fight family, wielding secret grudges, hurt feelings, and minor betrayals. Karen Jaehne's interview with actor Mary Steenburgen about Henley's work is instructive. Steenburgen says, "I respond more than most people to Beth's humor, because I'm Southern. She writes about what I am. My humor is very Southern, and it's as hard to describe as Jewish humor" (Jaehne 12–13). Jaehne surmises that "[i]n fact, it's the humor of the vanquished, who secretly believe they have won" (12–13).

Amidst these skirmishes of the Magraths, Henley refigures another serious issue, racism, still unresolved after all these years. Babe's affair with a fifteen-year-old black youth, Willie Jay (Greg Travis), incites her racist husband Zackery (Beeson Carroll) to proclaim that he holds "blackening evidence," damning photos of Babe and Willie Jay, which he will use against the "lily-white" Babe. Henley offers this scene in the film as comic relief, for Zackery makes his threat while a nurse jabs a needle into his buttock. In addition to showing us Zackery, Henley brings to the screen another character absent from the play—Willie Jay. This addition proves both good and bad, for by realizing Willie Jay on screen, Henley allows us to feel sympathy for this innocent victim of racism when Babe's husband curses at him and throws him off the premises, calling him "boy." A later glimpse of Willie Jay, which is not in the play, poignantly follows him as he boards a bus to leave Hazlehurst. Whereas in the play Willie Jay escapes town at midnight, as Babe's lawyer informs her, the film devotes a full scene to his daytime departure, the camera zooming in for a shot of Babe's young lover peering out a Greyhound bus window, a tear staining his cheek. Babe hovers across the street with her lawyer, watching from a distance. Audiences rightly attribute this painful departure to Zackery Botrelle; racial injustice still thrives in the South. Heightening the effect of the parting, the film focuses on the dark tinted bus window, a symbolic barrier that separates the black man from the white woman.

Does Henley mean her audiences to view this scene as southern quirkiness? No. Willie Jay, marginalized in life, will escape to the North, but no underground railway will assure his transfer or safety. Henley's penchant for truth telling continues, again giving audiences pause. A young black man in the South involved with a married (or even unmarried) white woman risks being escorted from town regardless of whether the woman's husband is abusive. Racism often perverts justice, corrupting a system designed to protect the innocent.

Justice, it seems, does prevail in the film's most hilarious scene when Henley again dallies with the theme of southern honor. When Chick extends her condolences to Lenny for having to claim such a trashy sister as Meg, a tormented Lenny explodes:

LENNY: Get out of here—
CHICK: Don't you tell me to get out! What makes you think you can order me around? Why, I have just about had my fill of you trashy Magraths and your trashy ways; hanging yourselves in cellars; carrying on with married men; shooting your own husbands! (*CPI* 57)

For the first time, Lenny the caregiver transforms from a passive mouse to a roaring lioness. Not only does she look different physically as an assertive, even aggressive, woman, but she thinks differently. No longer thinking herself a charity case, she even claims ownership of the house, demanding that a shocked and stammering Chick get off the premises. Audiences applaud her action. Wielding a broom, she chases Chick around the kitchen, out the door, and into the backyard, then up a mimosa tree, a sequence the filmmakers successfully prolong as Chick scrambles, squirrel-like, up a pile of logs to reach the tree's protection. All the while, Lenny wildly swings. Not only does Lenny claim ownership of the house in this scene but also she takes control of her life. Transformed, she finally musters the courage to call Memphis and speak to the man she has continued to love from the Lonely Hearts Club. She focuses on what she wants, thus breaking Old Granddaddy's control over her.

The director of the film *Crimes of the Heart* adeptly casts David Carpenter as Barnette Lloyd, Babe's lawyer, a one-man battalion. Emerging as Babe's love interest, Barnette epitomizes the true southern gentleman. Unlike the play, in which he wages a "personal vendetta" against Botrelle for having ruined his father (*CPI* 24), the modern equivalent of the old southern feud, the film dispenses with this aspect of Barnette's character, making him less intriguing. Indeed, the play *Crimes* indicates that the lawyer may be as unstable as his client, Babe.

MEG: Hmmm. A personal vendetta . . . I think I like that. So you have some sort of a persona vendetta to settle with Zackery?

BARNETTE: Precisely. Just between the two of us, I not only intend to keep that sorry S.O.B. from ever being re-elected to the state senate by exposing his shady, criminal dealings; but I also intend to decimate his personal credibility by exposing him as a bully, a brute, and a red-neck thug!

MEG: Well; I can see that you're—fanatical about this. (*CPI* 24)

Focusing on this pivotal moment, the director films a scene at Zackery's hospital bed in which Babe's husband, surrounded by his entourage and sister, Lucille, meets with Babe's lawyer. Barnette's strategy, correctly, is that Botrelle would be too ashamed to let gossip flurry in Hazelhurst that his wife had taken as her lover a fifteen-year-old black youth. Certainly citizens would question the senator's leadership qualities, an obvious allusion to his southern manhood, equated with sexual virility.

The metamorphoses of the three sisters, Lenny, Meg, and Babe not only figure crucially in the play's main action but also factor importantly in the transformation of Barnette Lloyd. At the play's end, he too changes, setting aside his personal vendetta for the greater good of Babe's case. No longer content to let vengeance rule him, Barnette makes a shrewd deal to free Babe while at the same time, relinquishing the hatred which once gave his life purpose. This ability to care for another, even at the expense of losing one's advantage, complicates and intensifies the theme of rehabilitative love. Unfortunately, the film deletes all references to Barnette's vendetta. Carpenter, the film's lawyer turned knight armed for combat, carries no grudges or hatreds, unlike his counterpart in the play. Thus, the film's Barnette Lloyd seems but a man of good deeds, in no need of transformation. Likeable, but not peaking our interest, Carpenter's acting cannot add complexity to a script that rewrites Henley's knight, Barnette Lloyd, into a pretty ordinary lawyer who once bought a cake from Babe at the bazaar.

In another case, the film succeeds in indicating transformation, matching Meg with her old love, Doc Porter, played by Sam Shepard. Since they last met, Doc has married a "Yankee" from the East and has two children, whom Meg mockingly refers to as "half-Yankees" (*CPI* 16). With these offspring, Doc obviously has tainted his southern bloodline. Reunited and whole again, Meg figuratively undergoes a metamorphosis, a revitalized ability to care for someone. The camera highlights the two of them on a moonlit walk, a romantic golden moon hovering in the night sky. Thus reinvigorating and reinvesting in a relationship once thought dead, Meg can get past her fear and pain, and love again, even without sex. A jubilant Meg emerges from this reunion singing, her voice restored. As she later confesses to Lenny and Babe, she has gained strength: "I realized I could care about someone. I could want someone. And I sang! I sang all night long! I sang right up into the trees! But not for Old Granddaddy. None of it was to please Old Granddaddy!" This poignant moment disintegrates in the film when Meg begins to sing, unfortunately off key. Nevertheless, Meg's transformation makes her whole, ready to confront Old Granddaddy, to demand that he accept her for what she is. In the play and the film, she also reclaims her voice, which audiences learn has special powers. Indeed, Meg has a witness to this miraculous voice that defies limitations and knows all possibilities:

BARNETTE: I came to hear you five different times when you were singing at that club in Biloxi. Greeny's I believe was the name of it.
MEG: Yes, Greeny's.
BARNETTE: You were very good. There was something sad and moving about how you sang those songs. It was like you had some sort of vision. Some special sort of vision. (*CPI* 23)

Attributing to Meg a voice with a quality of sight, "special vision," Henley endows her favorite character with a mythic vision, making her at once distinctive, seeing, and powerful.[3]

Henley's screenplay *Crimes of the Heart* does justice to her Pulitzer Prize–winning play, winning for Sissy Spacek the New York Film Critics Circle Award for Best Actress in 1986 and a Golden Globe award (1987) for

Best Performance by an Actress in a Motion Picture, as well as Academy Award nominations for Best Actress in a Leading Role (Sissy Spacek), Best Actress in a Supporting Role (Tess Harper), and Best Screenplay Based on Material from Another Medium (Beth Henley), all in 1987. Henley's themes, both universal and particular, played to audiences successfully across the country. Though not winning an Oscar for *Crimes of the Heart*, Henley, the screenwriter, appears content. Asked if she were satisfied with the film *Crimes*, the native Mississippian merely replied, "Yes, I was happy with it. I can't watch it because it hurts me to watch my own things, but I really was when I saw it. I was very moved and very pleased; I have it on video, and someday I'm going to watch it again" (Wimmer-Moul 114).

Miss Firecracker, Henley's next film after *Crimes of the Heart*, again captivated audiences. As with *Crimes*, the screenwriter adds and subtracts, shifts and rearranges, thus telling new stories to old audiences. Yet, Henley remains true to her original vision. With her second film, Henley again foregrounds themes of transformation and autonomy, endeavoring to capture the spirit of the original play, *The Miss Firecracker Contest*.

In *Miss Firecracker*, the screenwriter transposed the title from its original emphasis upon the beauty contest to one almost exclusively concentrating on a single, heroic figure, Carnelle Scott. With a new title, *Miss Firecracker,* Henley further delved into Carnelle's complex relationship Elain, the beautiful cousin whose rivalry with Carnelle complicates her love. *Miss Firecracker* parades passions across the screen, and what more talented and passionate actor than Holly Hunter could Henley bring to the starring role of her heroine, Carnelle? A natural progression to follow the playwright from the stage to screen, Hunter, who starred in the Manhatten Theatre Club's premiere production of the play, seemed a logical choice for the role: " 'Holly has a strange ability to be passionate and vulnerable, but extremely tough and rageful,' Henley says of her longtime collaborator. 'Also, she knows how to walk the edge between truth and humor. Holly hears the music of what I write' " (Renner 18). Given the new, concentrated focus on Carnelle, the screenplay produces a rather different sort of story than that of the original play. Rather than a carnival of funny, bizarre, and touching characters, the film develops and displays a certain faintheartedness about her character as well. Whereas *The Miss Firecracker Contest* makes clear that Carnelle has been a bad girl, actually contracting syphilis and transmitting it, most notably, to her friend and previous lover, Mac Sam, the film slashes all references to Carnelle's association with disease, acknowledging nothing coarser than the protagonist's nickname of "Miss Hot Tamale." In the original play version, Carnelle sheepishly apologizes to Mac Sam for giving him syphilis. Not only does the film forfeit this apology but also it deletes Mac Sam's easy dismissal of it. Instead, the pair appears like reunited lovers, with no major hint, at first, that for Carnelle, the flame has died. Despite Mac Sam's tubercular coughing attacks, evidence of at least one of his diseases, the couple has a hearty spin on the tilt-a-whirl, smooching and cuddling, whirling to the carnival music. Indeed, this romantic scene, obviously designed for a Hollywood sell, deletes grotesque elements that frequent the play. Note the contrast between film and play when Mac Sam treats Carnelle to a glimpse of one of his blood:

MAC SAM: Yeah. (*Cough, cough.*) Yeah. (*Cough, cough, cough, cough, cough.*) He spits up blood.
CARNELLE: Mac Sam, what's wrong? Are you choking?
MAC SAM: Nah. I'm just spitting up clots of blood.
CARNELLE: What?
MAC SAM: It's nothing. Happens all the time. Look at that clot there; it's a nice pinkish-reddish sorta color.
CARNELLE: You're making me sick, here. Sick (*CPI* 189)

Though still likeable, the film versions of Carnelle and Mac Sam lack the complexity that Henley incorporates into her play's characters. Thus, the film loses something distinctive in the relationship, becoming a simpler version of the stereotypical dying-but-sexy-man-supports-idealistic-girl.

Perhaps the key to unlocking the strengths of *Miss Firecracker*, and surprisingly overlooked by critics of both the play and the film, is by exploiting the fairy tale motif which inspires Henley's characters and themes. Fairy tale threads, intertwined with codes of southern chivalry, portraits of family disintegration and transformation, and searches for identity stitch Henley's characters tightly to her audiences. On some level, we already know these characters from their fairy tale counterparts, and here Henley makes us care about them all over again. This film is not simply a retelling of the familiar tale, with handsome princes (Tim Robbins as Delmount in the film), would-be princesses (the Miss Firecracker contestants), and dark, sinister stepmothers and wicked stepsisters (Ronelle and Elain) intent on beguiling or belittling a traditional heroine. Henley's psychologically complex fairy tale inverts the traditional stories, adding a contradictory quality to them. When asked if her work allowed her to write about repression buried "in [her] own life," Henley quipped,

> I don't know. I write about things I'm concerned with, that are troubling me; and I suppose some of what you write is unconscious and subliminal. That's sort of where the magic comes from: it's not plotted logically like "This is something I want to explore." But it does come from inside you. (Wimmer-Moul 108)

As evidenced in *Crimes of the Heart*, Henley's fragmented, and even dysfunctional characters—what one movie reviewer characterizes as "half crazy people" (Hinson D7)—sometimes exhibit exquisite powers for making others whole, functional human beings.

In both play and film, Henley subverts traditional fairy tale plots by a series of inversion and appropriations. Thomas Schlamme directs Hunter as the exuberant, orphaned misfit, Carnelle Scott, a young woman craving acceptance, worrying about being ugly, and aspiring to the coveted title of Miss Firecracker, the fairy tale equivalent of attending the ball. Mary Steenburgen, cast as Carnelle's cousin Elain, encapsulates the idea of the southern belle, graced with beauty and charm, but is similar to the queen of "Snow White" fame, who fears displacement and time's passage. References to Elain's ownership of beautiful clocks indicate a figurative attempts to control time and the "mirror on the wall."

The film begins and ends with a flashback of a young Carnelle, a wooly hat atop her head in July to conceal head lice, gazing into the sun, awe-stricken by her cousin Elain's beauty: "Anyway, it was way back that first year when I came to live with them. She was a vision of beauty riding on that float with a crown on her head waving to everyone. I thought I'd drop dead when she passed by me," exclaims Carnelle. These lines, typically Henley, link beauty with death, a theme upon which Henley elaborates in her film. Carnelle admits being ready to "drop dead" at the sight of beauty.

Unrealized by Carnelle, a beautiful swan lies dormant beneath her ugly duckling exterior, but she needs visible proof of her value. As Robert L. McDonald submits in "A blaze of glory": Image and Self-Promotion in Henley's *The Miss Firecracker Contest*," only public affirmation will satiate Carnelle's thirst for respectability:

> For Henley's characters, the public arena is a place of magic, to be exploited rather than avoided for its potential to reveal what might otherwise remain hidden and silent in their private lives. In fact, Carnelle's admiration for the way Aunt Ronelle handled herself during the trial of her illness, even emerging as something of a local celebrity, points to her own basic motivation for wanting to enter The Miss Firecracker Contest: to provide for a similar kind of public metamorphosis, replacing her well-worn (and admittedly well-earned) vernacular title of "Miss Hot Tamale" with something more appropriate to her newly uplifted self. (152–153)

Elain's problem duplicates the one from which the evil queen of "Snow White" suffers. How does one maintain value in a patriarchal world which recognizes a woman only for her beauty? Elain combats this dilemma by preoccupying herself with beauty, by becoming narcissistic. In *The Culture of Narcissism*, Christopher Lasch observes that the "narcissist depends on others to validate h[er] self-esteem. [S]he cannot live without an admiring audience (10). Now married and with children, Elain, nevertheless, fears replacement. Her story, not unlike the wicked queen's in "Snow White," appears equally tragic:

> The real story begins when the Queen, having become a mother, metamorphoses also into a witch—that is, into a wicked "step" mother: ". . . when the child was born, the Queen died," and "After a year had passed the King took to himself another wife."
>
> When we first encounter this "new" wife, she is framed in a magic looking glass, just as her predecessor—that is, her earlier self—had been framed in a window. To be caught and trapped in a mirror rather than a window, however, is to be driven inward, obsessively studying self-images, as if seeking a viable self. (Gilbert and Gubar 37)

On another level, Elain seems the perfect "Cinderella," replete with ceremonial carriage and escort. Her charming "prince" of a husband, Franklin, however, turns out to be a self-absorbed, although rich, toad. In the play *The Miss Firecracker Contest*, he remains an absent character, which works effectively, powerful despite his absence (like Old Granddaddy's in *Crimes*), but, in the film, we glimpse a somewhat ordinary looking man as he exits the house, golf bag in tow. The aura of power dissipates considerably.

More in the play than in the film *Miss Firecracker*, audiences recognize in Elain one who has repressed the life force, and longs, Rapunzel-like, to "let down her hair." The play leaves the audience not knowing if Elain will return to her rich spouse, where she, assuredly, must settle for appearances, her beautiful home, and her clocks. Still, *The Miss Firecracker Contest* engages audiences in a fantasy that this Rapunzel likely will realize. Will she keep her rendezvous with a another prince, the blood-coughing Mac Sam, her new romantic interest who still carries a venereal disease? Elain of the *Firecracker* film would never contemplate, much less agree, to such an assignation. This difference makes her an altogether different kind of character from the one in the play, less ambiguous and less thought provoking. In his review of *Miss Firecracker*, Randy Parker castigates the film's Elain, labeling Steenburgen's "performance as Elain . . . adequate," but argues that "her character is so nauseating that you don't feel the least bit of sympathy for her" (Parker). The play does contain ambiguity as concerns Elain's future, however, revealed in a phone conversation with Franklin:

> . . . I—I don't want to come home . . . I mean not ever, or for awhile, or for not ever . . . I feel like I'm missing my life . . . I don't know about the children. They'll manage . . . Oh, for God's sake, Franklin, no one's going to bake them into a pie! . . . Oh, please! I don't want to discuss it anymore. I'm tired of it all, I'm through with it all. Good-bye! *(She hangs up the phone. She is stunned and shaken by what she has done).* (CPI 166)

The play indulges in multiple layers of ambiguity, unlike the film, thus pointing to Elain's complexity as well as her fairy tale antecedents: she wants excitement and yearns to step down from the pedestal, just once to engage in reckless behavior, but already her future has always been prescribed, determined, for her. In one of the play's heated confrontations with her brother, Delmount Williams, Elain screams, "Mama always loved you ten times better than me . . . I had to win contests and be in pageants before she'd give me any notice at all" (*CPI* 167). Indeed, audiences wonder why Elain's mother, Ronelle, dispossesses her only daughter, leaving the house and furnishings to her son. When Delmount, in the film, threatens to "give away" the family house if he "can't sell it," Elain angrily accuses him of having "everything" to her "nothing" even though she has tried outrageously hard to please their mother. Perhaps a believer in fairy tales, Ronelle assumed that young ladies marry wealth and success when they get a husband.

In the play as well as the film, Carnelle recounts that her Aunt Ronelle once proclaimed that Elain "had it all" up there, "just like a queen in a castle" (*CPI* 159). Figuratively trapped, however, Elain has moved merely from one type of prison to another (the fairy tale-like Atlanta estate). Thus, Aunt Ronelle leaves her touch not only on the house, but also on her children, and by extension, on her niece. Elain reminds Carnelle that Ronelle always said, "Pretty is as pretty does" (187). Though not literally making Elain spin gold, Ronelle teaches her daughter to value winning, getting the gold crown. The beautiful Elain learns well this lesson. As Lasch's examination of American culture suggests, "The narcissist admires and identifies [her]self with "winners"out of h[er] fear of being labeled a loser" (Lasch 85). The play, but not the film, of *Miss Firecracker* indicates that Ronelle equates winning with sustenance, food, for she preaches that beauty pageants are the "gravy" of life, a necessary prerequisite for winning a rich husband (*CPI* 167). Indeed, Ronelle shares some of the tendencies of Old Granddaddy in *Crimes of the Heart*, who wishes marriage for Babe to a rich husband. Both Elain and Carnelle digest the perverted message that beauty signals acceptance, and that, without it, woman will be denied a seat at the table of success, left to a bland diet of potatoes—with no "gravy"!

To Elain, Carnelle's obsession with winning the coveted crown of "Miss Firecracker" threatens her reality of the world, all that she accepts in life as truth. Now invited back to Yazoo City, Mississippi, *Miss Firecracker*'s replacement for the original locale of Brookhaven, Elain mounts a pedestal, quite literally, to deliver her speech, "My Life as a Beauty" (*CPI* 180). In the play, cousin Elain does bring the famous red dress that Carnelle insists upon wearing for the pageant, but, in the film, she hides it from Carnelle. This dress, that once gained Elain a metaphorical invitation to the ball, the winning of the Miss Firecracker title, must not be relinquished. Indeed, the dress in the play, *The Miss Firecracker Contest*, does not appear even to be the one that Elain wore to the Miss Firecracker contest. It has been worn by Elain instead to the Natchez Pilgrimage. Making this dress the one worn to capture the beauty title, Henley paints a portrait of *Miss Firecracker*'s Elain as a Cinderella turned into a wicked queen. In their analysis of "Snow White," Sandra

Sandra Gilbert and Susan Gubar point out that queens and Snow Whites (or Cinderellas) are, in a sense, one. Angels and monsters are often combined in the same character (Gilbert and Gubar 41). Appearing more complex, and worthy of our interest, the Elain of the play deserves the audiences' care, even sympathy, despite her having swallowed patriarchal prescriptions divvied out by her mother.

Also intent upon succeeding as a beauty, Carnelle hires her own seamstress, although she has just lost her job. Winning the Miss Firecracker Contest becomes her sole goal in life. In both the play and the film, Carnelle guides her new seamstress friend, Popeye, through the living room, praising along the way her Aunt Ronelle's "special touch," the antique spinning wheel that her celebrated aunt had "fixed . . . up" (*CPI* 151). Henley conjures in audiences' minds another fairy tale figure who pricked her finger on an old artifact like this, a spinning wheel owned by Rumpelstiltskin, the dwarfish villain who demanded that another beauty spin gold. Like Rumpelstiltskin and Old Granddaddy in *Crimes*, Ronelle, though an absent character in both the play and film, spawns resentment in her children: Delmount refers to his mother, in storybook fashion, as "mean," a spiteful monster, an "ape" (167). The film alludes to Ronelle's famous medical case, in which doctors had operated on her cancer, replacing her pituitary gland with a monkey's, thus causing her to "grow long, black hairs all over her body . . . just like an ape" (151), but only the play delves deeply into the sick relationship this monster-mother maintained with her children prior to her death. Certainly, the film humorously capitalizes on this supernatural description of Delmount and Elain's "ape" mother, but sadly, it ignores her significance to Henley's over all theme of transformation, one which the playwright threads into her main plot. Omitting in the film *Miss Firecracker* Delmount's claim that his mother "turned herself into a monkey to get at us—just to be mean" (*CPI* 167), Henley inspires her audiences to be less prepared to attach a negative motive to Aunt Ronelle's unusual metamorphosis.

In *Firecracker*, the play, Carnelle and Delmount undergo positive change, and so too does Elain to some extent, but Aunt Ronelle's metamorphosis proves faulty. This transformation does not heal or integrate, but is monstrous, dismembering. Her transformation, unlike her son's in which his dreams of fragmented women become whole, may have been stimulated by malice, or so Delmount charges. Again, Gregor Samsa's metamorphosis comes to mind. In transferring this play from the stage to the screen, Henley's Aunt Ronelle's story may echo Gregor's, for both of them metamorphose toward death, not life. Transformation through love remains one of Henley's dominant themes, but in Ronelle, the playwright and screenwriter reverses the order of positive metamorphoses. Indeed, the scenes in the film *Miss Firecracker* that introduce Ronelle's exploits seem superfluous, unengaging, and not noticeably or understandably connected to Henley's theme of transformation. The film refuses to challenge audiences, though the play does, to contemplate Aunt Ronelle or her motives. Thus, the bizarre details of the absent antagonist's metamorphosis instigate rollicking laughter, but not thoughtfulness.

With Delmount, however, a positive transformation occurs due to the influence of Popeye, who swears that her heart gets "hot" (*CPI* 170) at the sight of him and who appears unaffected by his reputation, his "checkered past" (153), which Carnelle details for her. To her, Delmount is Prince Charming, this southern gentleman who fights for woman's honor, no matter the consequence, even if it costs his freedom. Indeed, one such bout already landed him in an insane asylum:

DELMOUNT: ... I challenged that man to a duel! A duel! I can't help it if the weapons he chose were broken bottles! It was an honorable act in defense of a woman with beautiful, warm, bronze skin. I do not regret it. (162)

Cutting a "romantic figure" (153) with his Byronic poetry, his wild eyes and hair, Delmount, in both *The Miss Firecracker Contest* and *Miss Firecracker* is described as having a "strange, obsessive eye for beauty" (171). In the film we see him fight for the cause of beauty and woman by thrashing Ronnie Wayne for throwing popcorn and ice at Carnelle during one of her numbers at the beauty pageant.

Functioning as a defender as well as healer, Popeye becomes a helpmeet for several characters. Most noticeably she heals Delmount Williams. In both the play and the film, Henley endows her seamstress, Popeye, with magical powers. Hearing voices through her eyes, Popeye has abilities not unlike Meg's in *Crimes of the Heart*. Whereas society may consider Delmount a misfit, dysfunctional, insane, or just a vile "toad," as Elain calls him at one point, Popeye sees in him beauty. Under her positive influence, he is transformed, an action as miraculous as changing bullfrogs into doctors and nurses or frog queens donned with leaf capes. Indeed, this frog motif figures significantly in the film, but not to the complicated degree that it pervades the play. In the play, every major character carries with him or her "frog" connotations or associations. With Popeye, Delmount feels whole, as symbolically suggested by Delmount's dreams, which lose their terror as his visions of Popeye replace nightmares of fragmented women. In the play, and echoed in the film, Delmount announces his transformation:

DELMOUNT: Oh, Popeye! (*He grabs her and kisses her full on the mouth.*) I've been dreaming about you at night. I see you riding across the sea with a host of green whales. Popeye, I love you. (*CPI* 204)

Though the play complicates Delmount's character by romantically involving him with Popeye, Henley's *Miss Firecracker* the film adds an element of surprise by casting Alfre Woodard in the role of Popeye. Amazingly, and not very realistically, the film suggests no racial tension occurs as a result of this coupling. Ironically, and unbelievably, the film's characters ignore the possibility of miscegenation. Yazoo City appears blind to racism, but only with this one relationship. This oddity seems ironic, considering the film's periodic allusions to issues of race: Carnelle just knows that she will defeat black or Asian contestants, and Elain laments the quality of the pageant's "going down, down, down" once blacks enter as contestants (*CPI* 168). Racism as a theme in *Miss Firecracker*, however, remains relegated to the fringes of the film, treated somewhat similarly as wife battering in *Crimes*, yet audiences remain uncomfortably aware of its presence, thinking that at any moment an embarrassing incident will occur. Perhaps Ronnie Wayne may turn his attentions from throwing items at Carnelle to harassing Popeye.

Film audiences are made to feel uncomfortable also with the theme of incest, which Henley insinuates subtly into the plot of Miss Firecracker. This idea, more radical than Delmount's romantic interest in a black woman and more bizarre than Popeye's being an outfitter of bullfrogs, remains in audiences' minds. Though the play contain some intimations of incest between Delmount and his sister, Elain, the film exacerbates the problem by inserting a bedside scene in which Elain crawls onto her brother's bed to comfort him after one of his ghastly nightmares. What soothes Delmount, however, causes the audience anxiety and discomfort. Even the scene in which the pair dances may contribute to this angst. Delmount Williams appears to be a modern-day equivalent of Faulkner's Quentin Compson. Obsessively concerned with his sister's behavior and her supposed betrayal of him, especially as regards Elain's marriage, which she refuses to end, Delmount strikes an awkward chord with theater audiences. Why should a brother devote so much of his energy and thought to convincing his sister to end her marriage? Why then does Delmount repeatedly label Elain as unreliable, her "trademark" (*CPI* 166), when he rants about her marriage?

Unlike the beauty, Elain, Popeye earns "Cinderella" status in her own right, finding her Prince Charming in the character of Delmount. Their courtship, one of the funniest and most appealing in the film, retells other legends as well. When explaining to Carnelle that she learned to sew by making costumes for bullfrogs, Popeye presents herself as a kind-hearted princess, one not repelled by the frog-prince, Delmount, made ugly by his checkered past. In some ways, the casting of a black woman in this role complements Henley's vision that worth cannot be measured by one's face. Black skin is but another symbolic "dress" of the humanity within a person.

Intricately interweaving images and associations, Henley fashions "Cinderellas" from unusual angles and perspectives. Elain, as described above, seems to epitomize the fairy tale princess the morning (or decade) after the ball. In both the play and the film, she is the only character who really does get to go to the ball (having captured the Miss Firecracker title), but, now trapped with her prince, she remains disappointed. The Elain of the film will return to the castle and the clocks, stuck in time. The Elain of *The Miss Firecracker Contest*, however, may free herself, at least momentarily, by meeting her new but diseased prince, Mac Sam, underneath a mimosa tree. Mac Sam's disintegration parallels Gregor's, perhaps, for throughout the play, he noticeably loses his health and his body. Yet he is also the character to offer Carnelle "eternal grace" (*CPI* 202). With the play's audience privy to information of which Elain remains unaware, we realize that she may be inheriting something after all, a venereal disease, but at least, she may "have some real fun before [she] drop[s] dead off this planet" (199).

Carnelle, aided by her very own fairy godmother, Popeye, rises to the film's platform to present her routine, dressed in her red star-spangled costume and twirling a patriotic red, white, and blue wooden rifle. Carnelle, both an ugly duckling and a sort of frog prince herself, having lived metaphorically in rags, her soiled reputation finds redemption, ironically, in not winning the "Miss Firecracker" Contest. Only then do her inner strength and beauty emerge—interior beauty rather than a surface beauty. In the play, *The Miss Firecracker Contest*, Carnelle gets her chance to wear Elain's antebellum red dress, a metaphorical glass slipper, but it does not fit any more than Cinderella's stepsisters' feet can fit into the glass slipper. Other contestants also attempt to make their bodies fit into their own glass slippers, maiming themselves in the process. For instance, one contestant becomes permanently hunchbacked from incessant piano practice. In her resolve "to follow that float" (*CPI* 197), Henley's protagonist gains respect for herself, realizing that no dress should be worn for a lifetime. In the film, *Miss Firecracker*, Carnelle, wearing both the red dress that she found hidden in Elain's suitcase and her old yellowed cap from childhood, confronts a petrified Elain at the bottom of a staircase. When Carnelle asks for an explanation, Elain responds, "it just wouldn't do . . . because it's mine." Discarding from her head the yellowed, wooly cap, Carnelle adds, "And I guess this is mine . . . but I'm not gonna wear it forever." Thus, Carnelle requires no Cinderella masks, and certainly not the Mardi Gras mask that Elain presented to her earlier as a gift. "I just thought of you when I saw it. You'll have to wear it to a mask ball," Elain had joked (155). The scene indicates that Elain's Cinderella mask of beauty cakes her face, forever locking her in a beauty pose, a position that brittles over time.

The fairy tales discussed here as background to *Miss Firecracker* evince dark and menacing threads. In particular, these stories contain ideas of family cruelty and betrayal, as does *Crimes of the Heart*. Elain, the adored cousin, portrays something close to the "Snow White" queen, bringing the dress with her, but lying, and refusing to relinquish it. Sharing even the possibility of beauty with another woman threatens Carnelle's cousin. The play, however, takes a more generous, more focused view of its characters. In *The*

Miss Firecracker Contest, Elain, more subtly, first forgets to bring the dress, self-centered creature that she is, but then has it sent. Unfortunately, or perhaps fortunately, Carnelle looks terrible in it. Thus, the fault lies not directly with Elain that Carnelle will fail to emerge a fairy tale "Miss Firecracker," for she does deliver the dress. In the play, Henley's protagonist does get her chance with the glass slipper—the red dress—but cannot wear it successfully. Thus, Henley's depiction of Carnelle symbolically suggests elements of both the ugly stepsister as well as the beautiful Cinderella. Though older and less appealing as a character, Elain remains in both the play and the film, ironically, the true story princess after all, the only woman audiences meet who wins the Miss Firecracker contest. Her fate in the film, however, Henley seals with no storybook romance. Finally, by examining these characters in light of their fairy tale counterparts, one appreciates the mythic depth with which Henley crafts her Miss Firecrackers. Both play and film audiences delight in recognizing a familiar story pattern, as they do here. These tales, which appear and reappear in *Miss Firecracker*, have been altered, blended in a way that casts new light on the original tales, marked by their rigidity and pervasive cruelty. They tell stories of regeneration, rebirth, and autonomy.

Being a heroine *may* mean marrying the man of one's dreams; or, it *may* not. Henley's world has room for both kinds of endings, and for the prince charming, who is also a frog prince, and the princess who thinks herself a frog. *Crimes of the Heart* and *Miss Firecracker* prove transformation possible. Whereas the metamorphosis of Kafka's Gregor Samsa leads to death—only a hollow shell evidence that a life existed—Henley's stories predominantly reveal positive changes: new ways of seeing, hearing, becoming whole. Other types of transformations, those from the stage to the screen, open up new avenues for Henley's audiences to explore. Her films teach us the value of the human spirit and inspire us to get through those "real bad days."

Notes

1. Pat Graham's review of the movie characterizes it as "[no]t exactly heavyweight" and charges that the director, Bruce Beresford, "pushed the brittle humor toward coarse cartoon." Paul Attanasio, likewise, asserts that Henley's effort as a screenwriter, though "well-intentioned," proves "misguided," his advice: "Never hire a playwright to do a screen writer's job" (C11).
2. In her interview with Wimmer-Moul, Henley praises Holly Hunter's ability at one time to be "violently enraged" or "real sweet": "I know Holly has the technical facility and the emotional guts," the playwright/screenwriter notes (116). Henley further discusses her technique of fusing a "dark side and a comic side, maintaining that life can be "complicated and beautiful and horrible" at the same time" "To deny either of these is such a loss," says Henley (117).
3. Henley has said that her "favorite characters are the ones who screw up most." When asked to name some, Henley promptly responded, "Well, I do love Meg, and she's insane you know" (Dellasega 257).

Works Cited

Attanasio, Paul. " 'Crime' Doesn't Play." *Washington Post*, 12 December 1986, C11, final edition.
Betsko, Kathleen, and Rachel Koenig. "Beth Henley." *Interviews with Contemporary Women Playwrights*. New York: Beech Tree Books, 1987. 211–222.
Dellasega, Mary. "Beth Henley." *Speaking on Stage*. Eds. Philip Kolin and Colby Kullman. Tuscaloosa: University of Alabama Press, 1996. 251–259.
Ebert, Roger. "Crimes of the Heart." Rev. of *Crimes of the Heart*. 12 December 1986. www.suntimes.com/ebert/ebertreviews/1986/12/121910.html. 26 June 2001.
Gilbert, Sandra M., and Susan Gubar. *The Madwoman in the Attic: The Woman Writer and the Nineteenth-Century Literary Imagination*. New Haven, Conn.: Yale University Press, 1984.
Graham, Pat. "Crimes of the Heart." Film Rev. capsule of *Crimes of the Heart*. 2001. onfilm.chireader.com/MovieCaps/C/CR/02268_CRIMES_OF_THE_HEART.html. 26 June 2001.
Guerra, Jonnie. "Beth Henley: Female Quest and the Family-Play Tradition." *Making a Spectacle: Feminist Essays on Contemporary Women's Theatre*. Ed. Lynda Hart. Ann Arbor: University of Michigan Press, 1989. 118–130.
Haedicke, Janet V. " 'A Population and Theater at Risk': Battered Women in Henley's *Crimes of the Heart* and Shepard's *A Lie of the Mind*." *Modern Drama* 36 (1993): 83–95.
Henley, Beth, adapt. *Crimes of the Heart*. Dir. Bruce Beresford. De Laurentiis Entertainment, 1986.
———. adapt. *Miss Firecracker*. Based on her play, *The Miss Firecracker Contest*. Dir. Thomas Schlamme. Corsair Pictures. 1989.
Hinson, Hal. " 'Firecracker' Ignited by Hunter, Robbins." *Washington Post*, 12 May 1989, D7, final edition.
Jaehne, Karen. "Beth's Beauties." *Film Comment* 25 (May–June 1988): 9–14.
Kullman, Colby H. "Beth Henley's Marginalized Heroines." *Studies in American Drama, 1945–Present* 8 (1993): 21–28.
Lasch, Christopher. *The Culture of Narcissism: American Life in an Age of Diminishing Expectations*. New York: W. W. Norton, 1978.
Lerner, Harriet Goldhor. *The Dance of Anger: A Woman's Guide to Changing the Patterns of Intimate Relationships*, New York: Harper and Row, 1985.
McDonald, Robert L. " 'A Blaze of Glory': Image and Self-Promotion in Henley's *The Miss Firecracker Contest*." *Southern Quarterly* 37.2 (1999): 151–157.
Parker, Randy. "Miss Firecracker." Rev. of *Miss Firecracker*. 1989. Netscape, Internet Movie Database, 1996 us.imdb.com/Reviews/51/5131. 26 June 2001.
Renner, Pamela. "The Mellowing of *Miss Firecracker*." *American Theatre* 15.9 (1998): 18–19.
Toscan, Richard. "Themes and the Meanings of Plays." *The Playwriting Seminars: The Full-Length Play, 1995–99*. Virginia Commonwealth University. www.vcu.edu./artweb/playwriting/ theme.html. 26 June 2001
Wimmer-Moul, Cynthia. "Beth Henley." *The Playwright's Art: Conversations with Contemporary American Dramatists*. Ed. Jackson R. Bryer. New Brunswick, N.J.: Rutgers University Press, 1995. 102–122.

Bibliography

Primary Sources

Plays

Abundance. New York: Dramatists Play Service, 1991.

Am I Blue. New York: Dramatists Play Service, 1982.

Collected Plays: Volume I, 1980–1989. Lyme, N.H.: Smith and Kraus, 2000.

Collected Plays: Volume II, 1990–1999. Lyme, N.H.: Smith and Kraus, 2000.

Crimes of the Heart. New York: Dramatists Play Service, 1982.

The Debutante Ball. New York: Dramatists Play Service, 1991.

Four Plays [*The Wake of Jamey Foster*, *The Miss Firecracker Contest*, *The Lucky Spot*, *Abundance*]. Portsmouth, N.H. and London: Heinemann/Methuen, 1992.

Impossible Marriage. New York: Dramatists Play Service, 1999.

The Lucky Spot: A Play. New York: Dramatists Play Service, 1987.

The Miss Firecracker Contest: A Play. New York: Dramatists Play Service, 1985.

The Wake of Jamie Foster. New York: Dramatists Play Service, 1983.

Motion Pictures

Come West with Me. Dir. Marleen Gorris. Screenplay by Beth Henley, based on her play *Abundance*. Twentieth-Century Fox, 1998.

Crimes of the Heart. Dir. Bruce Beresford. Screenplay by Beth Henley, based on her play. De Laurentiis Entertainment, 1986.

Miss Firecracker. Dir. Thomas Schlamme. Screenplay by Beth Henley, based on her play *The Miss Firecracker Contest.* Corsair Pictures, 1989.

Nobody's Fool. Dir. Evelyn Purcell. Screenplay by Beth Henley. Island Pictures, 1986.

True Stories. Dir. David Byrne. Screenplay by David Byrne, Beth Henley, and Stephen Tobolowsky. Warner Bros., 1986.

Interviews and Secondary Sources

Interviews and Profiles

Berkvist, Robert. "Act I: the Pulitzer, Act II: Broadway." *New York Times,* 25 October 1981, sec. 2: 4+, late city final edition.

Betsko, Kathleen, and Rachel Koenig. "Beth Henley." *Interviews with Contemporary Women Playwrights.* New York: Beech Tree Books, 1987. 211–221.

Corliss, Richard. "I Go with What I'm Feeling." *Time,* 8 February 1982, 80.

Dellasega, Mary. "Beth Henley." *Speaking on Stage: Interviews with Contemporary American Playwrights.* Eds. Philip C. Kolin and Colby H. Kullman. Tuscaloosa and London: University of Alabama Press, 1996. 250–259.

Green, Alexis, ed. *Women Who Write Plays: Interviews with Contemporary American Dramatists.* Lyme, N.H.: Smith and Kraus, 2000.

Haller, Scot. "Her First Play, Her First Pulitzer Prize." *Saturday Review* 8 (November 1981): 40–44.

Isenberg, Barbara. "She'd Rather Do It Herself." *Los Angeles Times,* 11 July 1993, Calendar, 5+, home edition.

Jones, John Griffin, ed. "Beth Henley." *Mississippi Writers Talking: Interviews with Eudora Welty, Shelby Foote, Elizabeth Spencer, Barry Hannah, Beth Henley.* Jackson: University Press of Mississippi, 1982. 169–190.

Pogrebin, Robin. "Sharing a History as Well as a Play." *New York Times,* 11 October 1998, sec. 2, 5, late edition.

Renner, Pamela. "The Mellowing of *Miss Firecracker.*" *American Theatre* 15 (1998): 18–19.

Rosenfeld, Megan. "Beth Henley's World of Southern Discomfort: The Comic Perspective Behind the Playwright's Crimes of the Heart." *Washington Post*, 12 December 1986, C1, final edition.

Shirley, Don. "Crossroads: Beth Henley. Looking into the Future with Influential Figures in the World of Arts and Entertainment; Stage-Struck in Screen City." *Los Angeles Times*, 5 January 1999. F1.

Weiss, Hedy. "Beth Henley Takes the Director's Chair for *Control Freaks*. *Chicago Sun-Times*, 20 September 1992, Show, 1, five star sports final.

Wimmer-Moul, Cynthia. "Beth Henley." *The Playwright's Art: Conversations with Contemporary American Dramatists*. Ed. Jackson R. Bryer. New Brunswick, N.Y.: Rutgers University Press, 1995. 102–122.

Performance Reviews (Reviews are grouped by play as shown)

Am I Blue

Am I Blue (first produced in Dallas, Texas, at Southern Methodist University Margo Jones Theatre, fall 1974; produced by Circle Repertory Company, New York, 10 January 1982).

Beaufort, John. "Sensitive One-Act Plays at the Circle Rep." Review of *Am I Blue*, Circle Repertory Company, New York. *Christian Science Monitor*, 19 January 1982, 19, midwestern edition.

Crimes of the Heart

Crimes of the Heart (first produced in Louisville, Kentucky, at Actors Theatre, 18 February 1979; produced off-Broadway by Manhattan Theatre Club, New York, New York, 21 December 1980; produced on Broadway at John Golden Theatre, New York, New York, 4 November 1981; revived off-Broadway at Second Stage Theatre, New York, New York, 17 April 2001).

Barnes, Clive. " 'Crime' Is a Prize Hit That's All Heart." Review of *Crimes of the Heart*, John Golden Theatre, New York. *New York Post*, 5 November 1981. Rpt. in *New York Theatre Critics Reviews* 42 (1981): 137–138.

Beaufort, John. "A Play That Proves There's No Explaining Awards." Review of *Crimes of the Heart*, John Golden Theatre, New York. *Christian Science Monitor*, 9 November 1981. Rpt. in *New York Theatre Critics Reviews* 42 (1981): 137.

Brantley, Ben. "Granddaddy Is in a Coma, and That's the Good News." Review of *Crimes of the Heart*, Second Stage Theatre, New York. *New York Times*, 17 April 2001, B1+, national edition.

Brustein, Robert. "Broadway Inches Forward." Review of *Crimes of the Heart*, Manhattan Theatre Club, New York. *New Republic*, 23 December 1981, 25–27.

Cunningham, Dennis. Review of *Crimes of the Heart*, John Golden Theatre, New York. WCBS-TV2, November 1981. Rpt. in *New York Theatre Critics Reviews* 42 (1981): 141.

Dominguez, Robert. " 'Crimes' Does Pay, in Wit & Feeling." Review of *Crimes of the Heart*, Second Stage Theatre, New York. *New York Daily News*, 17 April 2001, 38, sports final edition.

Gardner, Elysa. " 'Crimes' Is an Apt Title for Revival." Review of *Crimes of the Heart*, Second Stage Theatre, New York. *USA Today*, 17 April 2001, 4D, final edition.

Gutman, Les. Review of *Crimes of the Heart*, Second Stage Theatre, New York. CurtainUp.com, April 2001. www.curtainup.com/crimesoftheheart.html.

Kalem, T. E. "Southern Sibs." Review of *Crimes of the Heart*, John Golden Theatre, New York. *Time*, 16 November 1981, 122. Rpt. in *New York Theatre Critics Reviews* 42 (1981): 140.

Kissel, Howard. "Crimes of the Heart." Review of *Crimes of the Heart*, John Golden Theatre, New York. *Women's Wear Daily*, 6 November 1981. Rpt. in *New York Theatre Critics Reviews* 42 (1981): 140.

Kroll, Jack. "Theatre." Review of *Crimes of the Heart*, John Golden Theatre, New York. *Newsweek*, 16 November 1981. Rpt. in *New York Theatre Critics Reviews* 42 (1981): 139.

Nelsen, Don. " 'Crimes' Is Heartwarming." Review of *Crimes of the Heart*, John Golden Theatre, New York. *New York Daily News*, 5 November 1981. Rpt. in *New York Theatre Critics Reviews* 42 (1981): 139.

Oliver, Edith. "The Theatre Off Broadway." Review of *Crimes of the Heart*, Manhattan Theatre Club, New York. *New Yorker*, 12 January 1981, 81–82.

Rich, Frank. "Beth Henley's *Crimes of the Heart*." Review of *Crimes of the Heart*, John Golden Theatre, New York. *New York Times*, 5 November 1981, C21. Rpt. in *New York Theatre Critics Reviews* 42 (1981): 136–137.

———. " 'Crimes of Heart' Comedy about 3 Sisters." Review of *Crimes of the Heart,* Manhattan Theatre Club, New York. *New York Times*, 22 December 1980, C1, final late city edition.

Sauvage, Leo. "On Stage: Reaching for Laughter." Review of *Crimes of the Heart*, John Golden Theatre, New York. *New Leader*, 30 November 1981, 19–20.

Snow, Leida. Review of *Crimes of the Heart*, John Golden Theatre, New York. WABC-TV7, 4 November 1981. Rpt. in *New York Theatre Critics Reviews* 42 (1981): 141.

Wilson, Edwin. "Beth Henley: Aiming for the Heart." Review of *Crimes of the Heart*. John Golden Theatre, New York. *Wall Street Journal*, 6 November 1981. Rpt. in *New York Theatre Critics Reviews* 42 (1981): 138.

Winer, Linda. "Another Bad Day for the Sisters Magrath." Review of *Crimes of the Heart*, Second Stage Theatre, New York. *Newsday*, 17 April 2001, B2.

The Miss Firecracker Contest

The Miss Firecracker Contest (first produced in Burbank, California, at Victory Theatre, Spring, 1980; produced off-Broadway at Manhattan Theatre Club, New York, 1 May 1984).

Beaufort, John. " 'Miss Firecracker Contest': Beth Henley's Latest Is Lush, Wacky Drama." Review of *The Miss Firecracker Contest*, Manhattan Theatre Club, New York. *Christian Science Monitor*, 6 June 1984, 22, arts and leisure section.

Jones, Welton. "New York Theater Fare." Review of *The Miss Firecracker Contest*, Manhattan Theatre Club, New York. *San Diego Union-Tribune*, 24 June 1984, E6, entertainment section.

Nightingale, Benedict. "A Landscape That Is Unmistakably by Henley." Review of *The Miss Firecracker Contest*, Manhattan Theatre Club, New York. *New York Times*, 3 June 1984, sec. 2, 3, final late city edition.

Oliver, Edith. "The Theatre Off Broadway." Review of *The Miss Firecracker Contest*, Manhattan Theatre Club, New York. *New Yorker*, 11 June 1984, 112.

Rich, Frank. " 'Firecracker,' a Beth Henley Comedy." Review of *The Miss Firecracker Contest*, Manhattan Theatre Club, New York. *New York Times*, 28 May 1984, A11, final late city edition.

Ringel, Eleanor. "*Miss Firecracker* Doesn't Have Spark despite Stellar Cast." *Atlanta Constitution*, 12 May 1989, C1.

Schickel, Richard. "Jagged Flashes of Inspiration." Review of *The Miss Firecracker Contest*, Manhattan Theatre Club, New York. *Time*, 11 June 1984, 80.

The Wake of Jamey Foster

The Wake of Jamey Foster (first produced in Hartford, Connecticut, at Hartford Stage Theatre, 1 Jan. 1982; produced on Broadway at Eugene O'Neill Theatre, 14 October 1982).

Rich, Frank. "Beth Henley, 'Wake of Jamey Foster.' " Review of *The Wake of Jamey Foster*, Eugene O'Neill Theater, New York. *New York Times*, 15 October 1982, C3 final late city edition.

Sauvage, Leo. "On Stage: Dark and Shallow Visions." Review of *The Wake of Jamey Foster*, Eugene O'Neill Theater, New York. *New Leader*, 15 November 1982, 20.

The Debutante Ball

The Debutante Ball (first produced in Costa Mesa, California, at South Coast Repertory, April 1985; produced by Manhattan Theatre Club, New York, 26 April 1988; produced at the Powerhouse Theater at Vassar College, Poughkeepsie, New York, 28 July 1988).

Billington, Michael. "A Cracked Belle." Review of *The Debutante Ball*. *Guardian*, 1 June 1989, 24.

Hagen, Bill. "Coast Rep Plays: 'Ball' Needs Work; 'Rum' Uninspired." Review of *The Debutante Ball*, South Coast Repertory, Costa Mesa, Calif. *San Diego Union Tribune*, D6.

Jones, Welton. "Henley's Southern Voice Is Shrill in 'Debutante Ball.' " Review of *The Debutante Ball*, South Coast Repertory, Costa Mesa, Calif. *San Diego Union-Tribune*, 13 April 1985, D10.

Sullivan, Dan. "All Odds, No Evens at the 'Ball.' " Review of *The Debutante Ball*, South Coast Repertory, Costa Mesa, Calif. *Los Angeles Times*, 11 April 1985, part 6, 3, home edition.

The Lucky Spot

The Lucky Spot (first produced in Williamstown, Massachusetts, at Williamstown Theatre Festival, summer, 1986; produced on Broadway at City Center Theatre, 9 April 1987).

Beaufort, John. " 'Lucky Spot': Offbeat Comedy by Beth Henley." Review of *The Lucky Spot*, Manhattan Theatre Club, New York. *Christian Science Monitor*, 30 April 1987, 30, arts and leisure section.

Fein, Esther B. "Role Call: Waif, Wife, Drummer Girl." Review of *The Lucky Spot*, Manhattan Theatre Club, New York. *New York Times*, 26 April 1987, sec. 2, 5, final late city edition.

Oliver, Edith. "The Theatre." Review of *The Lucky Spot*, Manhattan Theatre Club, New York. *New Yorker*, 11 May 1987, 80–82.

Rich, Frank. "*Lucky Spot* by Beth Henley." Review of *The Lucky Spot*, Manhattan Theatre Club, New York. *New York Times*, 29 April 1987, C22, final late city edition.

Simon, John. Review of *Lucky Spot*, Manhattan Theatre Club, New York. *New Yorker*, 11 May 1987, 82–84.

Abundance

Abundance (first produced by the South Coast Repertory, Costa Mesa, California, 21 April 1989; produced by the Manhattan Theatre Club, New York, 4 October 1990).

Brustein, Robert. "She-Plays, American Style." Review of *Abundance*, Manhattan Theatre Club, New York. *The New Republic*, 17 December 1990, 28–29. Rpt. in *Reimagining American Theatre*. New York: Hill and Wang, 1991. 104–108.

Drake, Sylvie. "Henley's 'Abundance' Goes West with a New-Found Maturity." Review of *Abundance*, South Coast Repertory, Costa Mesa, Calif. *Los Angeles Times*, 24 April 1989, part 6, 1, home edition.

Jones, Welton. "Two Mail-Order Brides Are 'Abundance'; Premier Work at South Coast through May 25." Review of *Abundance*, South Coast Repertory, Costa Mesa, Calif. 26 April 1989, E4.

Kirkpatrick, Melanie. "Asians in America." Review of *Abundance*, Manhattan Theatre Club, New York. *Wall Street Journal*, 9 November 1990, A8.

Kramer, Mimi. "Picturing Abundance." Review of *Abundance*, Manhattan Theatre Club, New York. *New Yorker*, 12 November 1990, 105–106.

Rich, Frank. " 'Abundance,' Beth Henley's Revisionist Women." Review of *Abundance*, Manhattan Theatre Club, New York. *New York Times*, 31 October 1990, C15, final late city edition.

Scher, Valerie. " 'Abundance' Blends Western Melodrama, Feminism." Review of *Abundance*, South Coast Repertory, Costa Mesa, Calif. *San Diego Union-Tribune*, 24 April 1989, C7.

Simon, John. "Yo, Kay!" Review of *Abundance*, Manhattan Theatre Club, New York. *New York*, 12 November 1990, 92–93.

Sterns, Daniel Patrick. "Two Powerful Tales of Greed Gone Wild." Review of *Abundance*, South Coast Repertory, Costa Mesa, Calif. *USA Today*, 25 May 1989, 5D.

Winer, Linda. "Beth Henley's 'Abundance' in a Bizarre Old West." Review of *Abundance*, Manhattan Theatre Club, New York. *Newsday*, 31 October 1990, part II, 2, final edition.

Signature

Signature (first produced by New York Stage and Film Company, Poughkeepsie, New York, 1990; produced by Charlotte Repertory Theatre, Charlotte, North Carolina, 1995; produced by Passage Theater Company, Mill Hill Playhouse, Trenton, New Jersey, May 1996).

Klein, Alvin. "Hooray for Hollywood? More like 'Horrors!' " Review of *Signature*, Passage Theater Company, Mill Hill Playhouse, Trenton, N.J. *New York Times*, 12 May 1996, B12, national edition.

Control Freaks

Control Freaks (first produced by Center Theater, Chicago, Illinois, 20 September 1992; produced by the Met Theatre, Los Angeles, California, 19 July 1993).

Christianson, Richard. " 'Control Freaks' Deviates from Taste, Subtlety." Review of *Control Freaks*, Center Theater, Chicago, Ill. *Chicago Tribune*, 22 November 1992, 22, final sports edition.

Jacobs, Tom. Review of *Control Freaks*, Met Theater, Los Angeles, Calif. *Daily Variety*, 21 July 1993.

Shirley, Don. " 'Freaks' Slips at End but It's a Fun Ride." Review of *Control Freaks*, Met Theater, Los Angeles, Calif. *Los Angeles Times*, 19 July 1993, F1, home edition.

Smith, Sid. "Playwright's Progress: Beth Henley Makes a Reluctant Debut as a Director with *Control Freaks*." *Chicago Tribune*, 20 September 1992, sec. 13, 12.

Weiss, Hedy. "Henley's 'Control Freaks' Doesn't Deserve a Stage." Review of *Control Freaks*, Center Theater, Chicago, Ill. *Chicago Sun-Times*, 22 September 1992, sec. 2, 32, five star sports final edition.

Revelers

Revelers (first produced by New York Stage and Film company, Poughkeepsie, New York, 1994; produced by Center Theater, Chicago, Ill, 1996).

Weiss, Hedy. "Henley's 'Revelers' No Fun at All." Review of *Revelers*, Center Theater, Chicago, Ill. *Chicago Sun-Times*, 10 1996, 34, late sports final edition.

L-Play

L-Play (produced by the Berkshire Theatre Festival, Stockbridge, Massachusetts, 1995; benefit performance at Met Theatre, Los Angeles, California, 1996).

Seligsohn, Leo. "The L in Confusion, Beth Henley Veers into the Theater of the Absurd." Review of *L-Play*, Berkshire Theatre Festival, Stockbridge, Mass. *Newsday*, 27 August 1996, part II, B7.

Siegel, Ed. "*L-Play* Is a Lifeless Lemon, Largely Lackluster, Leaden." Review of *L-Play*, Berkshire Theatre Festival, Stockbridge, Mass. *Boston Globe*, 28 August 1996, C5, city edition.

Sommer, Elyse. "Going Places in the Berkshires: A New Theater, a New Play by Beth Henley." 25 August 1996. Review of *L-Play*, Berkshire Theatre Festival, Stockbridge, Mass. *CurtainUp: The Internet Theater Magazine of Reviews, Features, Annotated Listings*. www.geocities.com/Broadway/1068/lplays.html.

Impossible Marriage

Impossible Marriage (produced off-Broadway by Roundabout Theatre Company, New York, 15 October 1998).

Brantley, Ben. "Fairies Adrift in Love's Garden." Review of *Impossible Marriage*, Roundabout Theatre Company, Laura Pels Theater, New York. *New York Times*, 16 October 1998, E1, final late edition.

Isherwood, Charles. Review of *Impossible Marriage*, Roundabout Theatre Company, Laura Pels Theater, New York. *Variety*, 19 October 1998, 84.

Karem, Edward. "Verdict Misadventure." Review of *Impossible Marriage*, Roundabout Theatre Company, Laura Pels Theater, New York. *Times* (London), 4 November 1998, features.

Kilian, Michael. "Perfect Marriage Collaboration of Playwright Henley and Actress Hunter Brings Big Rewards." Review of *Impossible Marriage*. *Chicago Tribune*, 3 December 1998, sec. 5, 10B.

Lyons, Donald. "Theater: No Faith in Love and Charity." Review of *Impossible Marriage*, Roundabout Theatre Company, Laura Pels Theater, New York. *Wall Street Journal*, 21 October 1998, A20.

O'Toole, Fintan. "New Georgia Play Is Just Peachy; Hunter's a Hoot Is Henley's Latest." Review of *Impossible Marriage*, Roundabout Theatre Company, Laura Pels Theater, New York. *New York Daily News*, 16 October 1998, 59.

Ridley, Clifford A. "Eccentrics Draped in Wisteria." Review of *Impossible Marriage*, Roundabout Theatre Company, Laura Pels Theater, New York. *Philadelphia Inquirer*, 18 October 1998, F10.

Simon, John. "The Boys in the Sand." Review of *Impossible Marriage*, Roundabout Theatre Company, Laura Pels Theater, New York. *New York*, 26 October 1998, 82–83.

Sommer, Elyse. "A *CurtainUp* Review of *Impossible Marriage*." Review of *Impossible Marriage*, Roundabout Theatre Company, Laura Pels Theater, New York. 18 October 1998. *CurtainUp: The Internet Theater Magazine of Reviews, Features, Annotated Listings.* geocities.com/Broadway/1068/imposs.html

Stearns, David Patrick. "Star Power Can't Save Henley's Troubled *Impossible Marriage*." Review of *Impossible Marriage*, Roundabout Theatre Company, Laura Pels Theater, New York. *USA Today*, 20 October 1998, D4, final edition.

Winer, Linda. "A Perky Personality Marries." Review of *Impossible Marriage*, Roundabout Theatre Company, Laura Pels Theater, New York. *Newsday*, 16 October 1998, B2.

Family Week

Family Week (produced by Century Theater, New York, 10–16 April 2000).

Henderson, Kathy. "Best Beth: Playwright Beth Henley Celebrates *Family Week*." 11 April 2000. *TheatreMania.com*. www.theatermania.com/news/feature/index.cfm?story=484&cid=1.

Isherwood, Charles. Review of *Family Week*, Century Center, New York. *Variety*, 17 April 2000, 34.

Paller, Michael. "Getting the Family Together; a Clan Converges on One of Its Casualties." Review of *Family Week*, Century Center, New York. *Newsday*, 11 April 2000, B9.

Sommer, Elyse. "A *CurtainUp* Review of *Family Week*." April 2000. *CurtainUp: The Internet Theater Magazine of Reviews, Features, Annotated Listings.* www.curtainup.com/familyweek.html.

Weber, Bruce. "Plan Your Family Reunion in Rehab." Review of *Family Week*, Century Center, New York. *New York Times*, 11 April 2000, B1(N).

Film Reviews

Crimes of the Heart

Crimes of the Heart. Dir. Bruce Beresford. Screenplay by Beth Henley, based on her play. De Laurentiis Entertainment, 1986.

Ansen, David. "When Ditsyness Was in Flower." *Newsweek*, 22 December 1986, 75.

Attansio, Paul. " 'Crimes' Doesn't Play." *Washington Post*, 12 December 1986, C11, final edition.

Canby, Vincent. "Henley's 'Crimes of the Heart.' " *New York Times*, 12 December 1986, C19, final late city edition.

Ebert, Roger. "Crimes of the Heart." *Roger Ebert on Movies*, 12 December 1986. www.suntimes.com/ebert/ebertreviews/1986/12/121910.html.

Kauffmann, Stanley. "The Three Sisters." *The New Republic*, 2 February 1987, 26–27.

Schickel, Richard. "Once a Comedy, Now an Elegy." *Time*, 22 December 1986, 70.

Sterritt, David. "Performances Give Lift to 'Crimes of the Heart.' " *Christian Science Monitor*, 19 December 1986, 25, arts and leisure section.

Nobody's Fool

Nobody's Fool. Dir. Evelyn Purcell. Screenplay by Beth Henley. Island Pictures, 1986.

Base, Ron. "Portrait of Life in the Weird Lane." *Toronto Star*, 14 November 1986, D14, final edition.

Canby, Vincent. "Nobody's Fool." *New York Times*, 7 November 1986, C18, final late city edition.

Ebert, Roger. "Nobody's Fool." *Roger Ebert on Movies*, 7 November 1986. www.suntimes.com/ebert/ebertreviews/1986/11/115858.html.

Freedman, Samuel G. "Beth Henley Writes a 'Real, Real Personal' Movie." *New York Times*, 2 November 1986, sec. 2, 1+, final late city edition.

Hagen, Bill. "Henley's 'Nobody's Fool" Captures Small-Town Ways." *San Diego Union-Tribune*, 10 November 1986, D9.

Kauffmann, Stanley. "Nobody's Fool." *The New Republic*, 15 December 1986, 22–23.

Rafferty, Terrence. "Nobody's Fool." *Savvy*, 8 January 1987, 67.

True Stories

True Stories. Dir. David Byrne. Screenplay by David Byrne, Beth Henley, and Stephen Tobolowsky. Warner Bros., 1986.

Ebert, Roger. "True Stories." *Roger Ebert on Movies*, 31 October 1986. www.suntimes.com/ebert/ebertreviews/1986/10/114718.html.

Elliott, David. " 'True Stories' Appear to Byrne with Fresh Charm." *San Diego Union-Tribune*, 10 November 1986, C4.

Hagen, Bill. "Byrne's 'True Stories' Rings False." *San Diego Union-Tribune*, 18 November 1986, D9.

Kauffmann, Stanley. "True Stories." *The New Republic*, 10 November 1986, 26.

Sterritt, David. " 'True Stories': Another Plus for David Byrne." *Christian Science Monitor*, 9 October 1986, 25, arts and leisure.

Miss Firecracker

Miss Firecracker. Dir. Thomas Schlamme. Screenplay by Beth Henley, based on her play *The Miss Firecracker Contest*. Corsair Pictures, 1989.

Clark, Mike. " 'Miss Firecracker': Pixilated in Dixieland." *USA Today*, 28 April 1989, 4D.

Corliss, Richard. "Dreams to Avoid." *Time*, 1 May 1989, 68.

Darling, Lynn. " 'Miss Firecracker' Crackles with Charm." *Newsday*, 28 April 1989, 3, weekend.

Ebert, Roger. "Miss Firecracker." *Roger Ebert on Movies*, 28 April, 1989. www.suntimes.com/ebert/ebertreviews/1989/04/351213.html.

Hinson, Hal. " 'Firecracker': Ignited by Hunter, Robbins." *Washington Post*, 12 May 1989, D7, final edition.

Jaehne, Karen. " 'Miss Firecracker' Goes Pow! Beth's Beauties." *Film Comment*, 25.3 (1989): 9–15.

James, Caryn. "Seeking Redemption in a Beauty Pageant." *New York Times*, 28 April 1989, C12, final late city edition.

Kael, Pauline. "The Current Cinema." *New Yorker*, 19 May 1989, 102–104.

Kroll, Jack. "Southern Discomfort." *Newsweek*, 1 May 1989, 75.

Stein, Jeannie. "Into the Night." *Los Angeles Times*, 28 April 1989, sec. 5, 8, home edition.

Sterritt, David. " 'Miss Firecracker' Fizzles—Despite Its Potential." *Christian Science Monitor*, 16 May 1989, 11, arts.

Wilmington, Michael. " 'Miss Firecracker': Beauty in Bursts of Affection." *Los Angeles Times*, 28 April 1989, sec. 6, 16, home edition.

Scholarly Criticism

Burke, Sally. "Beth Henley: Crimes of the Patriarchy." *American Feminist Playwrights: A Critical History*. New York: Twayne, 1996. 193–197.

Gagen, Jean. " 'Most Resembling Unlikeness, and Most Unlike Resemblance': Beth Henley's *Crimes of the Heart* and Chekhov's *Three Sisters*." *Studies in American Drama, 1945–Present* 4 (1989): 119–128.

Guerra, Jonnie. "Beth Henley: Female Quest and the Family-Play Tradition." *Making a Spectacle: Feminist Essays on Contemporary Women's Theater*. Ed. Lynda Hart. Ann Arbor: University of Mich. Press, 1989. 118–130.

Haedicke, Janet V. "A Population (and Theater) at Risk": Battered Women in Henley's *Crimes of the Heart* and Shepard's *A Lie of the Mind*." *Modern Drama* 36 (1993): 83–96.

Harbin, Billy J. "Familial Bonds in the Plays of Beth Henley." *Southern Quarterly* 25.3 (1987): 81–94.

Hargrove, Nancy D. "The Tragicomic Vision of Beth Henley's Drama." *Southern Quarterly* 22.4 (1984): 54–70.

Karpinsky, Joanne B. "The Ghosts of Chekhov's *Three Sisters* Haunt Beth Henley's *Crimes of the Heart*." *Modern American Drama: The Female Canon*. Ed. June Schlueter. London: Associated University Press, 1990. 229–245.

Keyssar, Helene. "Success and Its Limits: Mary O'Malley, Wendy Wasserstein, Nell Dunn, Beth Henley, Catherine Hayes, Marsha Norman." *Feminist Theatre*. New York: Grove, 1985. 148–166.

Kullman, Colby H. "Beth Henley's Marginalized Heroines." *Studies in American Drama, 1945–Present* 8.1 (1993): 21–28.

Laughlin, Karen L. "Criminality, Desire, and Community: A Feminist Approach to Beth Henley's *Crimes of the Heart*." *Women and Performance: A Journal of Feminist Theory* 3:1 (1986): 35–51.

McDonald, Robert L. " 'A Blaze of Glory': Image and Self-Promotion in Henley's *The Miss Firecracker Contest.*" *Southern Quarterly* 37.2 (1999): 151–157.

McDonnell, Lisa J. "Diverse Similitude: Beth Henley and Marsha Norman." *Southern Quarterly* 25.3 (1987): 95–104.

Morrow, Laura. "Orality and Identity in *'Night, Mother* and *Crimes of the Heart.*" *Studies in American Drama, 1945–Present* 3 (1988): 23–39.

Porter, Laurin R. "Women Re-conceived: Changing Perceptions of Women in Contemporary American Drama." *Conference of College Teachers of English Studies* 54 (1989): 53–59.

Shepard, Alan Clarke. "Aborted Rage in Beth Henley's Women." *Modern Drama* 39 (1993): 96–108. Rept. in *States of Rag, Emotional Eruption, Violence, and Social Change.* Eds. Renée R. Curry and Terry L. Allison. New York and London: New York University Press, 1996. 179–194.

Thompson, Lou. "Feeding the Hungry Heart: Food in Beth Henley's *Crimes of the Heart.*" *Southern Quarterly* 30.2–3 (1992): 99–102.

Whited, Lana A. "Suicide in Beth Henley's *Crimes of the Heart* and Marsha Norman's *'Night, Mother.*" *Southern Quarterly* 36.1 (1997): 65–74.

Contributors

Miriam M. Chirico teaches in the Department of English and Foreign Languages at the University of North Florida, where she specializes in dramatic literature. Dr. Chirico has written on other contemporary playwrights such as Wendy Wasserstein and Jose Rivera. The juncture between women and comedy particularly interests her, as does modern retellings of ancient myths.

Julia A. Fesmire is an associate professor of English at Middle Tennessee State University, where she specializes in nineteenth- and twentieth-century English literature. Having practiced law in an earlier life, she also teaches courses in law and literature and legal writing and research. Dr. Fesmire's scholarship focuses primarily on contemporary literature and women's studies.

Rebecca King, assistant professor of English at Middle Tennessee State University, teaches courses in nineteenth- and twentieth-century British and American literature, women's studies, professional writing, and literary theory. Dr. King is currently working on a book about William Godwin, Mary Wollstonecraft, and George Eliot, which examines their responses to the Modern Liberal Project.

Karen L. Laughlin is an associate professor of English at Florida State University where she specializes in modern and American drama, critical theory, and women's studies. Dr. Laughlin's 1986 essay "Criminality, Desire, and Community: A Feminist Approach to Beth Henley's *Crimes of the Heart*" was among the first critical studies of this Henley play. She is also the author of the entry on Henley in the *History of Southern Women's Literature*, forthcoming from LSU Press. Her other publications include *Theatre and Feminist Aesthetics* (1995) and articles on American

Feminist Theatre as well as on the plays of Samuel Beckett, Susan Glaspell, Bertolt Brecht, and others.

Larry G. Mapp, professor of English at Middle Tennessee State University, teaches courses in computer-assisted instruction, southern literature, nineteenth-century American literature, composition, and Romantic literature. Dr. Mapp is currently creating a literature textbook for Mayfield Publishing and continues to write the workbooks that accompany the *Harbrace Handbook*. In 1997 he won the South Atlantic Modern Language Association Outstanding Teaching Award.

Linda Rohrer Paige, associate professor of English, teaches women's literature and modern drama in the Department of Literature and Philosophy, Georgia Southern University. Coeditor of *Southern Women Playwrights: New Essays in Literary History and Criticism* (University of Alabama Press, 2002), Dr. Paige's interests include women playwrights and women in film. Some of her essays appear in *Papers on Language and Literature*, the *Literature/Film Quarterly*, *Studies in Short Fiction*, and the *Journal of Popular Film and Television*.

Gene A. Plunka is professor of English at the University of Memphis, where he teaches courses on modern and contemporary drama. His books include *Peter Shaffer: Roles, Rites, and Rituals in the Theater* (1988); *Jean Genet: The Art and Aesthetics of Risk Taking* (1992); *Antonin Artaud and the Modern Theater* (1994); *Jean-Claude van Itallie and the Off-Broadway Theater* (1999); and, *The Black Comedy of John Guare* (2002). He is currently working on a book about the theater of Beth Henley.

Gary Richards is an assistant professor of English at the University of New Orleans where he teaches southern, American, and African-American literature. His scholarship focuses on gender and sexuality in southern literary production and includes publications on Truman Capote, William Goyen, Carson McCullers, and Alfred Uhry.

Index

Note: Literary works are listed under their authors' names, except for plays by Beth Henley.

Absurdist Theater xvii, 22, 107
Abundance xi, xv, xvi, 44, 58–59, 88–104
Adler, Jacob 49
Adler, Thomas P. 116
Albee, Edward 107
Allison, Dorothy, *Bastard out of Carolina* 45
Am I Blue xi, xii, xv, xviii, 33–34, 35, 48
Andrews, William L, *The Literature of the American South* 45–46
Arquette, Rosanna xii

Beckett, Samuel 107
Berry, Wendell 40
Billington, Michael 15
Bottoms, Stephen J. 94
Brustein, Robert 58, 89, 96
Bryer, Jackson 3

Caldwell, Erskine 45, 46
Camus, Albert 107
Carpenter, David 141
Carroll, Beeson 140
Chase, Truddi, *When Rabbit Howls* 28
Chekhov, Anton xvii, 107, 108–109
    Cherry Orchard, The 3, 108
    Three Sisters, The 108
Chesnut, Mary Boykin, xv, 37, 40

Chirico, Miriam, xiv, 1–31
Chopin, Kate xv, 40
Control Freaks xii, xv, xviii, 2, 19, 20, 24–28, 29, 44, 51–57, 58, 59
Cooks, John W. 10
Coward, Rosalind 99
Crimes of the Heart (film) xvii, 129, 130–144
Crimes of the Heart (play) xi, xii, xiv, xv, xvii, xviii, 1, 2, 6–7, 8, 15, 25, 33, 34, 44, 48, 57, 58, 59, 88, 105–127, 133–134, 136–137, 139, 141–142
Cross, Christopher xi

Debutante Ball, The xii, xv, xviii, 2, 15–19, 20, 24, 36–37, 48
Dellasega, Mary xii
Demastes, William W. 108
Depressive Personality Disorder 118–120
Durham, Ayne Cantrell 107

Early, Tony xiv, 47
Ebersole, Gary 97
Ebert, Roger 131
Elam, Diane xvii, 88, 89, 92, 95
Eliot, George xvi, 89
eternal grace 11, 36, 39, 130

171

Family Week xviii
Faulkner, William xiv, xv, 32, 42, 43, 47, 150
  Light in August 41
Forster, E. M. 49
Freud, Sigmund xvii, 27, 107, 109–115
  Civilization and Its Discontents 105–106, 109
  Jokes and Their Relation to the Unconscious 12

Gagen, Jean 108
Genet, Jean 107
Gilbert, Sandra 146, 148
Glasgow, Ellen 32
Gordon, Caroline 32
Gomez, Christine 117
grotesque, definition 3, 4
  and theology 10
Gubar, Susan 146, 148
Guerra, Jonnie xiii, xvii, 5, 14, 106, 129

Haedicke, Janet 88, 99, 106, 137–138
Harbin, Billy J. 7, 111, 112, 114, 120
Harper, Tess 132, 143
Harpham, Geoffrey Galt 2, 20
Hargrove, Nancy D. 5, 117
Hatfield, Hurd 133
Heilman, Robert B. 45
Henley, Beth
  on Chekhov 3, 107, 109–110
  on *Collected Plays* 47
  on *Control Freaks* 24
  on *Crimes* (film) 143
  on *Crimes* (play) xii, 108, 123
  on death
  on *Debutante Ball* 16, 18
  on film adaptations 130
  on Holly Hunter 143
  on human condition 109–110
  on humor 108–109
  on *Impossible Marriage* 50
  on James Earl Jones 3–4
  on *L-Play* 49
  on paradox 1
  on screenplays 132
  on *Signature* 20, 23
  on split images 3, 131
  on theater 29, 107
  on themes 128–129
  on writing 144
Hobbes, Thomas xvi, 64, 75–78
Hucheon, Linda 51
Hucheson, Francis 64, 74, 77
Hunter, Holly 143
Hurston, Zora Neale xv, 40

Ibsen, Henrik 110
  A Doll's House 1
Ionesco, Eugène 107
Impossible Marriage xii, xv, xvii, 44, 50, 57, 58, 59

Jameson, Fredric 91

Kachur, Barbara 107
Kafka, Franz, "The Metamorphosis" 128, 129, 133, 139, 148, 151, 152
Kane, Carol 24
Karpinsky, Joanne B. 7, 108
Kayser, Wolfgang 3, 10, 24
Keaton, Diane xviii, 132
Keyssar, Helene 106
King, Rebecca xvi, 64–87
Klein, Alvin xii, 24
Kullman, Colby H. 138
Kuryluk, Ewa 14, 16–17, 26, 27
Kushner, Tony 60

Lasch, Christopher 115, 117, 145, 147
Lange, Jessica xviii, 132
Laughlin, Karen L. xiii, xvi-xvii, 7, 88–104, 106, 116
Lerner, Harriet Goldhor 134–136
L-Play xv, xviii, 44, 49, 51, 57, 59
Locke, John xvi, 64, 68, 71, 74, 75–79
Lucky Spot, The xii, xv, xvi, xviii, 1, 36, 48, 64–87

MacPherson, C. B. 64
McCullers, Carson 32
McDonald, Robert L. 145
McDonnell, Lisa 6, 117
Manning, Carol 32

Mapp, Larry G. xv, 32–41
Miller, Arthur 42
Miss Firecracker (film) xi, xvii-xviii, 129, 130, 143–152
Miss Firecracker Contest, The (play) xii, xv, xvii, 2, 5, 8–11, 15, 16, 24, 35–36, 38–39, 40, 48, 57, 143–152.
Mitchell, Margaret, *Gone with the Wind* 45, 46, 66, 69, 70
Morrow, Laura 117, 118, 119, 122

narcissism 115–118, 145–146
Noble, Donald R. 43
Nobody's Fool xii

O'Connor, Flannery xi, xiv, 1, 32, 45, 46, 47, 49, 107
O'Neill, Eugene 107, 111

Paige, Linda Rohrer xvii-xviii, 128–153
paradox 2
parody 75
  postmodern 51, 54, 56
pastiche (postmodern) 91, 99
Pinter, Harold 107
Plunka, Gene A. xvii, 105–127
Poe, Edgar Allan 45, 46, 50, 51
Porter, Katherine Anne 32
Porter, Laurin 106–107
Pullman, Bill 58

Ravenel, Shannon 45
Revelers xv, xviii, 44
Rich, Frank 89–90
Richards, Gary xiv, xv-xvi, 42–63
Robbins, Tim 144
Roberts, Eric xi
Roudané, Matthew C. 108
romance (postmodern) 89, 92–93, 95, 96, 98, 99
Rubin, Louis D., *The History of Southern Literature* 43

Sartre, Jean Paul 107
Sayre, Gordon M. 96
Schlame, Thomas 145
Scott, Sir Walter 92

Signature xii, xv, xvii, 2, 19, 20–24, 57, 59
Shaftesbury, Anthony Cooper, Third Earl of 64, 74, 77–78
Shepard, Alan Clarke 13, 14, 106, 110
Shepard, Sam 89, 110, 142
  Lie of the Mind, A 88
  True West xvi, 88–91, 93–94, 97, 100
Southern Renascence 43, 45
Smith, Adam 64, 73
Smith, Lee xv, 39, 40
Smith, Raynette Halvorsen 94
Spacek, Sissy xviii, 132, 142–143
St. Pierre, Ronald 93
Steenburgen, Mary 139–140, 145, 146

Tarantino, Quentin, *Pulp Fiction* 45
Taylor, Paul 18
Thompson, Lou 120, 122
Tobolowsky, Steven xii
Travis, Greg 140
True Stories xii

Uhry, Alfred 60

Viswanath, Ganga 117

Wake of Jamey Foster, The xii, xv, xvi, xviii, 2, 5, 11–15, 34–35, 48
Warren, Robert Penn 43
Welty, Eudora xi, xiv, xvi, 32, 42, 47, 107
  "Why I Live at the P.O." 55–57
Whited, Lana A. 111
Wilde, Oscar 50
  Importance of Being Earnest, The xii, 50, 51
Williams, Tennessee xi, 42, 48, 49, 50, 51–55, 107, 110
  Cat on a Hot Tin Roof 5
  Glass Menagerie, The 48, 51–55
Winer, Linda 89–90
Woodard, Alfre xii, 58, 150
Woods, Alan 106

Yeats, Wilson 4–5, 19–20, 22, 28

For Product Safety Concerns and Information please contact our EU
representative GPSR@taylorandfrancis.com
Taylor & Francis Verlag GmbH, Kaufingerstraße 24, 80331 München, Germany

www.ingramcontent.com/pod-product-compliance
Lightning Source LLC
Chambersburg PA
CBHW052121300426
44116CB00010B/1752